The U.S. Air Force in Korea

The USAF in Korea
Campaigns, Units, and Stations
1950–1953

Compiled by
Organizational History Branch
Research Division
Air Force Historical Research Agency

Judy G. Endicott, Editor

AIR FORCE HISTORY AND MUSEUMS PROGRAM
2001

For sale by the Superintendent of Documents, U.S. Government Printing Office
Internet: bookstore.gpo.gov   Phone: (202) 512-1800   Fax: (202) 512-2250
Mail: Stop SSOP, Washington, DC 20402-0001

ISBN 0-16-050901-7

Table of Contents

USAF Organizations at Korean Stations

Glossary

K-Site Map and Listings

Introduction

In commemoration of the Korean War, the U.S. Air Force History Program is publishing several works. One is this pamphlet, a companion volume to the air war chronology entitled *The USAF in Korea: A Chronology, 1950–1953*, which details monthly and daily USAF activities and operations in the theater. This pamphlet, *The USAF in Korea: Campaigns, Units, and Stations, 1950–1953*, provides information on the ten combat campaigns of the Korean War and gives an organizational view of tactical and support organizations carrying out combat operations. It also locates organizations or elements of organizations at their stations in Korea during the war and identifies designated K-Sites.

The first part of the pamphlet describes and illustrates the Korean service medal and service streamer and the ten designated campaigns of the Korean War. Accompanied by pertinent maps, the campaign narratives are general and selective rather than comprehensive, with each summary highlighting aerial combat. This section is extracted from Dr. A. Timothy Warnock's reference work *Air Force Combat Medals, Streamers, and Campaigns* (Washington: USGPO, 1990).

During World War II, the *group*, each with three or four flying squadrons, was the basic combat element of the Army Air Forces. This organization changed in 1947 when the new United States Air Force adopted the wing-base plan. Each combat group then active received a controlling parent wing of the same number and nomenclature. The new wing also controlled three additional groups with the same number to operate the air base, maintain the aircraft, and provide medical care at the base. When combat forces began to fight the war in Korea, the USAF units did so in various organizational forms. In some cases, the combat arm of the wing, plus a portion of the wing's supporting personnel, deployed to the Korean theater, leaving the rest of the wing to operate the home base, to which the group returned after its tour of combat ended. Early in the war, some combat groups deployed and operated under other wings, including temporary four-digit wings. In December 1950, those groups' aligned (same number) parent wings *moved on paper* from their previous bases and *replaced* the temporary wings in combat. The personnel of the temporary wing's headquarters were reassigned to the headquarters of its replacement. In 1951, the Strategic Air Command began to eliminate its combat groups by reducing the group headquarters to token strength and attaching the flying squadrons directly to the wing; therefore, wings replaced the medium bombardment groups attached to Far East Air Forces (FEAF) Bomber Command for combat. The groups were either inactivated or reduced in strength to one officer and one enlisted. In most cases, the personnel assigned to the group headquarters were simply reassigned to the wing headquarters, which had moved on paper to the location of the group headquarters. Most other combat organizations in-theater continued to operate with both wing and group headquarters or with group headquarters only. In a few cases, individual squadrons, such as the 319th Fighter-Interceptor Squadron, were directly controlled by an organization higher than either wing or group level.

The second section comprises briefs on the combat flying organizations and a selected number of combat support organizations that operated in the theater. In instances where the tactical group and wing of the same number began combat at different times, the first to enter combat is summarized first; if both began operational missions at the same time, information on the parent wing is given first. Each brief in section two contains an operational summary of a given organization's activities in the war, but specific information in the *Chronology* is not repeated here. Next, where pertinent, is a listing of flying or mission components. Following that is an organization's station list based on information in the organization's histories; in some cases, the station shown in the brief will not agree with the station listings found in the third section of this pamphlet. The commanders of groups and wings are listed next, and where applicable, Korean War campaign streamers, Korean War decorations, and Medal of Honor recipients are identified. The organizations' official emblems at the time of the Korean War appear with their descriptions or blazons.

The third part of the pamphlet contains the available official lists of Air Force units and organizations located in Korea, extracted directly from the bimonthly publication, *Directory of USAF Organizations*, issued by HQ USAF DCS/Comptroller. These listings date from July 1, 1950, which showed no USAF unit or organization located in Korea, to July 1, 1953, which listed stations and organizations located in Korea just before the end of the conflict. Unfortunately, we were not able to locate two issues of this series — May 1, 1951, and July 1, 1951. The issue of April 1952 was a special edition; then, the series reverted to bimonthly issues. *These lists appear exactly as shown in the directories.* The data contained in each issue reflects information provided by FEAF and other commands to the HQ USAF, Directorate of Statistical Services, Machine Accounting Division, through the end of the previous month. In some instances, the inputs did not specifically identify the location of an organization, leaving the reader to guess whether an organization was located in the town or at a nearby air base or airdrome. Rendering Korean place names in English inevitably results in a variety of spellings, and these lists are no exception. For example, the location generally known in USAF documents as Kangnung is in these lists consistently spelled as Kangnumg.

The directories have several additional unfortunate shortcomings. The appearance in the *Directory* of an organization at a new location usually followed that organization's actual move by several months. The bimonthly nature of the publication totally missed the movement of USAF organizations into North Korean bases in November 1950; conversely, it continued to show organizations located in the North Korean capital well after the invasion by

Chinese Communist Forces restored Pyongyang to Communist control. Occasionally an organization would unaccountably or inadvertently drop out of a *Directory*, only to reappear in following issues. Despite the discrepancies contained in the directories, these lists chart the ebb and flow of the war, demonstrate the buildup of air power in the campaign zone, identify the type of units supporting the operational organizations, and name the Korean bases at which USAF organizations were located at any given approximate time in the war. Included at the end of this part is a glossary of abbreviations and acronyms used in the directories.

The final section is a listing, both numerically and alphabetically, of locations in Korea identified as K-Sites. The place name spellings used are those found in Fifth Air Force general orders designating the K-Sites and other official Fifth Air Force documents. Also included is a map of Korea that approximately locates each K-Site.

Personnel of AFHRA's Organizational History Branch wrote and edited the organizational briefs and the K-Site lists. We wish to acknowledge our gratitude to Ms. Susan Beasley for scanning the initial section of the pamphlet and adding the unit emblem representations to the second part; to Ms. Barbara Robertson and Technical Sergeant Andrea Johnson, USAFR, for extracting from the publication *Directory of USAF Organizations* the Korean station lists that appear in the in the third part; and to Dr. Forrest L. Marion for locating the K-Sites on the map of Korea in the final section. Ms. Barbara Wittig of AFHSO's Production Team formatted the material and prepared, with the assistance of Dr. Richard Wolf, the pamphlet for publication.

Korean Service, 1950–1954

Korean Service Medal

A gateway encircled with the inscription KOREAN SERVICE is embossed in the center of the obverse side of the Korean Service Medal. Centered on the reverse side is the Korean symbol that represents the unity of all beings, as it appears on the national flag of the Republic of Korea. Encircling this symbol is the inscription UNITED STATES OF AMERICA. A spray of oak and laurel graces the bottom edge. The medal is worn with a suspension ribbon, although a ribbon bar may be worn instead. Both the suspension ribbon and ribbon bar are blue, representing the United Nations, with a narrow, white stripe on each edge and a white band in the center.

Executive Order No. 10179, November 8, 1950, established the Korean Service Medal. A member of the U.S. Armed Forces earned the medal if he or she participated in combat or served with a combat or service unit in the Korean Theater on permanent assignment or on temporary duty for 30 consecutive or 60 nonconsecutive days anytime between June 27, 1950, and July 27, 1954. Service with a unit or headquarters stationed outside the theater but directly supporting Korean military operations also entitled a person to this medal. An individual also received a Bronze Service Star for each campaign in which he or she participated, or a Silver Service Star in place of five Bronze Stars. These stars are worn on the suspension ribbon or the ribbon bar. Service members who participated in at least one airborne or amphibious assault landing are entitled to wear an arrowhead on the ribbon or ribbon bar.

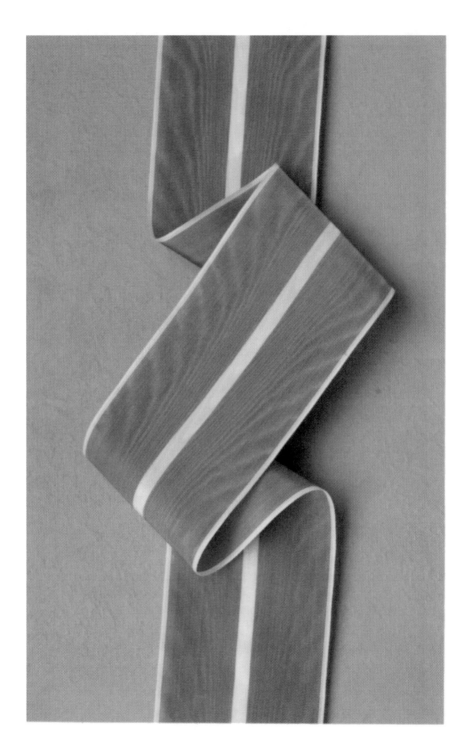

Korean Service Streamer

The Korean Service Streamer is identical to the ribbon in design and color. Air Force units received a service streamer if they were based in Korea between June 27, 1950, and July 27, 1954, or based in adjacent areas of Japan and Okinawa, where they actively supported other units engaged in combat operations. A campaign streamer is a service streamer with the name and dates of the campaign embroidered on it. A unit received a campaign streamer instead of a service streamer if it served in, or flew combat missions into, the combat zone during a particular campaign. Units participating in amphibious or airborne assault landings received the campaign streamer with an embroidered arrowhead preceding the name and dates.

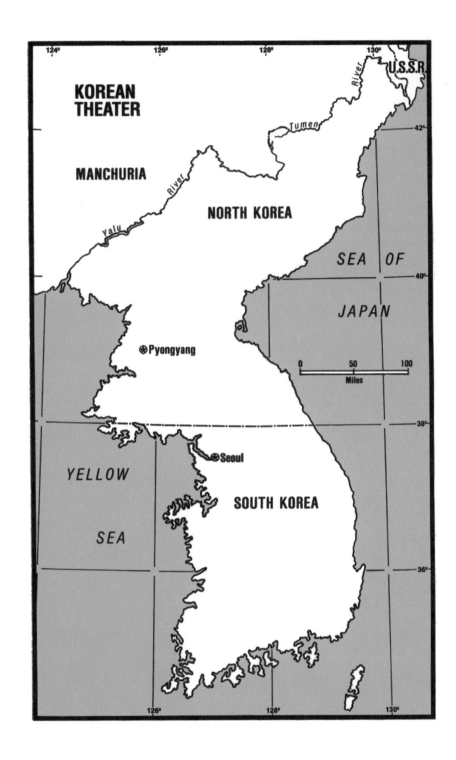

KOREAN THEATER

MANCHURIA

NORTH KOREA

U.S.S.R.

Tumen River

Yalu River

SEA OF JAPAN

⊕Pyongyang

0   50   100
Miles

38°

YELLOW SEA

⊕Seoul

SOUTH KOREA

124° 126° 128° 130°

42°

40°

36°

126° 128° 130°

Korean Campaigns
June 27, 1950–July 27, 1953

Designated Campaigns of Korean Service

The U.S. Army designated ten campaigns, adopted by the U.S. Air Force, for Korean Service. The first campaign began on June 27, 1950, when elements of the U.S. Air Force first countered North Korea's invasion of South Korea; the last ended on July 27, 1953, when the Korean Armistice cease-fire became effective. In all designated campaigns, the combat zone for campaign credit is the Korean Theater of Operations, which encompassed North and South Korea, Korean waters, and the airspace over these areas. The Secretary of Defense extended the period of Korean Service by one year from the date of the cease-fire. During this time, units and individuals earned no campaign credits but received either the Korean Service Streamer or the Korean Service Medal and Ribbon if stationed in Korea. The first campaign for Korean service is the UN Defensive.

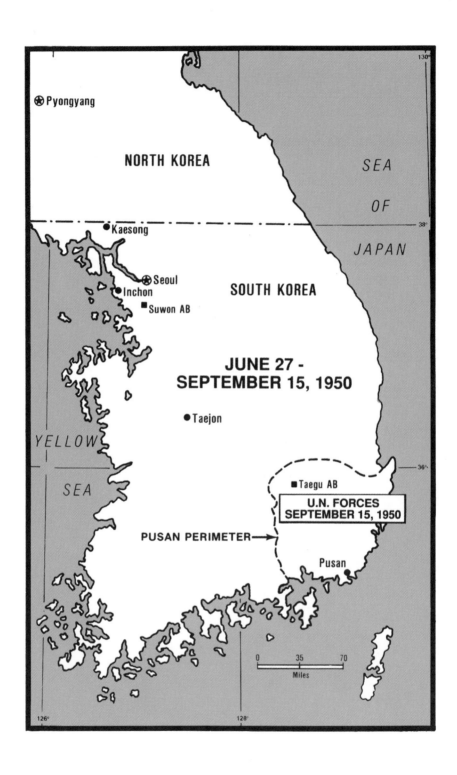

UN Defensive:
June 27–September 15, 1950

Early on June 25, 1950, North Korean forces crossed the 38th parallel near Kaesong to invade the Republic of Korea (ROK).* During the afternoon, North Korean fighter aircraft attacked South Korean and U.S. Air Force (USAF) aircraft and facilities at Seoul airfield and Kimpo Air Base (AB), just south of Seoul. The next day, FEAF fighters flew protective cover while ships evacuated American citizens from Inchon, a seaport on the Yellow Sea, 20 miles west of Seoul.

With the Communists at the gates of Seoul, on June 27 FEAF transport aircraft evacuated Americans from the area. Fifth Air Force fighters escorting the transports destroyed three North Korean fighters to score the first aerial victories of the war. Meanwhile, the United Nations (UN) Security Council in New York, with the Soviet Union's delegate absent and unable to veto the resolution, recommended that UN members assist the Republic of Korea. President Harry S. Truman then ordered the use of U.S. air and naval forces to help counter the invasion.

Commanded by Lt. Gen. George E. Stratemeyer, FEAF responded immediately. On June 28 FEAF began flying interdiction missions between Seoul and the 38th parallel; photoreconnaissance and weather missions over South Korea; airlift missions from Japan to Korea; and close air support missions for the ROK troops. North Korean fighters attacked FEAF aircraft that were using Suwon airfield, 15 miles south of Seoul, as a transport terminal and an emergency airstrip. The next day the 3d Bombardment Group made the first American air raid on North Korea, bombing the airfield at Pyongyang. The FEAF Bomber Command followed this raid with sporadic B–29 missions against North Korean targets through July. Then in August the B–29s made

*The Republic of Korea, established by the United Nations on August 15, 1948, had Seoul as its capital city. North Korea, the Democratic Republic of Korea, was established on September 9, 1948, under a Communist regime, with its capital at Pyongyang. In June 1950 the boundary between North and South Korea was the 38th degree, north latitude, i.e., the 38th parallel.

concerted and continuous attacks on North Korean marshaling yards, railroad bridges, and supply dumps. These raids made it difficult for the enemy to resupply, reinforce, and move its frontline troops.

As Communist troops pushed southward, on June 30, 1950, President Truman committed U.S. ground forces to the battle. Shortly afterward, on July 7, the UN established an allied command under President Truman, who promptly named U.S. Army Gen. Douglas MacArthur as UN Commander. A few weeks later, on July 24, General MacArthur established the United Nations Command (UNC). Meantime, the Fifth Air Force, commanded by USAF Maj. Gen. Earle E. Partridge, established an advanced headquarters in Taegu, South Korea, 140 miles southeast of Seoul. Headquarters, Eighth U.S. Army in Korea, under U.S. Army Lt. Gen. Walton H. Walker, was also established at Taegu.

During July 1950, as UN forces continued to fall back, most FEAF bombers and fighters operated from bases in Japan, over 150 miles from the battlefront. This distance severely handicapped F–80 jet aircraft because of their very short range, even when equipped with wing fuel tanks. After only a short time over Korean targets, the F–80s had to return to Japan to refuel and replenish munitions. Cooperating with naval aviators, the USAF pilots bombed and strafed enemy airfields, destroying much of the small North Korean Air Force on the ground. During June and July, Fifth Air Force fighter pilots shot down 20 North Korean aircraft. Before the end of July, the U.S. Air Force and the Navy and Marine air forces could claim air superiority over North and South Korea.

UN ground forces, driven far to the south, had checked the advance of North Korean armies by August 5. A combination of factors—air support from FEAF, strong defenses by UN ground forces, and lengthening North Korean supply lines—brought the Communist offensive to a halt. The UN troops held a defensive perimeter in the southeastern corner of the peninsula, in a 40- to 60-mile arc about the seaport of Pusan. American, South Korean, and British troops, under extensive and effective close air support, held the perimeter against repeated attacks while the UNC built its combat forces and made plans to counterattack.

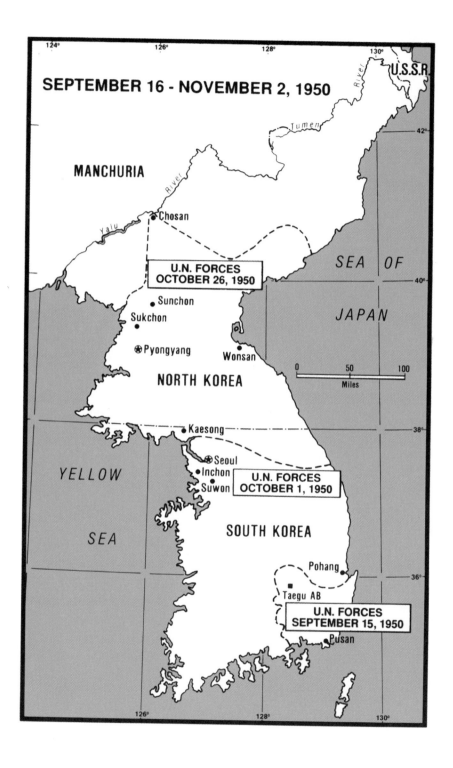

SEPTEMBER 16 - NOVEMBER 2, 1950

MANCHURIA

Chosan

U.N. FORCES
OCTOBER 26, 1950

Sunchon

Sukchon

Pyongyang

Wonsan

SEA OF

JAPAN

NORTH KOREA

0   50   100
        Miles

Kaesong

Seoul
Inchon
Suwon

U.N. FORCES
OCTOBER 1, 1950

YELLOW

SEA

SOUTH KOREA

Pohang

Taegu AB

U.N. FORCES
SEPTEMBER 15, 1950

Pusan

U.S.S.R.

Tumen

Yalu River

River

UN Offensive:
September 16–November 2, 1950

The first UN offensive against North Korean forces began on September 15, 1950, with the U.S. X Corps, under Army Maj. Gen. Edward M. Almond, making an amphibious assault at Inchon, 150 miles north of the battlefront. In the south the Eighth U.S. Army, made up of U.S., ROK, and British forces, counterattacked the next day. The 1st Marine Air Wing provided air support for the landing at Inchon while the Fifth Air Force likewise supported the Eighth Army. On September 16, as part of a strategic bombing campaign, FEAF bombed Pyongyang, the capital of North Korea, and Wonsan, an east coast port 80 miles north of the 38th parallel.

U.S. Marines attached to X Corps captured Kimpo AB near Seoul on September 17. Two days later the first FEAF cargo carrier landed there, inaugurating an around-the-clock airlift of supplies, fuel, and troops. C–54s returned wounded personnel to hospitals in Japan, and C–119s airdropped supplies to frontline forces. Bad weather hindered close air support of the Eighth Army, but on the 26th the U.S. 1st Cavalry Division forged out of the Pusan Perimeter north of Taegu and within a day thrust northward to link up with 7th Infantry Division forces near Osan, 25 miles south of Seoul. Air controllers, using tactics similar to those developed in France during World War II, accompanied the advancing tank columns, supported tank commanders with aerial reconnaissance, and called in close air support missions as needed. On September 26 General MacArthur announced the recapture of Seoul, but street fighting continued for several more days.

For a time in August and September 1950, before the recapture of Kimpo, all FEAF flying units had to fly from bases in Japan. The only continuously usable tactical base in Korea was Taegu, which FEAF used as a staging field to refuel and arm tactical aircraft. On September 28 fighter-bombers returned permanently to Taegu. As UN forces swept North Korean troops from South Korea, aviation engineers rebuilt the airfields, beginning with Pohang on the east coast 50 miles northeast of Taegu. USAF flying units returned on October

7 to Pohang, and to other rebuilt airfields at Kimpo, near Seoul, and at Suwon, 20 miles south of Seoul.

Supported by a UN resolution. President Truman directed the U.S. Joint Chiefs of Staff to authorize pursuit of the retreating North Korean forces, and on October 9 the Eighth Army crossed the 38th parallel near Kaesong. American and South Korean forces entered the North Korean capital of Pyongyang on October 19. FEAF B–29s and B–26s continued to bomb surface transport lines and military targets in North Korea while B–26s, F–51s, and F–80s provided close air support to ground troops. FEAF also furnished photographic reconnaissance, airlift, and air medical evacuation. For example, on October 20 the air force's troop carriers delivered 2,860 paratroopers and more than 301 tons of equipment and supplies to drop zones near Sukchon and Sunchon, 30 miles northeast of Pyongyang. The airborne troops bypassed strong defenses established by the North Koreans, and taken by surprise, the enemy troops abandoned their positions to retreat further northward.

Meantime, on the east coast of Korea, the ROK forces crossed the 38th parallel on October 1 and ten days later captured Wonsan. On October 26 South Korean forces reached the Yalu River at Chosan, 120 miles north of Pyongyang. Communist forces counterattacked within two days along the ROK lines near Chosan, forcing the South Koreans to retreat. The People's Republic of China had entered the conflict against the U.S. Eighth Army in Korea in the west and the U.S. X Corps in the east. At this point, the war in Korea took on an entirely different character as the tide turned against the UN forces.

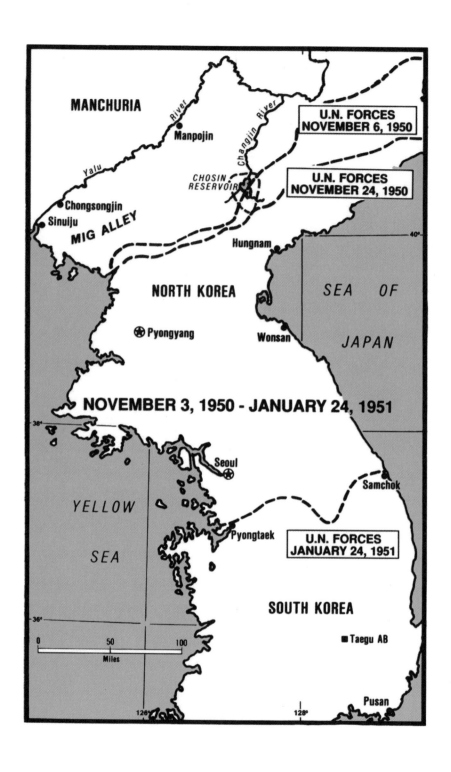

MANCHURIA

Yalu River

Changjin River

Manpojin

CHOSIN RESERVOIR

U.N. FORCES NOVEMBER 6, 1950

U.N. FORCES NOVEMBER 24, 1950

Chongsongjin

Sinuiju

MIG ALLEY

Hungnam

40°

NORTH KOREA

SEA OF JAPAN

⊛ Pyongyang

Wonsan

NOVEMBER 3, 1950 - JANUARY 24, 1951

38°

Seoul ⊛

Samchok

YELLOW

SEA

Pyongtaek

U.N. FORCES JANUARY 24, 1951

SOUTH KOREA

36°

0   50   100
Miles

■ Taegu AB

126°

128°

Pusan

CCF* Intervention:
November 3, 1950–January 24, 1951

Confronted by Chinese troops in North Korea, on November 3, 1950, UN troops, with the protection of Fifth Air Force close air support, began to withdraw to the Chongchon River in northwest Korea. On November 8, FEAF bombed the city of Sinuiju, the gateway from Korea to Manchuria on the Yalu River. Chinese MiG–15 jet aircraft engaged F–80 jets flying cover for the U.S. bombers, and in the first all-jet aerial combat, an American pilot scored a victory against a MiG.

During the remainder of November, FEAF medium and light bombers, along with U.S. Navy aircraft, attacked bridges over the Yalu River and supply centers along the Korean side of the river. Operations against bridges were usually unsuccessful because the bombers had to fly parallel to the river to avoid violating Chinese air space. The B–29s also dropped their bombs from at least 20,000 feet to avoid flak. Nevertheless, the bombers destroyed a span of a railroad bridge on November 25 at Manpojin, 150 miles north of Pyongyang, and two spans of a highway bridge on November 26 at Chongsongjin, 110 miles northwest of Pyongyang. The Communists simply built pontoon bridges or, as winter set in, crossed the Yalu on the ice. The B–29s did destroy North Korean supply centers, which forced the enemy to disperse its supplies or to hold them in Manchuria until needed.

The UNC planned a new offensive, unaware of the extent of the Chinese involvement. Even as General MacArthur kicked off the offensive on November 25–26, 1950, Communist forces also launched a major attack, driving both the Eighth Army in northwest Korea and the X Corps in northeast Korea southward. In the Chosin Reservoir area, the U.S. 1st Marine Division was surrounded. Between December 1 and 11, FEAF Combat Cargo Command, commanded by Maj. Gen. William H. Tunner, airlifted over 1,500 tons of supplies to the embattled Marines. FEAF pilots even dropped eight bridge spans so that the Marines could build a bridge across a gorge. The division finally broke through the Chinese troops to UN lines near Hungnam, an east coast

*Chinese Communist Forces

seaport 100 miles northeast of Pyongyang. The U.S. Navy, with some assistance from FEAF airlifters, evacuated the X Corps from Wonsan on December 5–15, and from Hungnam on December 15–24, leaving northeast Korea to the Communist forces. On the 27th the X Corps passed to the control of the Eighth Army, and by the end of the month, General MacArthur, UN Commander, had placed Lt. Gen. Matthew B. Ridgway, newly arrived in Korea and replacing General Walker, in control of all UN ground forces in Korea.

Meanwhile, FEAF had brought additional C–54s to Korea to meet the demands of the ground forces for theater airlift, and the air force began moving its fighter units, including a squadron of South African Air Force fighters, to airfields in North Korea to meet the close air support needs of UN troops. The appearance of the MiG–15 jet fighter in November 1950 threatened UN air superiority over Korea because the MiG outperformed available U.S. aircraft. FEAF requested the newest and best jet fighters, and on December 6, less than a month later, the 27th Fighter-Escort Wing, flying F–84 Thunderjets, arrived at Taegu. Then, on December 15 the 4th Fighter-Interceptor Wing flew its first mission in Korea in F–86 Sabres. Less than a week later, on the 22d, F–86 pilots shot down six MiG–15s, losing only one Sabre. The newer jet fighters permitted the UNC to maintain air superiority.

During December 1950 FEAF flew interdiction and armed reconnaissance missions that helped slow the advancing Chinese armies. B–29s and B–26s bombed bridges, tunnels, marshaling yards, and supply centers. When the Chinese troops resorted to daytime travel north of Pyongyang in pursuit of the Eighth Army, Fifth Air Force pilots killed or wounded an estimated 33,000 enemy troops within two weeks. By mid-December Communist forces were moving only at night, though still advancing.

On January 1, 1951, Communist forces crossed the 38th parallel and three days later entered Seoul behind retreating UN troops. Finally, on January 15 UN forces halted the Chinese and North Korean armies 50 miles south of the 38th parallel, on a line from Pyongtack on the west coast to Samchok on the east coast.

JANUARY 25 - APRIL 21, 1951

MANCHURIA

NORTH KOREA

Tumen River

Yalu River

MIG ALLEY

Sinuiju

Chongchon River

Hamhung AB

Sunan AB
Kangdong AB
⊛ Pyongyang

Wonsan

Sariwon AB
Anak AB
Sinmak AB

SEA

OF

JAPAN

40°

U.N. FORCES
APRIL 21, 1951

Yonchon
Munsan

38°

38°

⊛ Seoul
Kimpo AB
Suwon AB

YELLOW

SEA

U.N. FORCES
JANUARY 25, 1951

SOUTH KOREA

0   25   50
Miles

36°

Taegu AB

126°

128°

First UN Counteroffensive: January 25–April 21, 1951

Taking the offensive on January 25, 1951, the UNC began military operations directed toward wearing down the enemy rather than capturing territory. For two weeks UN forces, with close air support provided by Fifth Air Force fighter-bombers, advanced slowly northward against inconsistent but often stubborn resistance. On February 10 the troops captured Kimpo AB near Seoul. When thawing roads made ground transport virtually impossible, Brig. Gen. John P. Henebry's 315th Air Division airdropped supplies to the ground forces. For example, between February 23 and 28 the 314th Troop Carrier Group, flying C–119s, dropped 1,358 tons of supplies to troops north of Wonju, a town 50 miles southeast of Seoul. UN forces reoccupied Seoul on March 14.

A few days later, on March 23, FEAF airdropped a reinforced regiment at Munsan, 25 miles north of Seoul. In preparation, fighter-bombers and medium bombers, under direction of airborne tactical controllers, bombed enemy troops and positions near the drop zones. The C–119s continued the airdrop of supplies until March 27, as the paratroopers advanced from Munsan to Yonchon, 35 miles north of Seoul.

By this time, Communist forces had established such a strong air presence between the Chongchon and Yalu Rivers in northwestern Korea that Fifth Air Force pilots began to refer to this region as "MiG Alley." The Fifth, unable to challenge the enemy's temporary air superiority in northwestern Korea from bases in Japan, returned its tactical fighter units to Korean airfields recently wrested from Communist control. By March 10, F–86 Sabres were once again battling Chinese and North Korean pilots in MiG Alley while flying cover for FEAF Bomber Command's B–29s against targets in the area. Through the rest of March and April, FEAF bombed bridges over the Yalu River and other targets under the protection of escorting jet fighters. In spite of the escorts, MiG pilots on April 12 destroyed 3 of 38 B–29s attacking bridges at Sinuiju, causing the FEAF Bomber Command to put Sinuiju temporarily off-limits to B–29s.

On the eastern side of the peninsula. Bomber Command executed an interdiction campaign against railroads, tunnels, and bridges. U.S. naval aviators also were conducting missions against targets in the northeastern section of Korea between Wonsan and the Siberian border. From April 12 to 23 FEAF Bomber Command attacked rebuilt airfields on the outskirts of Pyongyang, at Sariwon 40 miles south of Pyongyang, and at Hamhung, on the east coast 110 miles northeast of Pyongyang.

On the ground, the Eighth Army pushed north of Seoul to reach the 38th parallel on March 31. Soon after, on April 11, President Harry S. Truman removed the UN Commander, Gen. Douglas MacArthur, because of his outspoken criticism of the President's prosecution of the war. Gen. Matthew B. Ridgway replaced General MacArthur, and Lt. Gen. James A. Van Fleet inherited the Eighth Army command. With close air support from the Fifth Air Force, UN ground forces pushed north beyond the 38th parallel between April 17 and 21, until halted by a North Korean and Chinese counterattack.

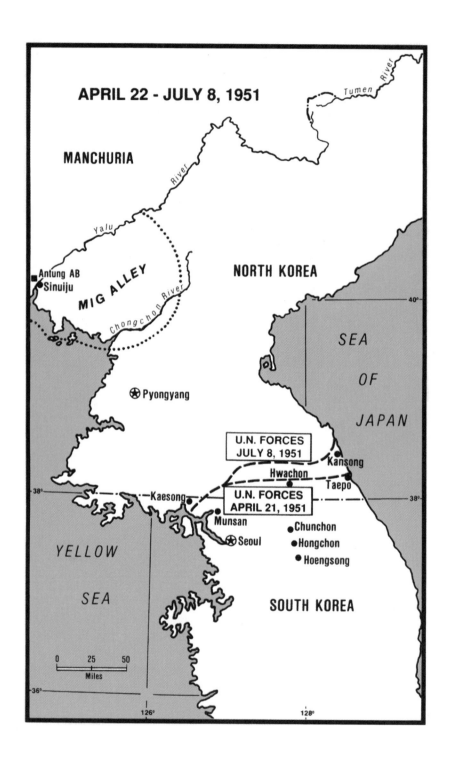

APRIL 22 - JULY 8, 1951

MANCHURIA

NORTH KOREA

Tumen River

Yalu River

Antung AB
Sinuiju

MIG ALLEY

Chongchon River

Pyongyang

SEA

OF

JAPAN

40°

U.N. FORCES
JULY 8, 1951

Kansong

Hwachon

Taepo

38°

Kaesong

38°

U.N. FORCES
APRIL 21, 1951

Munsan

Seoul

Chunchon

Hongchon

Hoengsong

YELLOW

SEA

SOUTH KOREA

0   25   50
Miles

36°

126°

128°

CCF Spring Offensive: April 22–July 8, 1951

The CCF's spring offensive began on April 22, 1951, with an assault on ROK Army positions 40 to 55 miles northeast of Seoul. U.S. Army and Marine Corps forces joined a United Kingdom brigade to plug the gap opened in UN lines north of Seoul, and by May 1 the Communist drive had lost momentum. For the next two weeks the Chinese and North Koreans built their strength before attacking in the vicinity of Taepo, between the east coast and Chunchon, 45 miles northeast of Seoul. By May 20 Eighth Army forces had stopped the Communist troops just north of Hongchon, 50 miles east of Seoul.

The UNC launched a counterattack two days later, on the 22d, along most of the battle line, except for a holding action just north of Munsan. ROK forces on the east coast quickly advanced northward to Kansong, 25 miles north of the 38th parallel. Advance in the center of the peninsula was slower, but by May 31 the Communist forces had their backs to Hwachon, 65 miles northeast of Seoul. Farther west, UN troops had pushed the enemy troops to Yonchon, 40 miles north of Seoul.

During the CCF Spring Offensive, FEAF and the U.S. Navy maintained air superiority over Korea through aerial combat and continued bombing of North Korean airfields. The Fifth Air Force and a Marine Corps air wing extended airfield attacks on May 9 to include Sinuiju airfield in the northwest corner of Korea. MiG fighters from Antung airfield just across the Yalu River in Manchuria offered little resistance to the American raid. Jet fighter-bombers destroyed antiaircraft positions, followed by Marine Corsairs and Air Force Mustangs that bombed and rocketed targets around Sinuiju airfield. F–86s protected the attack aircraft from MiGs. This mission destroyed all North Korean aircraft on the field, most buildings, and several fuel, supply, and ammunition dumps. All U.S. aircraft returned safely from the Sinuiju raid.

General Stratemeyer, Commander of FEAF, suffered a heart attack in May 1951, and General Partridge became Acting Commander while Gen. Edward

J. Timberlake temporarily took over the Fifth Air Force. Maj. Gen. Frank F. Everest succeeded to the command of the Fifth Air Force on June 1, and ten days later, Lt. Gen. O. P. Weyland took over FEAF.

Through most of May the Chinese pilots stayed on the Manchurian side of the Yalu River, but on the 20th 50 MiGs engaged 36 Sabres in aerial combat. During this fight Capt. James Jabara destroyed two MiGs. Added to his four previous victories, these credits made him the first jet ace in aviation history. MiG pilots again challenged Sabre flights escorting B–29 bombers on May 31 and June 1, but the Communists lost six more aircraft.

FEAF, Marine Corps, and Navy close air support of the UN ground forces. coupled with extensive artillery fire, forced the North Korean and Chinese forces during the spring of 1951 to restrict their movements and attacks to periods of darkness and bad weather. In addition, the air force used ground-based radar with considerable success to direct B–29 and B–26 night attacks against Communist positions and troop concentrations. FEAF also supplemented sealift with its cargo aircraft by flying supplies, mostly artillery ammunition and petroleum products, from Japan to Korea. Transports usually landed at Seoul or Hoengsong, 55 miles southeast of Seoul. The 315th Air Division delivered 15,900 tons in April; 21,300 tons in May; and 22,472 tons in June 1951. Also, whenever rains slowed overland transport to the front lines, C–119s airdropped supplies to UN troops. In late May FEAF initiated Operation Strangle, an interdiction campaign aimed at highways south of the 39th parallel. The next month the campaign was extended, with somewhat greater success, to railroads.

On June 23, 1951, the North Koreans, through the Soviet Union, proposed a cease-fire, and in July delegations began negotiations at Kaesong, North Korea, on the 38th parallel 35 miles northwest of Seoul. UN forces continued pushing the Communist troops northward until by July 8 the front line correlated closely with the armistice line established two years later.

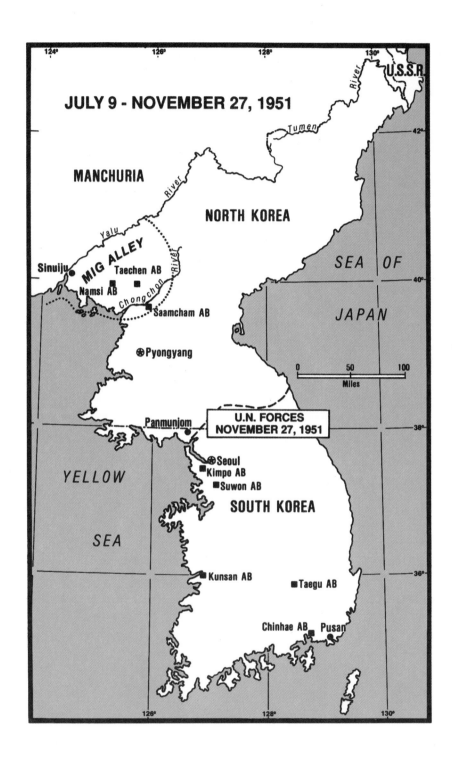

JULY 9 - NOVEMBER 27, 1951

MANCHURIA

NORTH KOREA

SEA OF

JAPAN

MIG ALLEY

Sinuiju

Taechen AB

Namsi AB

Chongchon

Saamcham AB

Pyongyang

0   50   100
Miles

Panmunjom

U.N. FORCES
NOVEMBER 27, 1951

Seoul
Kimpo AB
Suwon AB

YELLOW

SOUTH KOREA

SEA

Kunsan AB

Taegu AB

Chinhae AB Pusan

U.S.S.R.

Tumen

River

Yalu

River

UN Summer-Fall Offensive: July 9–November 27, 1951

Although truce negotiations began on July 10, 1951, hostilities continued. When the parties suspended negotiations on August 23, the UNC conducted an offensive in central Korea, to gain an important tactical position. But overall the UN ground forces fought a war of attrition. When the ground action subsided, FEAF began to improve its Korean airfields.

The Allies distributed their air power on the improved airfields throughout South Korea. In July 1951 the Royal Australian Air Force sent a squadron of jet fighters to Kimpo airfield, on the western outskirts of Seoul. U.S. Air Force units assigned to Kimpo included a fighter-interceptor group and a tactical reconnaissance group. A South African Air Force fighter-bomber squadron, flying Mustangs, operated from Chinhae AB on the south coast, ten miles west of Pusan. The USAF also stationed a fighter-bomber group at Chinhae. Other major UN airfields in Korea included two at Pusan, one with a Marine Corps air wing assigned and the other hosting a USAF light bomber group. The USAF had stationed two fighter-bomber groups at Taegu, 140 miles southeast of Seoul; a fighter-bomber group and a fighter-interceptor group at Suwon, 15 miles south of Seoul; and a light bomber group at Kunsan, on the west coast 110 miles south of Seoul. FEAF and Fifth Air Force used other airfields in South Korea primarily as staging bases from which to rearm and refuel aircraft, make emergency landings, and fly in supplies for frontline troops. The B–29s and cargo carriers operated from bases in Japan.

The Chinese Air Force implemented an air campaign in late July to test UN air superiority. Through August the Communist pilots tried their tactics in scattered air battles, then in September they challenged Fifth Air Force pilots in earnest. During the month, UN pilots engaged 911 Communist aircraft in aerial combat and shot down 14 MiGs, while suffering six losses. Aggressive Communist pilots nonetheless forced the Fifth Air Force to suspend fighter-bomber interdiction attacks in MiG Alley until the winter, and on October 28 FEAF Bomber Command restricted the vulnerable B–29s to night operations.

UN fighter-bombers, no longer able to attack targets in MiG Alley, turned to the destruction of railway lines in the area between Pyongyang and the Chongchon River. On August 18 the UNC expanded its railway interdiction campaign. Fifth Air Force attacked railroads and bridges in the northwest but outside MiG Alley; FEAF Bomber Command hit transportation targets, especially bridges, in the center of North Korea; and U.S. Navy aerial units bombed railroads and bridges on the northeast coast. This campaign forced the Communists to resort to motor vehicles and move supplies and troops at night. Thus, in August and September night-flying B–26s found lucrative targets on the roads of North Korea. Stronger flak defenses and worsening weather in October and November permitted the Communists to repair damaged railroads.

Meantime, in October 1951, the North Koreans began to construct within a few miles of each other three new airfields at Saamcham, Taechon, and Namsi, all 50 to 70 miles north and northwest of Pyongyang. American B–29s attempted to destroy the newly constructed airfields. During the night of October 13 FEAF Bomber Command unsuccessfully raided the field at Saamcham. The Bomber Command staff subsequently planned daytime raids under the escort of F–84s and F–86s. The B–29s made successful raids on October 18, 21, and 22, damaging the landing strips and other facilities at all three airfields. However, on the 23d MiG interceptors attacked the bombers and their escorts, shooting down three B–29s and an F–84, while losing four MiGs. The B–29s returned to night raids but failed to destroy the North Korean airfields, and the MiG pilots flying from these fields continued to intercept and shoot down UN aircraft.

On November 12, 1951, truce negotiations resumed at a new site— Panmunjom—and UN ground forces ceased all offensive action. By November 27 the UN had established defensive positions, and the Allies settled into a war of containment, although the Communists still pursued their effective air offensive.

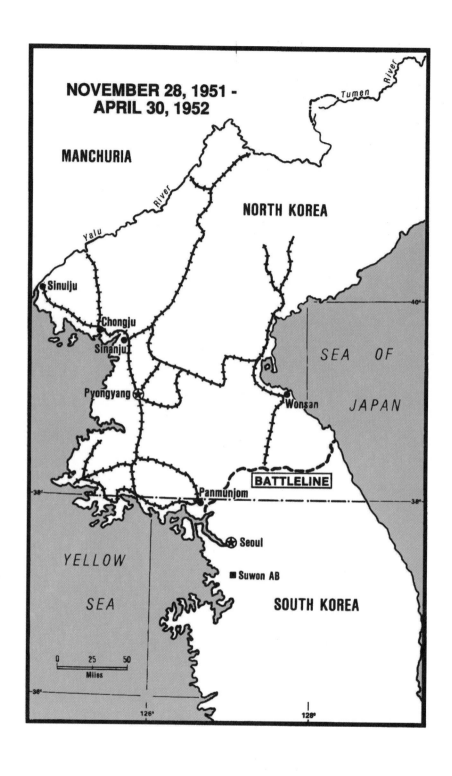

NOVEMBER 28, 1951 -
APRIL 30, 1952

MANCHURIA

NORTH KOREA

Tumen River

Yalu River

• Sinuiju

Chongju

Sinanju

Pyongyang

Wonsan

SEA OF JAPAN

BATTLELINE

Panmunjom

⊗ Seoul

■ Suwon AB

SOUTH KOREA

YELLOW SEA

0   25   50
Miles

40°

38°   38°

36°

126°   128°

Second Korean Winter:
November 28, 1951–April 30, 1952

USAF officials recognized the need for more F–86s to counter the Chinese Air Force in Korea. The 51st Fighter-Interceptor Wing at Suwon AB, 15 miles south of Seoul, consequently received F–86s from the United States to replace its F–80s. On December 1, 1951, the wing flew its first combat missions in the new Sabres. Members of the 51st and 4th Fighter-Interceptor Wings shattered the Communists' air offensive, downing 26 MiGs in two weeks, while losing only six F–86s. The Sabres achieved in the air results that had eluded the B–29s when they bombed the enemy airfields near Pyongyang. For the rest of the winter, the MiG pilots generally avoided aerial combat; nevertheless, Fifth Air Force pilots between January and April 1952 destroyed 127 Communist aircraft while losing only nine in aerial combat.

In spite of increasing vulnerability to flak damage, Fifth Air Force continued its raids against railways. In January 1952 FEAF Bomber Command's B–29s joined this interdiction campaign. Although the Communists managed to build up supply dumps in forward areas, the UN air forces damaged the railways enough to prevent the enemy from supporting a sustained major offensive. The interdiction missions also forced the North Koreans and Chinese to divert materiel and troops from the front lines to protect and repair the railways. As the ground began to thaw, between March 3 and 25, the Fifth Air Force bombed key railways, but with limited success. For example, on the 25th fighter-bombers attacked the railway between Chongju, on the west coast 60 miles northeast of Pyongyang, the North Korean capital, and Sinanju, 20 miles farther southeast. This strike closed the railway line for only five days before the Communists repaired it. The B–29s were somewhat more successful during the last week in March, knocking out bridges at Pyongyang and Sinanju. Fifth Air Force continued the interdiction campaign through April while looking for more effective means to block North Korean transport systems.

In the winter of 1951–1952, with the establishment of static battle lines, the need for close air support declined drastically. To use the potential firepower of the fighter-bombers, in January 1952 the UN commander alternated aerial bombardment of enemy positions on one day with artillery attacks of the same positions the next day. The Chinese and North Korean troops merely dug deeper trenches and tunnels that were generally invulnerable to either air or artillery strikes. After a month the UN Commander, General Ridgway, ordered the strikes stopped.

With peace talks at Panmunjom stalemated and ground battle lines static, on April 30 UN air commanders prepared a new strategy of military pressure against the enemy by attacking targets previously exempted or underexploited.

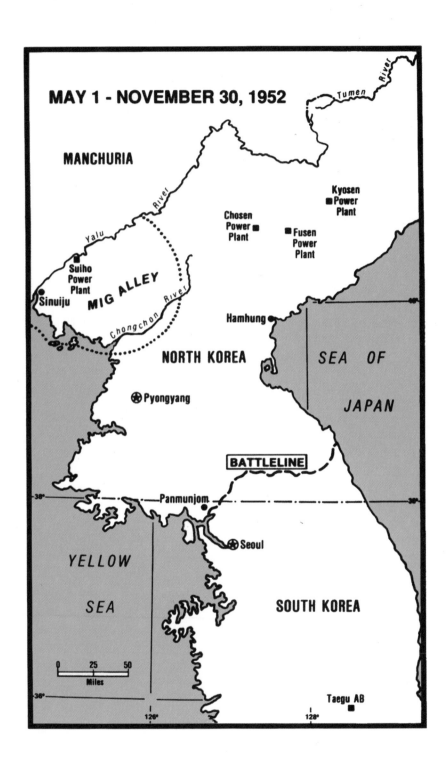

MAY 1 - NOVEMBER 30, 1952

MANCHURIA

Tumen River

Yalu River

Kyosen
Power
Plant

Chosen
Power
Plant

Fusen
Power
Plant

Suiho
Power
Plant

MIG ALLEY

Sinuiju

Chongchon River

Hamhung

NORTH KOREA

SEA OF

JAPAN

Pyongyang

BATTLELINE

38°   38°

Panmunjom

Seoul

YELLOW

SEA

SOUTH KOREA

0   25   50
Miles

36°   36°

Taegu AB

126°   128°

Korea, Summer-Fall 1952:
May 1–November 30,1952

The new UN strategy sought to increase military pressure on North Korea and thus force the Communist negotiators to temper their demands. In May 1952 the Fifth Air Force shifted from interdiction missions against transportation networks to attacks on North Korean supply depots and industrial targets. On May 8 UN fighter-bombers blasted a supply depot and a week later destroyed a vehicle-repair factory at Tang-dong, a few miles north of Pyongyang. The Fifth Air Force, under a new Commander, Maj. Gen. Glenn O. Barcus, also destroyed munitions factories and a steel-fabricating plant during May and June. Meanwhile, Gen. Mark W. Clark took over the UNC. Beginning on June 23, U.S. Navy and Fifth Air Force units made coordinated attacks on the electric power complex at Sui-ho Dam, on the Yalu River near Sinuiju, followed by strikes against the Chosin, Fusen, and Kyosen power plants, all located midway between the Sea of Japan and the Manchurian border in northeastern Korea.

The aerial reconnaissance function, always important in target selection. became indispensable to the strategy of increased aerial bombardment, since target planners sought the most lucrative targets. One inviting target was the capital city of Pyongyang. It remained unscathed until July 11 when aircraft of the U.S. Seventh Fleet, 1st Marine Air Wing, Fifth Air Force, British Navy, and ROK Air Force struck military targets there. That night, after daylong attacks, FEAF Bomber Command sent a flight of B–29s to bomb eight targets. Poststrike assessments of Pyongyang showed considerable damage inflicted to command posts, supply dumps, factories, barracks, antiaircraft gun sites, and railroad facilities. The North Koreans subsequently upgraded their antiaircraft defenses, forcing UN fighter-bombers and light bombers (B–26s) to sacrifice accuracy and bomb from higher altitudes. Allied air forces returned to Pyongyang again on August 29 and 30, destroying most of their assigned targets. In September, Fifth Air Force sent its aircraft against troop concentrations and barracks in northwest Korea while Bomber Command bombed similar targets near Hamhung in northeast Korea.

Along the front lines, throughout the summer and fall of 1952, FEAF joined the U.S. Navy and Marine Corps to provide between 2,000 and 4,000 close air support sorties each month. For example, FEAF Bomber Command not only flew nighttime interdiction missions but also gave radar-directed close air support (10,000 or more meters from friendly positions) at night to frontline troops under Communist attack. During the daytime, Mustang (F–51) pilots flew preplanned and immediate close air support missions.

The 315th Air Division also supported the ground forces, flying supplies and personnel into Korea and returning wounded, reassigned, and furloughed personnel to Japan. C–124s, more efficient on the long haul, carried personnel and cargo. C–47s provided tactical airlift to airfields near the front lines, and C–119s handled bulky cargo and airborne and airdrop operations.

During the summer of 1952, the 4th and 51st Fighter-Interceptor Wings replaced many of their F–86Es with modified F–86Fs. The new Sabre aircraft had more powerful engines and improved leading wing-edges which allowed them to match the aerial combat performance of the MiG–15 jet fighters of the North Korean and Chinese air forces. Even though the Communists had built up their air order of battle, they still tended to restrict their flights to MiG Alley and often avoided aerial combat with the F–86 pilots. By August and September, however, MiG pilots showed more initiative, and aerial engagements occurred almost daily. Even though the Communist pilots improved their tactics and proficiency, U.S. pilots destroyed many more MiGs, achieving at the end of October a ratio of eight enemy losses to every U.S. loss.

The Communists, in spite of the pressure of the air campaign, remained stubborn in the truce talks. On October 8, 1952, the UN negotiators at Panmunjom recessed the talks because the Chinese would not agree to non-forced repatriation of prisoners of war. (Only those POWs who wanted repatriation would return to Communist control. Many enemy POWs preferred to remain in South Korea, but the Communist authorities insisted that these POWs also be returned.). As winter set in, UN forces in Korea remained mired in the stalemated conflict.

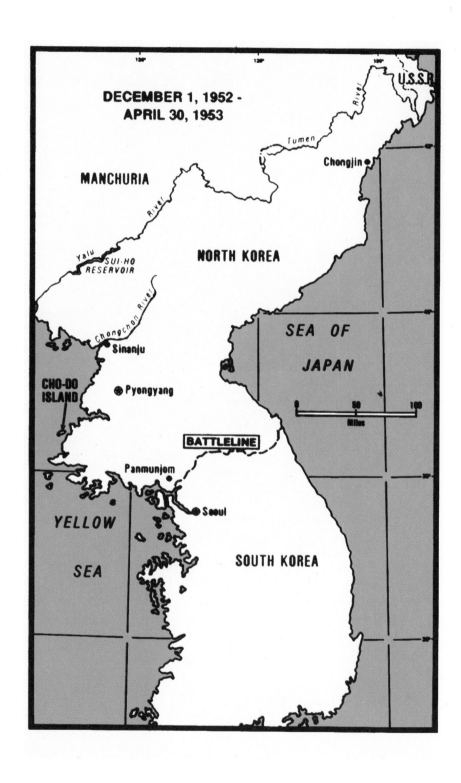

DECEMBER 1, 1952 -
APRIL 30, 1953

U.S.S.R.

MANCHURIA

Tumen River

Chongjin

River

NORTH KOREA

Yalu
SUI-HO
RESERVOIR

SEA OF

JAPAN

Chongchon River

Sinanju

Miles

CHO-DO
ISLAND

Pyongyang

BATTLELINE

Panmunjom

Seoul

YELLOW

SOUTH KOREA

SEA

Third Korean Winter: December 1, 1952–April 30, 1953

The military stalemate continued throughout the winter of 1952–1953. Allied Sabre pilots, meantime, persisted in destroying MiGs at a decidedly favorable ratio. In December the Communists developed an ambush tactic against F–86 pilots patrolling along the Yalu River: MiG pilots would catch the UN aircraft as they ran short of fuel and headed south to return to base. During these engagements, some of the F–86 pilots exhausted their fuel and had to bail out over Cho-do, an island 60 miles southwest of Pyongyang. UN forces held the island and maintained an air rescue detachment there for such emergencies. To avoid combat while low on fuel, Sabre pilots began to fly home over the Yellow Sea. MiG pilots at this time generally sought the advantages of altitude, speed, position, and numbers before engaging in aerial combat. The UN pilots, on the other hand, relied on their skills to achieve aerial victories, even though they were outnumbered and flying aircraft that did not quite match the flight capabilities of the MiG–15s. One memorable battle occurred on February 18, 1953, near the Sui-ho Reservoir on the Yalu River, 110 miles north of Pyongyang; four F–86Fs attacked 48 MiGs, shot down two, and caused two others to crash while taking evasive action. All four U.S. aircraft returned safely to their base.

While the Fifth Air Force maintained air superiority over North Korea during daylight hours, FEAF Bomber Command on nighttime missions ran afoul of increasingly effective Communist interceptors. The aging B–29s relied on darkness and electronic jamming for protection from both interceptors and antiaircraft gunfire, but the Communists used spotter aircraft and searchlights to reveal bombers to enemy gun crews and fighter-interceptor pilots. As B–29 losses mounted in late 1952, Bomber Command compressed bomber formations to shorten the time over targets and to increase the effectiveness of electronic countermeasures. Fifth Air Force joined the Navy and Marine Corps to provide fighter escorts to intercept enemy aircraft before they could attack the B–29s. Bomber Command also restricted missions along the

Yalu to cloudy, dark nights because on clear nights contrails gave away the bombers' positions. FEAF lost no more B–29s after January 1953 although it continued its missions against industrial targets. On March 5 the B–29s penetrated deep into enemy territory to bomb a target at Chongjin in northeastern Korea, only 63 miles from the Soviet border.

While Bomber Command struck industrial targets throughout North Korea during the winter of 1952–1953, Fifth Air Force cooperated with the U.S. Navy's airmen in attacks on supplies, equipment, and troops near the front lines. In December 1952 the Eighth Army moved its bombline from 10,000 to 3,000 meters from the front lines, enabling Fifth Air Force and naval fighter-bombers to target areas closer to American positions. Beyond the front lines, Fifth Air Force focused on destroying railroads and bridges, allowing B–26s to bomb stalled vehicles. In January 1953 Fifth Air Force attempted to cut the five railroad bridges over the Chongchon Estuary near Sinanju, 40 miles north of Pyongyang. Expecting trains to back up in marshaling yards at Sinanju, Bomber Command sent B–29s at night to bomb them, but these operations hindered enemy transportation only briefly. As the ground thawed in the spring, however, the Communist forces had greater difficulty moving supplies and reinforcements in the face of the Fifth Air Force's relentless attacks on transportation.

At the end of March 1953, the Chinese Communist government indicated its willingness to exchange injured and ill prisoners of war and to discuss terms for a cease-fire in Korea. On April 20, Communist and UN officials began an exchange of POWs, and six days later they resumed the sessions at Panmunjom.

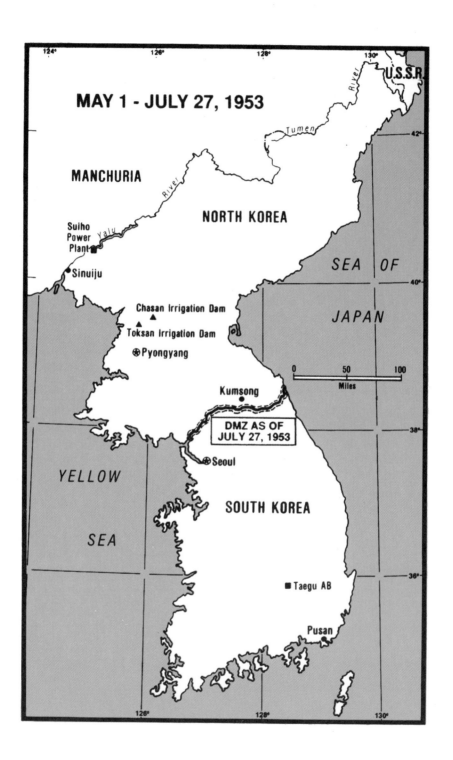

MAY 1 - JULY 27, 1953

U.S.S.R.

MANCHURIA

NORTH KOREA

Suiho Power Plant

Sinuiju

Chasan Irrigation Dam

Toksan Irrigation Dam

Pyongyang

SEA OF

JAPAN

Kumsong

DMZ AS OF JULY 27, 1953

Seoul

YELLOW

SEA

SOUTH KOREA

Taegu AB

Pusan

0   50   100
Miles

Korea, Summer 1953:
May 1–July 27, 1953

Although Communist leaders showed a desire to negotiate an armistice, they would not do so before trying to improve their military positions. During May 1953 Fifth Air Force reconnaissance revealed that the Chinese and North Koreans were regrouping their frontline forces. On the last day of the month, Lt. Gen. Samuel E. Anderson took command of the Fifth Air Force.

Communist forces directed a major assault on June 10 against the ROK's II Corps near Kumsong, a small town in central Korea, 110 miles southeast of Pyongyang. With American aid, the South Koreans stopped the Communist drive by June 19 with little loss of territory. During the enemy offensive, UN pilots broke previous records in flying close air support sorties, with FEAF flying 7,032, the Marine Corps, 1,348, and other UN air forces, 537. Also during June FEAF devoted about one-half of its combat sorties to close air support. Communist troops attacked again in central Korea on July 13, forcing the ROK II Corps to retreat once more. But by the 20th Allied ground forces had stopped the foe's advance only a few miles south of previous battle lines. During July, FEAF once again devoted more than 40 percent of its 12,000 combat sorties to close air support missions.

During the Communist offensives, the 315th Air Division responded to demands of Eighth Army, and between June 21 and 23 it airlifted an Army regiment (3,252 soldiers and 1,770 tons of cargo) from Japan to Korea. From June 28 through July 2, the airlifters flew almost 4,000 more troops and over 1,200 tons of cargo from Misawa and Tachikawa ABs in Japan to Pusan and Taegu airfields in Korea. These proved to be the last major airlift operations of the Korean conflict.

In aerial combat, meanwhile, Fifth Air Force interceptors set new records. Sabre pilots fought most aerial battles in May, June, and July 1953 at 20,000 to 40,000 feet in altitude, where the F–86F was most lethal, and during these three months they claimed 165 aerial victories against only three losses—the best quarterly victory-to-loss ratio of the war.

Fifth Air Force and FEAF Bomber Command also continued to punish the enemy through air interdiction, making attacks on the Sui-ho power complex and other industrial and military targets along the Yalu River. In addition, the Fifth Air Force in May attacked irrigation dams that had previously been excluded from the list of approved targets. On May 13 U.S. fighter-bombers broke the Toksan Dam about 20 miles north of Pyongyang, and on the 16th they bombed the Chasan Dam, a few miles to the east of Toksan Dam. The resulting floods extensively damaged rice fields, buildings, bridges, and roads. Most importantly, two main rail lines were disabled for several days. Between July 20 and 27 the UNC bombed North Korean airfields to prevent extensive aerial reinforcement before the armistice ending the Korean conflict became effective on July 27, 1953.

Combat Organizations

Fighter-Bomber

8th Fighter-Bomber Group and Wing

Azure, a chevron nebule Or, all within a diminished bordure of the last. Motto: ATTAQUEZ ET CON-QUEREZ—Attack and Conquer. Approved for 8th Group on September 6, 1934, and for 8th Wing on July 3, 1952.

8th Fighter-Bomber Wing

Stationed at Itazuke AB, Japan, at the beginning of the Korean War and assigned to the Fifth Air Force, the 8th FBW controlled combat groups and attached squadrons that conducted combat operations in Korea, flying mostly interdiction and close air support missions. The 8th FBG and its squadrons moved to South Korea on August 11, 1950, while the wing remained in Japan and assumed operational control of other combat units. The wing replaced the 6131st Tactical Support Wing and reunited with its tactical group in Korea in December 1950. Until the end of the war, it remained in South Korea, performing a variety of missions, including some strategic bombardment, air cover for bombers, armed reconnaissance, and low-level bombing and strafing for interdiction and ground support.

Combat Components.
51st Fighter-Interceptor Wing: attached September 25–October 12, 1950.
452d Bombardment Wing: attached November 15–30, 1950.
8th Fighter-Bomber Group: duration, except detached August 14–November 30, 1950.
49th Fighter-Bomber Group: attached *c.* July 9–September 30, 1950.
9th Fighter-Bomber Squadron: attached *c.* June 27–*c.* July 9,1950.
68th Fighter–All Weather Squadron: attached March 1–December 1, 1950.
77th Squadron, Royal Australian Air Force: attached July 2–October 10, 1950, and June 25–August 22, 1951.
80th Fighter-Bomber Squadron: attached August 11–October 1, 1950.
339th Fighter–All Weather Squadron: attached June 26–July 5, 1950.

Stations.
Itazuke AB, Japan, to December 1, 1950; Pyongyang, North Korea, December

1, 1950; Seoul AB, South Korea, December 9, 1950; Itazuke AB, Japan, December 10, 1950; Kimpo AB, South Korea, June 25, 1951; Suwon AB, South Korea, August 23, 1951–.

Commanders.

Col. John M. Price, to December 9, 1950; Col. Charles W. Stark, December 9, 1950; Col. James B. Tipton, April 3, 1951; Col. Raymond K. Gallagher, February 20, 1952; Col. James J. Stone, Jr., January 24, 1953; Col. William E. Elder, May 29, 1953–.

Campaign Streamers.

UN Defensive; UN Offensive; CCF Intervention; First UN Counteroffensive; CCF Spring Offensive; UN Summer-Fall Offensive; Second Korean Winter; Korea, Summer-Fall 1952; Third Korean Winter; Korea, Summer 1953.

Decorations.

Two Republic of Korea Presidential Unit Citations for periods June 27, 1950–January 31, 1951, and February 1, 1951–March 31, 1953.

8th Fighter-Bomber Group

Assigned to the 8th Fighter-Bomber Wing at Itazuke AB, Japan, at the start of the Korean War, the 8th FBG participated in combat operations, June 1950–July 1953. On June 26, one day after the North Korean invasion, its F–80C pilots provided high-cover combat air patrols along the Han River near Seoul to protect the air evacuation of U.S. citizens from South Korea. The next day, pilots of the group's 35th Fighter-Bomber Squadron in aerial combat shot down four enemy aircraft. Early in July, as the North Koreans advanced down the Korean peninsula, the group began low-level close air support of UN ground forces. In August and September the 8th FBG converted to the propeller-driven F–51, which consumed less fuel and provided greater loiter time on target than the jet-powered F–80. Also in August, it was attached for operational control to one of Fifth Air Force's temporary wings, the 6131st Tactical Support Wing. The group began operating from Korean bases in October and moved to North Korea in late November 1950. It resumed operations from Japan under the 8th FBW in December, after Chinese Communist forces drove the UN troops southward beyond the 38th parallel. Also in December, the group's pilots began once again to fly the F–80. The 8th FBG returned to forward bases in Korea some six months later, continuing to provide close air support to UN ground forces but increasingly flying interdiction missions against enemy transportation systems, airfields, troop concentrations, and supply areas. By January 1952, rail interdiction missions had become such a regular activity that the men chose as their theme song, "We've Been Working on the Railroad." By mid-1952, the group had returned to close air support of UN ground troops, but in November its pilots began flying night interdiction missions. As combat operations wound down in the spring of 1953, the group converted to the F–86 Sabre, using it effectively against ground targets, particularly enemy airfields, just prior to the armistice in July.

Combat Components.

35th Fighter-Bomber Squadron: duration.

36th Fighter-Bomber Squadron: duration.

80th Fighter-Bomber Squadron: duration.

Stations.

Itazuke AB, Japan, to August 11, 1950; Tsuiki, Japan, August 11, 1950; Suwon AB, South Korea, October 7, 1950; Kimpo AB, South Korea, October 28, 1950; Pyongyang, North Korea, November 25, 1950; Seoul AB, South Korea, December 3, 1950; Itazuke AB, Japan, December 10, 1950; Kimpo AB, South Korea, June 25, 1951; Suwon AB, South Korea, August 24, 1951–.

Commanders.

Col. William T. Samways, to May 19, 1951; Col. Edward O. McComas, May 19, 1951; Col. Harvey L. Case, Jr., July 31, 1951; Col. Levi R. Chase, January 22, 1952; Col. Walter G. Benz, Jr., September 12, 1952–.

Medal of Honor Recipient.

Maj. Charles J. Loring, Jr. (80th FBS), November 22, 1952.

Campaign Streamers.

UN Defensive; UN Offensive; CCF Intervention; First UN Counteroffensive; CCF Spring Offensive; UN Summer-Fall Offensive; Second Korean Winter; Korea, Summer-Fall 1952; Third Korean Winter; Korea, Summer 1953.

Decorations.

Distinguished Unit Citation for actions September 16–November 2, 1950.

Two Republic of Korea Presidential Unit Citations for periods June 27, 1950–January 31, 1951, and February 1, 1951–March 31, 1953.

18th Fighter-Bomber Group and Wing

Or, a fighting cock with wings displayed Sable, wattled and combed Gules. Motto: UNGUIBUS ET ROSTRO—With Talons and Beak. Approved for the 18th Group on February 21, 1931, and for the 18th Wing on April 17, 1953.

18th Fighter-Bomber Group

At the outbreak of the Korean War, the 18th FBG's 12th FBS provided personnel to form the "Dallas" fighter squadron, which rushed into battle. In late

July, the group headquarters with two of its squadrons (the 12th and 67th FBSs) deployed with F–80s from the Philippines to Taegu AB, South Korea. From July 28 to August 3, the 18th Group operated directly under Fifth Air Force and then passed to the control of the 6002d Fighter (later, Tactical Support) Wing. Pilots exchanged their F–80s for F–51 Mustangs. Combat targets included tanks and armored vehicles, locomotives and trucks, artillery and antiaircraft guns, fuel and ammunition dumps, warehouses and factories, and troop concentrations. In August, advancing enemy forces and insufficient aircraft parking at Taegu AB forced the group to move to Japan, but it returned to South Korea the following month to support UN forces in a counteroffensive. Because the front advanced so rapidly, operations from Pusan soon became impractical, and the group moved in November to an airstrip near Pyongyang, North Korea. The 2d South African Air Force Squadron joined the 18th in mid-November. The CCF intervention caused the group to move twice in as many weeks, first to Suwon AB, South Korea, then to Chinhae. From there the 18th FBG continued to support ground forces and carry out armed reconnaissance and interdiction missions. From November 1950 through January 1951, it earned a Distinguished Unit Citation for destroying roughly 2,400 enemy vehicles and severely damaging almost 500 more. From early 1951 until January 1953, the group and its tactical squadrons, moving from base to base in South Korea, operated separately from the rest of the 18th FBW. The group earned its second Distinguished Unit Citation from April 22 to July 8, 1951, when it flew 6,500 combat sorties while operating from sod, dirt-filled, and damaged runways to counter the enemy's 1951 spring offensive. When in January 1953 the group rejoined the wing at Osan-ni AB, its squadrons transitioned to F–86 Sabres without halting the fight against the enemy. It flew its first F–86 counterair mission on February 26, 1953. In the final days of the war, the 18th FBG attacked dispersed enemy aircraft at Sinuiju and Uiju Airfields.

Combat Components.

2d Squadron, South African Air Force: attached November 19, 1950–March 24, 1951, and *c.* April 22, 1951–.

12th Fighter-Bomber Squadron: duration.

39th Fighter-Interceptor Squadron: attached May 25, 1951–May 31, 1952.

67th Fighter-Bomber Squadron: duration.

Stations.

Taegu AB, South Korea, July 28, 1950; Ashiya AB, Japan, August 8, 1950; Pusan East AB, South Korea, September 8, 1950; Pyongyang East, North Korea, *c.* November 21, 1950; Suwon AB, South Korea, December 1, 1950; Chinhae, South Korea, December 9, 1950; Hoengsong, South Korea, June 2, 1952; Osan-ni AB, South Korea, January 11, 1953–.

Commanders.

Col. Ira L. Wintermute, to February 20, 1951; Lt. Col. Homer M. Cox, February 20, 1951; Col. William P. McBride, *c.* May 25, 1951; Col. Ralph H. Saltsman, Jr., June 5, 1951; Lt. Col. Henry W. Lawrence, by November

10, 1951; Col. Seymour M. Levenson, November 30, 1951; Col. Sheldon S. Brinson, May 17, 1952; Lt. Col. Albert J. Freund, Jr., November 25, 1952; Col. Maurice L. Martin, January 24, 1953–.

Medal of Honor Recipient.
Maj. Louis J. Sebille (67th FBS), August 5, 1950.

Campaign Streamers.
UN Defensive; UN Offensive; CCF Intervention; First UN Counteroffensive; CCF Spring Offensive; UN Summer-Fall Offensive; Second Korean Winter; Korea, Summer-Fall 1952; Third Korean Winter; Korea, Summer 1953.

Decorations.
Two Distinguished Unit Citations for actions November 3, 1950–January 24, 1951, and April 22–July 8, 1951.
Two Republic of Korea Presidential Unit Citations for periods July 24, 1950– January 31, 1951, and February 1, 1951–March 31, 1953.

18th Fighter-Bomber Wing

On December 1, 1950, the 18th FBW moved on paper from the Philippines to Pyongyang, North Korea, absorbing the personnel, F–51 aircraft, and responsibilities of the 6002d Tactical Support Wing. Under pressure from CCF advances, the 18th moved on December 4 to Suwon AB, South Korea, and six days later to Chinhae, near Pusan. The 35th FIG , also flying F–51s, was attached to the 18th FBW briefly from May 7 until it moved to Japan on May 25. The 18th Wing headquarters manned detachments with personnel drawn from all wing components to support the tactical components at South Korean bases until all wing personnel were reunited in January 1953 at Osan-ni AB. The 18th Wing's flying components continued combat to the end of the war.

Combat Components.
18th Fighter-Bomber Group: duration, except detached July28–November 30, 1950.
35th Fighter-Interceptor Group: attached May 7–24, 1951.

Stations.
Pyongyang East, North Korea, December 1, 1950; Suwon AB, South Korea, December 4, 1950; Chinhae, South Korea, December 10, 1950; Osan-ni AB, South Korea, December 26, 1952–.

Commanders.
Col. Curtis R. Low, December 1, 1950; Brig. Gen. Turner C. Rogers, February 1, 1951; Col. Ernest G. Ford, February 2, 1952; Col. William H. Clark, March 7, 1952; Col. Frank S. Perego, January 1, 1953; Col. John C. Edwards, June 15, 1953; Col. Maurice L. Martin, July 5, 1953–.

Campaign Streamers.
CCF Intervention; First UN Counteroffensive; CCF Spring Offensive; UN Summer-Fall Offensive; Second Korean Winter; Korea, Summer-Fall 1952; Third Korean Winter; Korea, Summer 1953.

Decorations.
Two Republic of Korea Presidential Unit Citations for periods December 1, 1950–January 31, 1951, and February 1, 1951–March 31, 1953.

49th Fighter-Bomber Group and Wing

A gyronny of three, Gules, Or, and Azure, a bolt of lightning, bend sinisterwise Argent, in chief, a knight's helmet, winged of the last, in dexter chief, five stars (Southern Cross) Argent, two on Gules, and three on Azure, in sinister base a covered wagon, trees, and road scene, all proper. Motto: TUTOR ET ULTOR—I Protect and Avenge. Approved for the 49th Group on December 29, 1951, and for the 49th Wing on July 2, 1953.

49th Fighter-Bomber Group

The 49th FBG and its tactical squadrons began operations in the Korean War with F–51s and F–80s in June 1950, first under its parent wing; then, the 8th FBW, July–September; and finally, the 6149th Tactical Support Wing, October–November. The group's first task in South Korea was to cover the evacuation of civilians from Kimpo and Suwon. Next, it flew close air support missions to help slow the advancing North Korean armies. Later, it turned to the interdiction of enemy troops, supplies, and lines of communication. Phasing out its F–51s for F–80s, the 49th FBG moved to Taegu AB on October 1, 1950, becoming the first jet fighter outfit to operate from bases in South Korea. It received a Distinguished Unit Citation (DUC) for its combat operations during the first five months of the war. On December 1, the group returned to its parent wing, the 49th. When the CCF offensive gained momentum in 1950–1951, the group again concentrated on ground support missions. It converted to F–84s, in June–September 1951, one squadron at a time, while the remaining squadrons continued combat operations. The 49th FBG earned another DUC for its contribution to the success of the UN Summer-Fall Offensive. Afterward, it engaged primarily in air interdiction operations against the main enemy channel of transportation: the roads and railroads between Pyongyang and Sinuiju. Also, it flew close air support missions for the ground forces and attacked high-value targets, including the Sui-ho hydroelectric plants in June 1952 and the Kumgang Political School in October 1952. On July 27, 1953, the 49th FBG joined the 58th FBG to bomb Sunan Airfield for the final action of F–84 fighter-bombers during the Korean War.

Combat Components.
7th Fighter-Bomber Squadron: duration, except detached July 9–August 17, 1950.
8th Fighter-Bomber Squadron: duration.

9th Fighter-Bomber Squadron: duration, except detached August 17–*c*. September 6, 1950, and December 17, 1952–.

Stations.

Misawa AB, Japan, to July 9, 1950; Itazuke AB, Japan, July 9, 1950; Taegu AB, South Korea, October 1, 1950; Kunsan AB, South Korea, April 1, 1953–.

Commanders.

Col. Stanton T. Smith, Jr., to October 21, 1950; Col. John R. Murphy, October 21, 1950; Col. Wilbur J. Grumbles, May 20, 1951; Col. William L. Mitchell, November 4, 1951; Lt. Col. Gordon F. Blood, May 20, 1952; Col. Charles G. Teschner, 1952; Col. Robert H. Orr, September 1952; Col. Richard N. Ellis, January 17, 1953; Col. Charles G. Teschner, April 1, 1953–.

Campaign Streamers.

UN Defensive; UN Offensive; CCF Intervention; First UN Counteroffensive; CCF Spring Offensive; UN Summer-Fall Offensive; Second Korean Winter; Korea, Summer-Fall 1952; Third Korean Winter; Korea, Summer 1953.

Decorations.

Two Distinguished Unit Citations for actions [June]–November 25, 1950, and July 9–November 27, 1951.

Two Republic of Korea Presidential Unit Citations for the periods [June] 1950–February 7, 1951, and February 8, 1951–March 31, 1953.

49th Fighter-Bomber Wing

The 49th FBW provided air defense of Japan until December 1, 1950, when it moved without personnel or equipment to Taegu AB, South Korea, replacing the 6149th Tactical Support Wing. The wing's non-tactical units returned to Japan for a month in January–February 1951, except for a wing detachment that stayed to refuel and rearm aircraft staging through Taegu—a vital mission maintained for most of the war. The 49th FBW was attached to the 58th FBW, March 16–31, 1953. On April 1, in a designation switch, the 49th moved without personnel or equipment to Kunsan AB, where it absorbed the resources of the 474th FBW and continued combat operations to July 27.

Combat Components.

49th Fighter-Bomber Group: duration, except detached July 9–November 30, 1950, and March 16–31, 1953.

543d Tactical Support Group: attached December 1, 1950–January 26, 1951.

9th Fighter-Bomber Squadron: attached August 17–*c*. September 6, 1950.

334th Fighter-Interceptor Squadron: attached February 24–March 1, 1951.

Stations.

Taegu AB, South Korea, December 1, 1950; Tsuiki AB, Japan, January 26, 1951; Taegu AB, South Korea, February 24, 1951; Kunsan AB, South Korea, April 1, 1953–.

Commanders.

Col. Aaron W. Tyer, December 1, 1950; Col. Kenneth W. Northamer, April 20, 1951; Col. Aaron W. Tyer, May 27, 1951; Col. Joe L. Mason, September 1, 1951; Col. David T. McKnight, February 1, 1952; Col. Robert J. Rogers, *c.* August 19, 1952–March 15, 1953; none (not manned), March 16–31, 1953; Col. William W. Ingenhutt, April 1, 1953; Col. Edwin A. Doss, April 24, 1953–.

Campaign Streamers.

CCF Intervention; First UN Counteroffensive; CCF Spring Offensive; UN Summer-Fall Offensive; Second Korean Winter; Korea, Summer-Fall 1952; Third Korean Winter; Korea, Summer 1953.

Decoration.

Republic of Korea Presidential Unit Citation for period [December 1] 1950–February 7, 1951.

58th Fighter-Bomber Group and Wing

Azure, on clouds in base a representation of the Greek mythological goddess Artemis with quiver and bow, in her chariot drawn by two deer, all Or, garnished Tan and Brown, all within a diminished bordure of the second. Motto: NON REVERTAR INULTUS—I Will Not Return Unavenged. Approved for the 58th Group on August 10, 1942, and for the 58th Wing on November 18, 1952.

58th Fighter-Bomber Wing

On July 10, 1952, the 58th FBW activated and absorbed the personnel and equipment of the 136th FBW. The 58th had some assets in Japan and some in South Korea until August, when the entire wing moved to Korea. The 58th FBW tested a "reinforced wing" concept in the spring of 1953, taking on the support and administrative functions of the 49th FBW while exercising direct control of both the 58th and 49th FBGs. In three months, the reinforced wing flew 10,422 combat sorties and delivered more firepower than two separate wings with a full complement of personnel.

Combat Components.

49th Fighter-Bomber Wing: attached March 16–31, 1953.

474th Fighter-Bomber Wing: attached April 1, 1953–.

49th Fighter-Bomber Group: attached March 16–31, 1953.

58th Fighter-Bomber Group: duration.

474th Fighter-Bomber Group: attached April 1, 1953–.

Stations.

Itazuke AB, Japan, July 10, 1952; Taegu AB, South Korea, August 1952–.

Commanders.
Col. James B. Buck, July 10, 1952; Col. Victor E. Warford, July 22, 1952; Col. Joseph Davis, Jr., July 1, 1953–.
Campaign Streamers.
Korea, Summer-Fall 1952; Third Korean Winter; Korea, Summer 1953.
Decorations.
Republic of Korea Presidential Unit Citation for the period July 10, 1952–March 31, 1953.

58th Fighter-Bomber Group

The 58th FBG flew F–84s in primarily close air support and ground attack missions from July 1952. Having entered the Korean War with the slow, short-ranged F–84D Thunderjets, the 58th transitioned in late 1952 to the new "G" model, designed with more speed and range. Targets were enemy ports, railroads, and airfields. The group attacked the major supply port of Sinuiju in September, inflicting heavy damage to the target area without loss of personnel or aircraft. Combining with other fighter-bomber units, it attacked the Kumgang Political School at Odong-ni in October 1952 and the North Korean tank and infantry school at Kangso in February 1953. In May, the 58th FBG bombed North Korean dams, flooding enemy lines of communication and rice fields. On July 27, 1953, the 58th FBG attacked the runway at Kanggye and, with the 49th FBG, bombed Sunan Airfield for the final action of fighter-bombers in the Korean War.

Combat Components.
69th Fighter-Bomber Squadron: July 10, 1952–.
310th Fighter-Bomber Squadron: July 10, 1952–.
311th Fighter-Bomber Squadron: July 10, 1952–.
Station.
Taegu AB, South Korea, July 10, 1952–.
Commander.
Col. Charles E. Jordan, 1952; Col. Frederick J. Nelander, 1953–.
Campaign Streamers.
Korea, Summer-Fall 1952; Third Korean Winter; Korea, Summer 1953.
Decorations.
Distinguished Unit Citation for actions May 1–July 27, 1953.
Republic of Korea Presidential Unit Citation for period July 10, 1952–March 31, 1953.

116 Fighter-Bomber Group

Per fess embattled debased Azure and Argent, three chevronels reversed of the second, the base chevronel fimbriated, forming a frazure at its apex over the embattlement Azure; in chief four darts of the second in formation chevron-wise points downward, one in fess point, two in sinister, all within a diminutive border Argent. Motto: VINCET AMOR PATRIAE—Love of Country Shall Conquer. Approved on June 6, 1952.

116th Fighter-Bomber Group

The 116th FBG, assigned to the 116th FBW, whose personnel came from Georgia, Florida, and California National Guard units, was ordered to active duty in October 1950. In early 1951, the group transitioned from F–80s to F–84 Thunderjets, and shortly thereafter received orders to deploy to Japan. Personnel and aircraft proceeded by ship to Japan, arriving near the end of July. After unloading, personnel found that 33 of the 75 aircraft shipped had structural damage or corrosion problems. While support personnel worked feverishly on the aircraft, the tactical elements resumed their training program. Most of the pilots had not flown for a month, and as the aircraft were repaired, the training in gunnery, rocketry, bombing, and instrument flying intensified. In August, the group began flying air defense alert missions in northern Japan. In November, elements of the tactical group and rotating squadrons deployed to South Korea for combat. Those rotating elements flew missions from Taegu AB to cut enemy rail lines; disrupt supply routes; destroy vehicles, equipment, and troop shelters; and support UN forces in close combat. Between rotations to South Korea, those squadrons remaining in Japan continued to fly air defense missions under control of the 116th Wing headquarters through the first half of 1952. On July 10, 1952, the 116th designation returned to control of the Air National Guard, with the 474th Fighter-Bomber Wing absorbing its personnel, equipment, aircraft, and other resources.

Combat Components.
158th Fighter-Bomber Squadron: duration.
159th Fighter-Bomber Squadron: duration.
196th Fighter-Bomber Squadron: duration.

Stations.
Misawa AB, Japan, *c.* July 25, 1951–July 10, 1952 (deployed to Taegu AB, South Korea, November 1951–*c.* June 1952).

Commanders.
Lt. Col. Ralph G. Kuhn, to January 1952; Lt. Col. Daniel F. Sharp, *c.* January 31, 1952–unknown.

Campaign Streamers.
UN Summer-Fall Offensive; Second Korean Winter; Korea, Summer 1952.

Decorations.
None.

136th Fighter-Bomber Wing

The 136th FBW of the Texas Air National Guard was ordered to active duty in October 1950. It transitioned to the F–84 Thunderjet in early 1951 and moved to Japan incrementally from May to July, integrating with, and then replacing, elements of the 27th Fighter-Escort Wing at Itazuke AB. The wing headquarters remained behind as most of its components moved to Taegu AB, South Korea, in late September. In November, the headquarters also moved to Taegu, leaving mostly rear-echelon maintenance elements in Japan. After almost a year of federal service, the 136th FBW was returned, without personnel or equipment, to the Air National Guard on July 10, 1952.

Combat Component.
136th Fighter-Bomber Group: duration
Stations.
Itazuke AB, Japan, May 1951; Taegu AB, South Korea, November 16, 1951–July 10, 1952.
Commanders.
Col. Albert C. Prendergast, to November 5, 1951; Col. Alfred G. Lambert, Jr., November 5, 1951; Col. James B. Buck, November 10, 1951–July 10, 1952.
Campaign Streamers.
UN Summer-Fall Offensive; Second Korean Winter; Korea, Summer-Fall 1952.
Decorations.
None.

136th Fighter-Bomber Group

The 136th FBG moved to Japan, May–July 1951, with the 182d FBS functioning by June 1, the 154th FBS by July 1, and the 111th FBS by August 1. The group engaged primarily in interdiction but it also flew close air support, escort, and armed reconnaissance missions. On June 26, 12 MiG–15s challenged a group of F–84 escort fighters that were screening a formation of B–29 bombers attacking a North Korean airfield. Although relatively new to combat, Thunderjet pilots of the 182d FBS successfully turned back the MiGs, shooting down one. The group, its flying squadrons, and essential support elements moved from Itazuke AB, Japan, to Taegu AB, South Korea, in late September. Despite battle damage, maintenance problems, and inclement weather, the 136th FBG hindered North Korean rail transportation and destroyed large quantities of supplies badly needed by the enemy's frontline troops. In the spring of 1952, it concentrated on close air support of frontline troops. On June 23, the 136th FBG and another unit successfully attacked the Sui-ho power plant on the Yalu River. This last major aerial assault for the

136th rendered the fourth largest power plant in the world unserviceable.
Combat Components.
111th Fighter-Bomber Squadron: duration.
154th Fighter-Bomber Squadron: duration.
182d Fighter-Bomber Squadron: duration.
524th Fighter-Escort Squadron: attached *c*. July 1–August 12, 1951.
Stations.
Itazuke AB, Japan, May 1951; Taegu AB, South Korea, *c*. September 26, 1951–July 10, 1952.
Commanders.
Lt. Col. Gerald E. Montgomery, *c*. May 10, 1951; Col. Dean Davenport, June 11, 1951; Col. William T. Halton, *c*. September 24, 1951; Lt. Col. Daniel F. Sharp, March 21–July 1952.
Campaign Streamers.
UN Summer-Fall Offensive; Second Korean Winter; Korea, Summer-Fall 1952.
Decorations.
None.

474th Fighter-Bomber Wing

On July 10, 1952, the 474th FBW activated at Misawa AB, Japan, taking over the personnel and F–84E Thunderjets of the 116th FBW. During the next three weeks, the 474th Wing moved to Kunsan AB on the western side of the Korean peninsula, while the 474th Maintenance Squadron moved to Itazuke AB, Japan, and integrated into the rear-echelon maintenance combined operations (REMCO) for Thunderjet fighters. Other wing-support units remained at Misawa AB, attached to the Japan Air Defense Force. The wing controlled its combat units until April 1, 1953, when its headquarters and support units were reduced to "paper status" and its tactical units attached to the 58th FBW.
Combat Component.
474th Fighter-Bomber Group: July 10, 1952–April 1, 1953.
Stations.
Misawa AB, Japan, July 10, 1952; Kunsan AB, South Korea, July 10, 1952; Taegu AB, South Korea, April 1, 1953–.
Commanders.
Col. William W. Ingenhutt, July 10, 1952–April 1, 1953.
Campaign Streamers.
Korea, Summer-Fall 1952; Third Korean Winter; Korea, Summer 1953.
Decoration.
Republic of Korea Presidential Unit Citation for period July 10, 1952–March 30, 1953.

474th Fighter-Bomber Group

The 474th Fighter-Bomber Group entered combat on August 1, 1952, joining the Fifth Air Force campaign against communist supply centers, transportation targets, and troop concentrations. During its first few weeks, the group's F–84s shredded a large troop concentration near the capital city of Pyongyang, broke up a MiG attack, hit a munitions factory ten miles south of the Yalu River, and destroyed a political–military instruction center. In November the 474th FBG started flying night interdiction missions to interfere with the enemy's movement of supplies. Its Thunderjets escorted B–26 Marauders on bombing operations in MiG Alley; flew flak suppression missions for strikes on heavily defended targets; conducted armed reconnaissance of the communist rear to gain intelligence information; and ranged over the front lines to strafe and bomb trenches, bunkers, troop shelters, and heavy weapons positions. In January 1953 the group's attention shifted to communications centers, training complexes, and strategic targets rebuilt after earlier raids. Over the next three months the F–84s struck the Sinanju rail facility on a major supply artery between the North Korean capital and the Manchurian border, an industrial area around Kyomipo located southwest of the capital, and the North Korean Tank and Infantry School west of Pyongyang. Effective April 1, 1953, in a name change only, the 474th and 49th Fighter-Bomber Groups switched places, with the 474th assuming the personnel and equipment of the 49th FBG at Taegu AB. Only the 430th FBS physically moved to Taegu. After April 1, the 474th FBG came under the operational control of the 58th FBW in a test of the "reinforced wing." On the day before the armistice went into effect, Thunderjets of the 474th Group bombed the Chunggangjin Airfield to prevent the buildup of enemy aircraft in the last hours of the war.

Combat Components.
428th Fighter-Bomber Squadron: July 10, 1952–.
429th Fighter-Bomber Squadron: July 10, 1952–.
430th Fighter-Bomber Squadron: July 10, 1952–.

Stations.
Misawa AB, Japan, July 10, 1952; Kunsan AB, South Korea, July 10, 1952; Taegu AB, South Korea, April 1, 1953–.

Commanders.
Lt. Col. William L. Jacobsen, July 10, 1952; Lt. Col. Francis J. Vetort, August 29, 1952; Col. Joseph Davis, Jr., December 16, 1952; Col. Richard N. Ellis, April 1953; Col. John S. Loisel, May 1953–.

Campaign Streamers.
Korea, Summer-Fall 1952; Third Korean Winter; Korea, Summer 1953.

Decorations.
Distinguished Unit Citation for actions December 1, 1952–April 30, 1953.
Republic of Korea Presidential Unit Citation for period July 10, 1952–March 30, 1953.

Fighter-Escort

27th Fighter-Escort Group and Wing

Per bend Azure and Or, in sinister chief a dexter hand clenched couped at the wrist; in dexter base a magnolia blossom, leave all Argent fimbriated and garnished Sable, all within a diminished bordure of the second. Motto: INTELLIGENT STRENGTH. Approved for the 27th Group on September 12, 1940, and for the 27th Wing on July 11, 1952.

27th Fighter-Escort Wing

To help meet the threat of the Soviet-built MiG–15 fighter in Korea, the USAF diverted Strategic Air Command's 27th FEW with its F–84 Thunderjets to the Far East instead of sending it as planned to England. In early December 1950 the wing established a rear echelon at Itazuke, Japan, and took its F–84s to Taegu AB, South Korea. Less than two months later, fearful that Chinese ground forces would overrun UN jet bases in South Korea, Fifth Air Force withdrew the 27th to Japan. The wing continued combat from Japan until the 136th FBW replaced it in late June 1951.

Combat Component.

27th Fighter-Escort Group: duration.

Stations.

Yokota AB, Japan, November 11–30, 1950; Taegu AB, South Korea (advanced echelon), December 1, 1950–January 31, 1951; Itazuke AB, Japan (rear echelon), December 9, 1950–January 31, 1951; Itazuke AB, Japan February 1–July 15, 1951.

Commanders.

Col. Ashley B. Packard, to May 1, 1951; Col. Raymond F. Rudell, May 1, 1951–.

Campaign Streamers.

CCF Intervention; First UN Counteroffensive; CCF Spring Offensive.

Decoration.

Republic of Korea Presidential Unit Citation for period November 9, 1950–May 31, 1951.

27th Fighter-Escort Group

The 27th FEG flew its first combat mission from Taegu AB, South Korea, on December 6, 1950. The F–84 crews, although trained in long-range escort, began combat by flying armed reconnaissance and close air support missions, and then added bomber escort, combat air patrol, flak suppression, and precise dive-bombing missions against bridges, tunnels, and airfield runways. An F–84 pilot destroyed the group's first MiG–15 in aerial combat on January 21, 1951. The group returned to Japan at the end of January to continue combat from Itazuke AB. In late June, it redeployed to Texas, but the 524th Squadron remained behind until early August to fly combat with the 136th FBG.

Combat Components.
522d Fighter-Escort Squadron: duration.
523d Fighter-Escort Squadron: duration.
524th Fighter-Escort Squadron: duration.

Stations.
Taegu AB, South Korea, December 5, 1950; Itazuke AB, Japan, January 31–July 2, 1951.

Commanders.
Col. Donald J. M. Blakeslee, December 1950; Lt. Col. William E. Bertram, March 3, 1951–.

Campaign Streamers.
CCF Intervention; First UN Counteroffensive; CCF Spring Offensive.

Decorations.
Distinguished Unit Citation for actions January 26–April 21, 1951.
Republic of Korea Presidential Unit Citation for period November 9, 1950–May 31, 1951.

Fighter-Interceptor

4th Fighter-Interceptor Group and Wing

Azure, on a bend Or, a spear garnished with three eagle feathers and shaft flammant to base all proper, all with a diminished bordure Or. Motto: FOURTH BUT FIRST. Approved for 4th Group on September 26, 1949, and for 4th Wing on October 7, 1952.

4th Fighter-Interceptor Wing

The 4th FIW, moving from the United States, arrived in Japan in late November with its F–86 Sabres aboard aircraft carriers. The primary mission of the wing was air superiority, and the Sabre was capable of battling the Soviet-built MiG–15 on equal terms. From Johnson AB, Japan, detachments deployed in mid-December to bases in South Korea, rotating between South Korea and Japan through February 1951. Then, the 4th FIW moved in stages to Korea, with all elements rejoined by May 1951. The 4th FIW was the deadliest interceptor wing of the Korean War. Wing, group, and squadron personnel accounted for 516 air-to-air victories, representing more than half of the enemy aircraft for which USAF credits were awarded. The wing boasted twenty-five aces by the end of the war.

Combat Components.

4th Fighter-Interceptor Group: duration.

77th Squadron, Royal Australian Air Force: attached August 23, 1951–.

Stations.

Johnson AB, Japan, November 28, 1950; Suwon AB, South Korea, May 7, 1951; Kimpo AB, South Korea, August 23, 1951–.

Commanders.

Brig. Gen. George F. Smith, to May 1951; Col. Herman A. Schmid, May 1951; Col. Harrison R. Thyng, November 1, 1951; Col. Charles E. King, October 2, 1952; Col. James K. Johnson, November 11, 1952–.

Campaign Streamers.

CCF Spring Offensive; UN Summer-Fall Offensive; Second Korean Winter; Korea, Summer-Fall 1952; Third Korean Winter; Korea, Summer 1953.

Decorations.

Two Republic of Korea Presidential Unit Citations for periods November 1, 1951–September 30, 1952, and October 1, 1952–March 31, 1953.

4th Fighter-Interceptor Group

A portion of the 4th FIG entered combat with F–86 Sabres from Taegu AB, South Korea, between December 15, 1950, and January 2, 1951. Another group detachment operated from Taegu, January 17–February 1. The entire group began operations in March 1951 from Suwon AB, South Korea. The 4th FIG's pilots primarily conducted counterair patrols, destroying enemy aircraft whenever possible. During April 1952, they confronted 540 MiG–15s and destroyed twenty. Besides combat air patrol and bomber escort missions, the group's Sabres attacked targets spread across the northwestern Korean landscape, from airfields at Sunuiju and Uiju on the Yalu to marshaling yards farther south at Kunu-ri. Its pilots also flew armed reconnaissance sorties and provided close support for ground forces.

Combat Components.

334th Fighter-Interceptor Squadron: duration, except detached May 1–June 26, 1951.

335th Fighter-Interceptor Squadron: duration, except detached September 20–November 3, 1951.

336th Fighter-Interceptor Squadron: duration, except detached June 27–September 19, 1951.

Stations.

Johnson AB, Japan, December 13, 1950; Suwon AB, South Korea, March 30, 1951; Kimpo AB, South Korea, August 23, 1951–.

Commanders.
Col. John C. Meyer, to May 8, 1951; Lt. Col. Glenn T. Eagleston, May 8, 1951; Lt. Col. Bruce W. Hinton, July 1, 1951 (acting); Lt. Col. Glenn T. Eagleston, July 10, 1951; Col. Benjamin S. Preston, Jr., July 26, 1951; Col. Walker M. Mahurin, March 18, 1952; Lt. Col. Ralph G. Kuhn, May 14, 1952; Col. Royal N. Baker, June 1, 1952; Col. Thomas D. DeJarnette, March 18, 1953–.

Medal of Honor Recipient.
Maj. George A. Davis, Jr. (334th FIS), for actions on February 10, 1952.

Campaign Streamers.
CCF Intervention; First UN Counteroffensive; CCF Spring Offensive; UN Summer-Fall Offensive; Second Korean Winter; Korea, Summer-Fall 1952; Third Korean Winter; Korea, Summer 1953.

Decorations.
Two Distinguished Unit Citations for actions in Korea during periods April 22–July 8, 1951, and July 9–November 27, 1951.
Two Republic of Korea Presidential Unit Citations for periods November 1, 1951–September 30, 1952, and October 1, 1952–March 31, 1953.

35th Fighter-Interceptor Group and Wing

Azure, a dexter cubit arm palewise Or grasping a dagger with point to base Gules, all within a diminished bordure of the second. Motto: ATTACK TO DEFEND. Approved for the 35th Group on March 24, 1941, and for the 35th Wing on December 16, 1953.

35th Fighter-Interceptor Wing

At the outbreak of the Korean War, the 35th FIW was flying F–80s on air defense missions from Yokota AB, Japan. Less its group and two squadrons detached for combat in Korea, the wing continued its air defense mission until December 1. It then moved without personnel and equipment (on paper) to Yonpo, North Korea, assuming the resources of the inactivated 6150th Tactical Support Wing. Almost immediately the 35th FIW moved again to Pusan AB, South Korea. On May 25, 1951, it moved without personnel and equipment to Johnson AB, Japan, to resume an air defense mission.

Combat Components.
35th Fighter-Interceptor Group: duration, except detached *c.* July 9–December 1, 1950, and May 7–24, 1951.
77th Squadron, Royal Australian Air Force: attached December 1, 1950–April 6, 1951.

339th Fighter–All Weather (later, 339th Fighter-Interceptor) Squadron: attached until December 1, 1950, and then May 25, 1951–.

Stations.

Yonpo, North Korea, December 1, 1950; Pusan AB, South Korea, *c.* December 7, 1950–May 25, 1951.

Commanders.

Col. Frederic C. Gray, December 1, 1950; Col. Brooks A. Lawhon, February 18, 1951–May 25, 1951.

Campaign Streamers.

CCF Intervention; First UN Counteroffensive; CCF Spring Offensive.

Decoration.

Republic of Korea Presidential Unit Citation for period September 7, 1950–February 7, 1951.

35th Fighter-Interceptor Group

In July 1950, the 35th FIG commenced combat from a base in southwestern Japan. It quickly converted from F–80s back to the rugged and longer-range F–51 Mustangs it had given up only a short time before. Group headquarters and the 40th FIS moved to Pohang AB on South Korea's eastern coast in mid-July, and the 39th Squadron followed on August 10. The precarious ground situation in Korea forced the 35th Group to return to Japan only days later, where it remained until early October. Attached to the 6131st Tactical Support Wing from August 1, then to the 6150th Tactical Support Wing from September 6, it supported UN ground forces moving north of the 38th parallel. The 35th FIG focused its attacks on fuel dumps, motorized transport, and enemy troop concentrations until it moved in mid-November to a forward airstrip at Yonpo near the North Korean port city of Hungnam to provide close air support to the U.S. Army X Corps. When Communist Chinese forces surrounded the 1st U.S. Marine Division at the Changjin Reservoir, the group provided close air support to the marines. Relocating to Pusan AB, South Korea in early December 1950, it continued supporting UN ground forces, eventually staging out of Suwon in March 1951 and Seoul Airport in April. The 35th FIG was attached to the 18th FBW, May 7–24, then rejoined its parent wing in Japan, leaving the 39th FIS behind, first with the 18th FBW and then the 51st FIW.

Combat Components.

39th Fighter-Interceptor Squadron: to May 7, 1951.

40th Fighter-Interceptor Squadron: duration.

Stations.

Yokota AB, Japan, to July 8, 1950; Ashiya AB, Japan, July 8, 1950; Pohang, South Korea, July 14, 1950; Tsuiki AB, Japan, August 13, 1950; Pohang, South Korea, October 3, 1950; Yonpo, North Korea, November 18, 1950; Pusan AB, South Korea, *c.* December 3, 1950–May 25, 1951.

Commanders.

Lt. Col. Jack D. Dale, Jr., to February 22, 1951; Col. William P. McBride, February 22–May 1951.

Campaign Streamers.
UN Defensive; UN Offensive; CCF Intervention; First UN Counteroffensive; CCF Spring Offensive.

Decoration.
Republic of Korea Presidential Unit Citation for period September 7, 1950–February 7, 1951.

51st Fighter-Interceptor Group and Wing

Per fess nebuly abased Azure and Or, issuing from partition line a demi-pegasus Argent with a machine gun in each wing bendwise Sable, gunfire proper. Motto: DEFTLY AND SWIFTLY. Approved for 51st Group on February 5, 1942. Not formally approved for the 51st Wing until 1956.

51st Fighter-Interceptor Wing

In September 1950, the 51st FIW moved from Okinawa to Japan and converted to F–80 Shooting Stars. Its pilots flew combat patrols, close air support, and armed reconnaissance missions in support of UN ground forces in Korea. The wing moved to South Korea in October only to return to Japan in December, leaving combat elements behind. In May 1951, the 51st FIW moved to Suwon AB, southwest of Seoul, but retained maintenance and supply elements at Tsuiki AB, Japan, to provide rear-echelon support. Transitioning in late 1951 to the F–86 Sabres, the wing assumed an air superiority mission for the rest of the war.

Combat Component.
51st Fighter-Interceptor Group: duration, except detached September 26–October 12, 1950.

Stations.
Itazuke AB, Japan, September 22, 1950; Kimpo AB, South Korea, October 10, 1950; Itazuke AB, Japan, December 10, 1950; Tsuiki AB, Japan, January 15, 1951 (operated detachment of wing elements at Suwon from May 1951); Suwon AB, South Korea, October 1, 1951–.

Commanders.
Col. John W. Weltman, to April 24, 1951; Col. Oliver G. Cellini, April 24, 1951; Col. William P. Litton, c. November 1, 1951; Col. George R. Stanley (interim), November 2, 1951; Col. Francis S. Gabreski, November 6, 1951; Col. John W. Mitchell, June 13, 1952; Col. William C. Clark, May 31, 1953–.

Campaign Streamers.
UN Offensive; CCF Intervention; First UN Counteroffensive; CCF Spring

Offensive; UN Summer-Fall Offensive; Second Korean Winter; Korea, Summer-Fall 1952; Third Korean Winter; Korea, Summer 1953.

Decorations.

Two Republic of Korea Presidential Unit Citations for periods September 20, 1950–June 30, 1951, and July 1, 1951–March 31, 1953.

51st Fighter-Interceptor Group

In September 1950, the 51st FIG and its 16th and 25th Squadrons moved to Japan under operational control of the 8th FBW. Within hours of arrival, group pilots began flying F–80s on combat air patrol, armed reconnaissance, and close air support missions over Korea. The 51st FIG moved to Kimpo AB, located just south of Seoul, in October. In December, it flew 763 sorties, including close air support for the 2d Infantry Division cut off by the enemy in the vicinity of Kunu-ri. The 51st FIG helped protect the division's flanks and destroyed enemy roadblocks halting southward movement. In early January 1951, it rejoined its parent wing in Japan but continued to fly missions over Korea, staging first through Taegu and then through Suwon AB. Returning to Korea in late July, the 51st FIG supported ground forces, and its pilots flew patrol, escort, interdiction, and armed reconnaissance missions. In September and October, the group devoted its major combat effort against railroads and other main supply routes in North Korea. After the 51st FIG transitioned to F–86 Sabres in November–December, its primary mission became air superiority.

Combat Components.

16th Fighter-Interceptor Squadron: duration.

25th Fighter-Interceptor Squadron: duration.

39th Fighter-Interceptor Squadron: attached June 1, 1952–.

68th Fighter–All Weather Squadron: attached September 25–October 9, 1950.

80th Fighter-Bomber Squadron: attached September 25–December 20, 1950.

Stations.

Itazuke AB, Japan, September 22, 1950; Kimpo AB, South Korea, October 24, 1950; Itazuke AB, Japan, January 3, 1951; Tsuiki AB, Japan, January 22, 1951; Suwon AB, South Korea, July 31, 1951–.

Commanders.

Col. Oliver G. Cellini, to November 7, 1950; Lt. Col. Irwin H. Dregne, November 7, 1950; Col. Oliver G. Cellini, December 16, 1950; Col. Irwin H. Dregne, April 24, 1951; Lt. Col. John M. Thacker, July 21, 1951; Lt. Col. George L. Jones, November 13, 1951; Lt. Col. William M. Shelton, c. March 17, 1952; Lt. Col. Albert S. Kelly, June 1952; Col. Robert P. Baldwin, January 1953–.

Campaign Streamers.

UN Offensive; CCF Intervention; First UN Counteroffensive; CCF Spring Offensive; UN Summer-Fall Offensive; Second Korean Winter; Korea, Summer-Fall 1952; Third Korean Winter; Korea, Summer 1953.

Decorations.

Distinguished Unit Citation for actions covering November 28, 1951–April 30, 1952.

Two Republic of Korea Presidential Unit Citations for periods September [22], 1950–June 30, 1951, and July 1, 1951–March 31, 1953.

319th Fighter-Interceptor Squadron

Over and through a light blue disc, a stylized brown and white falcon, beak and feet yellow, grasping a red aerial bomb in claws and carrying a caricatured black cat, wearing an orange aviator's helmet and white goggles, firing a "tommy" gun proper; all diving to base with white speed lines trailing. Approved on February 5, 1943.

319th Fighter-Interceptor Squadron

In December 1951, Fifth Air Force determined a need for additional nighttime all-weather air interceptors in the Seoul area. In response, the USAF provided the F–94-equipped 319th FIS, which moved from Moses Lake AFB, Washington, to Suwon AB in February and early March 1952. Until November, Fifth Air Force restricted the use of the Starfires to local air defense in order to prevent the possible compromise of its airborne intercept radar equipment in a loss over enemy-held territory. From November until the end of the conflict, the 319th used F–94s to maintain fighter screens between the Yalu and Chongchon Rivers, helping to protect B–29s from enemy interceptors.

Station.

Suwon AB, South Korea, March 10, 1952–.

Campaign Streamers.

Second Korean Winter; Korea, Summer-Fall 1952; Third Korean Winter; Korea, Summer 1953.

Decorations.

Distinguished Unit Citation for actions December 1, 1952–April 30, 1953.

Republic of Korea Presidential Unit Citation for period March 23–July 27, 1953.

Light Bombardment

3d Bombardment Group and Wing

Party per bend Vert and Sable a bend fimbriated Or in sinister Chief a prickly pear cactus of the like, all within a bordure Argent semi of nineteen crosses patee Black and fimbriated yellow. Motto: NON SOLUM ARMIS—Not by Arms Alone. Approved for 3d Group on January 17, 1922, and for 3d Wing on December 22, 1952.

3d Bombardment Wing, Light

On the first day of the war, the 3d BW's tactical units flew B–26s from Iwakuni AB, Japan, on combat missions in Korea. On July 20, 1950, the group was detached, and the wing assumed a supporting role at Yokota AB, Japan, until December 1. It then regained control of its combat units at Iwakuni AB and began night intruder missions to Korea. The 3d BW moved to South Korea in August 1951 and attacked main supply routes in western North Korea until the war's end. In the summer and autumn of 1952, the wing devised a "hunter–killer" B–26 tactic for nighttime interdiction of transportation targets.

Combat Component.

3d Bombardment Group: duration, except detached July 20–November 30, 1950.

Stations.

Johnson AB, Japan, to August 14, 1950; Yokota AB, Japan, August 14, 1950; Iwakuni, AB, Japan December 1, 1950; Kunsan AB, South Korea, August 22, 1951–.

Commanders.

Col. Thomas B. Hall, *c.* June–*c.* July 1950; Col. Strother B. Hardwick, Jr., *c.* July 1950; Col. Virgil L. Zoller, August 14, 1950; Col. Donald L. Clark, August 23, 1950; Col. Virgil L. Zoller, December 1, 1950; Col. Nils O. Ohman, July 24, 1951; Col. Marshall R. Gray, March 4, 1952; Col. Eugene B. LeBailly, August 14, 1952–.

Campaign Streamers.

UN Defensive; CCF Intervention; First UN Counteroffensive; CCF Spring Offensive; UN Summer-Fall Offensive; Second Korean Winter; Korea, Summer-Fall 1952; Third Korean Winter; Korea, Summer 1953.

Decoration.

Republic of Korea Presidential Unit Citation for period June 27–July 31, 1950.

3d Bombardment Group, Light

The 3d BG conducted its first combat missions in Korea on June 27, 1950. Its B–26 pilots flew reconnaissance sorties and protected allied shipping in Korean waters. The next day, the group attacked rail and road targets at Munsan. A day later, the B–26s attacked Pyongyang Airfield. On July 1, the group and its squadrons moved with a forward echelon of the wing to Iwakuni AB, Japan, to be closer to Korea. Fifth Air Force exercised direct operational control of the group from July 20, 1950, later attaching it to the 6133d Bomb (later, Tactical Support) Wing. After September, the 3d BG flew mostly at night against airfields, vehicles, and railways. Hindered by a lack of light over the target areas, the group's night intruders experimented with parachute-dropped flares, wing-mounted naval searchlights, and C–47 "Lightning Bugs." The "bugs," flown by the attached 731st BS, dropped flares from low altitudes, illuminating target areas. But B–26s soon replaced the C–47s, which flew too slowly to accompany the intruders to the target area. The 3d BG moved to Korea in August 1951 to continue combat missions, receiving three Distinguished Unit Citations before the armistice in July 1953.

Combat Components.

8th Bombardment Squadron: duration.

13th Bombardment Squadron: duration.

90th Bombardment Squadron: June 25, 1951–.

731st Bombardment Squadron: attached November 1950–June 25, 1951.

Stations.

Johnson AB, Japan, to July 1, 1950; Iwakuni AB, Japan, July 1, 1950; Kunsan AB, South Korea, August 22, 1951–.

Commanders.

Col. Donald L. Clark, to August 5, 1950; Lt. Col. Leland A. Walker, Jr., August 5, 1950; Col. Henry G. Brady, Jr., October 17, 1950; Col. Chester H. Morgan, January 4, 1952; Col. William G. Moore, Jr., January 17, 1952; Col. Sherman R. Beaty, by December 1952; Col. John G. Napier, April 1, 1953; Col. Straughan D. Kelsey, July 22, 1953–.

Medal of Honor Recipient.

Capt. John S. Walmsley, Jr. (8th BS), for actions on September 14, 1951.

Campaign Streamers.

UN Defensive; UN Offensive; CCF Intervention; First UN Counteroffensive; CCF Spring Offensive; UN Summer-Fall Offensive 1952; Second Korean Winter; Korea, Summer-Fall 1952; Third Korean Winter; Korea, Summer 1953.

Decorations.

Three Presidential Unit Citations for actions June 27–July 31, 1950; April 22–July 8, 1951; and May 1–July 27, 1953.

Republic of Korea Presidential Unit Citation for period June 27–July 31, 1950.

17th Bombardment Group and Wing

Or, seven crosses patee in pale Sable. Motto: TOUJOURS AU DANGER—Ever into Danger. Approved for 17th Group on November 2, 1937, and for 17th Wing on May 27, 1952.

17th Bombardment Wing, Light

The 17th BW activated in South Korea on May 10, 1952, replacing the Reserve 452d BW. Assigned to Fifth Air Force, it immediately began combat operations, conducting night intruder and light bombardment missions against enemy supply centers, communications, and transportation; interdicting North Korean railroads; flying armed reconnaissance; and providing close air support for ground forces until July 27, 1953.

Combat Component.
17th Bombardment Group: May 10, 1952–.

Station.
Pusan East AB, South Korea, May 10, 1952–.

Commanders.
Col. Albert W. Fletcher, May 10, 1952; Col. Glen C. Nye, June 3, 1952; Col. William C. Lindley, Jr., October 7, 1952; Col. Clinton C. Wasem, October 10, 1952–.

Campaign Streamers.
Korea, Summer-Fall 1952; Third Korean Winter; Korea, Summer 1953.

Decoration.
Republic of Korea Presidential Unit Citation for the period May 24, 1952–March 31, 1953.

17th Bombardment Group, Light

The 17th BG's B–26 light bombers saw initial night action against enemy communication centers, railroads, vehicles, bridges, gun emplacements, and troop concentrations. In 1953, the group engaged in interdiction operations designed to achieve the greatest destruction of enemy rail rolling stock, facilities, and supplies. In early February, equipped with glass-nose B–26s, it adopted new tactics for armed reconnaissance missions against railroads, locomotives, and boxcars. The 17th BG participated in Operation Spring Thaw in March 1953 against roads, and in April it repeatedly attacked the southbound route originating at Yangdok along the eastern coast of North Korea. By then, it was flying about a third of its sorties in close air support of ground troops. The 17th BG claimed the last enemy vehicle destroyed in the war.

Combat Components.
34th Bombardment Squadron: May 10, 1952–.
37th Bombardment Squadron: May 10, 1952–.
95th Bombardment Squadron: May 10, 1952–.
Stations.
Pusan East, South Korea, May 10, 1952; Pusan West, South Korea, October 1, 1952; Pusan East, South Korea, December 20, 1952–.
Commanders.
Col. James D. Kemp, May 10, 1952; Col. William C. Lindley, Jr., July 11, 1952; Col. Robert E. Keating, February 14, 1953; Col. Gordon D. Timmons, April 8, 1953–.
Campaign Streamers.
Korea, Summer-Fall 1952; Third Korean Winter; Korea, Summer 1953.
Decorations.
Distinguished Unit Citation for actions December 1, 1952–April 30, 1953.
Republic of Korea Presidential Unit Citation for the period May 24, 1952–March 31, 1953.

452d Bombardment Group and Wing

Azure, fimbriated Or, a bomb Gules, point downward superimposed on lightning flashes Or, shaded Gules, in saltire. Motto: LABOR AD FUTURUM—Work for the Future. Approved for 452d Wing and assigned groups on October 11, 1951.

452d Bombardment Wing, Light

The 452d BW, a Reserve wing ordered to active service in August 1950, moved from California to Japan during October–November. Arriving at Itazuke AB on October 25, the wing's air echelon began B–26 combat operations over Korea two days later. Its ground echelon arrived by ship in mid-November. The wing, under Fifth Air Force control, was briefly attached to the 8th FBW at Itazuke AB and to 314th Air Division while at Miho AB, Japan. The 452d BW inactivated on May 10, 1952 and returned to Reserve status.
Combat Component.
452d Bombardment Group: to May 10, 1952.
Stations.
Itazuke AB, Japan, October 25, 1950; Miho AB, Japan, December 12, 1950; Pusan East AB, South Korea, May 23, 1951–May 10, 1952.

Commanders.

Brig. Gen. Luther W. Sweetser, Jr., to May 12, 1951; Col. Brooks A. Lawhon, May 12, 1951; Col. Reginald J. Clizbe, by August 20, 1951; Col. Albert W. Fletcher, February 10–May 10, 1952.

Campaign Streamers.

UN Offensive; CCF Intervention; First UN Counteroffensive; CCF Spring Offensive; UN Summer-Fall Offensive; Second Korean Winter; Korea, Summer-Fall 1952.

Decoration.

Republic of Korea Presidential Unit Citation for period October 27, 1950–October 27, 1951.

452d Bombardment Group, Light

On October 27, 1950, the 452d BG with its B–26s entered combat against communist forces, flying medium-level armed reconnaissance, interdiction bombing, and close air support sorties. The group bombed and strafed buildings, tunnels, rail lines, switching centers, bridges, vehicles, supply dumps, and airfields. In one of its most important missions, the 452d BG supported the 187th Airborne Infantry Regiment's mass parachute drop over North Korean lines at Munsan-ni on March 23, 1951. Leading the troop carrier aircraft over the target area, the group dropped 500-pound bombs, fired rockets, and strafed the CCF front line. After the enemy launched its spring 1951 offensive, it added night missions, then it converted in early June solely to such operations until its inactivation on May 10, 1952.

Combat Components.

728th Bombardment Squadron: to May 10, 1952.
729th Bombardment Squadron: to May 10, 1952.
730th Bombardment Squadron: to May 10, 1952.
731st Bombardment Squadron: to November 1950.

Stations.

Itazuke AB, Japan, October 27, 1950; Miho AB, Japan, *c.* December 10, 1950; Pusan East AB, South Korea, May 17, 1951–May 10, 1952.

Commanders.

Col. Charles W. Howe, to May 17, 1951; Col. Frank L. Wood, Jr., May 17, 1951; Lt. Col. John A. Herrington, June 1951; Lt. Col. Harry C. Mailey, *c.* December 1951; Col. James D. Kemp, March 28–May 10, 1952.

Campaign Streamers.

UN Offensive; CCF Intervention; First UN Counteroffensive; CCF Spring Offensive; UN Summer-Fall Offensive; Second Korean Winter; Korea, Summer-Fall 1952.

Decorations.

Two Distinguished Unit Citations for actions July 9–November 27, 1951, and November 28, 1951–April 30, 1952.

Republic of Korea Presidential Unit Citation for period October 27, 1950–October 27, 1951.

Medium Bombardment

19th Bombardment Group and Wing

Azure, within the square of the constellation of Pegasus, a winged sword, point to base, all Or. Motto: IN ALIS VINCIMUS—On Wings We Conquer. Approved for the 19th Group on October 19, 1936, and for the 19th Wing on May 9, 1952.

19th Bombardment Group, Medium

Immediately after the communist invasion of South Korea, the 19th BG moved from Guam to Okinawa. Initially under the operational control of Twentieth Air Force, after July 8, 1950, it was attached to FEAF Bomber Command (Provisional). The first B–29 unit in the war, the group on June 28 attacked North Korean storage tanks, marshaling yards, and armor. In the first two months, it flew more than 600 sorties, supporting UN ground forces by bombing enemy troops, vehicles, and such communications points as the Han River bridges. In the north, its targets included an oil refinery and port facilities at Wonsan, a railroad bridge at Pyongyang, and an airfield at Yonpo. After UN ground forces pushed the communists out of South Korea, the 19th BG turned to strategic objectives in North Korea, including industrial and hydroelectric facilities. It also continued to attack bridges, marshaling yards, supply centers, artillery and troop positions, barracks, port facilities, and airfields. It inactivated on June 1, 1953.

Combat Components.
28th Bombardment Squadron: to June 1, 1953.
30th Bombardment Squadron: to June 1, 1953.
93d Bombardment Squadron: to June 1, 1953.

Stations.
Andersen AFB, Guam, to July 5, 1950; Kadena AB, Okinawa, July 5, 1950–
June 1, 1953.

Commanders.
Col. Theodore Q. Graff, to September 26, 1950; Col. Payne Jennings, Jr.,
September 26, 1950; Col. Donald O. Tower, March 29, 1951; Col. Adam K.
Breckenridge, July 26, 1951; Col. Julian M. Bleyer, February 6, 1952; Col.
Willard W. Smith, July 8, 1952; Col. Harvey C. Dorney, December 24,
1952– June 1, 1953.

Campaign Streamers.
UN Defensive; UN Offensive; CCF Intervention; First UN Counteroffensive;

CCF Spring Offensive; UN Summer-Fall Offensive; Second Korean Winter; Korea, Summer-Fall 1952; Third Korean Winter; Korea, Summer 1953.

Decorations.

Distinguished Unit Citation for actions June 28–September 15, 1950.

Republic of Korea Presidential Unit Citation for period July 7, 1950–[June 1] 1953.

19th Bombardment Wing, Medium

On June 1, 1953, the 19th BW moved on paper from Andersen AB, Guam, to Okinawa, absorbing the personnel and equipment of the 19th BG. Until the end of the war, the wing exercised control over the tactical squadrons, which maintained the B–29 interdiction program and provided some close air support for UN ground forces. In the course of the war, the 19th Group and 19th Wing flew almost 650 combat missions.

Combat Components.

28th Bombardment Squadron: June 1, 1953–.

30th Bombardment Squadron: June 1, 1953–.

93d Bombardment Squadron: June 1, 1953–.

Station.

Kadena AB, Okinawa, June 1, 1953–.

Commander.

Col. Harvey C. Dorney, June 1, 1953–.

Campaign Streamer.

Korea, Summer 1953.

Decoration.

Republic of Korea Presidential Unit Citation for period [June 1, 1953]–July 27, 1953.

22d Bombardment Group

Azure, a cougar's left gamb erased palewise claws to base Or armed Gules. Motto: DUCEMUS—We Lead. Approved on June 19, 1941.

22d Bombardment Group, Medium

Detached from the 22d BW, the 22d BG deployed its B–29s in early July 1950 from March AFB, California, to Okinawa, where it came under control of FEAF Bomber Command (Provisional). On July 13, the group flew its first mission, against the marshaling yards and oil refinery at Wonsan, North Korea. By October 21, it had amassed 57 missions against the enemy, attacking bridges, factories, industrial targets, troop concentrations, airfields, marshaling yards, communications centers, and port facilities. During four months of combat, the 22d BG flew 335 sorties with only 14 aborts and dropped over 6,500 tons of bombs. It redeployed to the United States in late October and November 1950.

Combat Components.
2d Bombardment Squadron: duration.
19th Bombardment Squadron: duration.
33d Bombardment Squadron: duration.

Station.
Kadena AB, Okinawa, early July–October 28, 1950.

Commander.
Col. James V. Edmundson, duration.

Campaign Streamers.
UN Defensive; UN Offensive.

Decorations.
None.

92d Bombardment Group

Azure, a pterodactyl (pteranodon) volant, in bend Or, langued Gules, eyed Vert. Motto: HIGHER, STRONGER, FASTER. Approved on March 9, 1943.

92d Bombardment Group, Medium

In early July 1950, 92d BG B–29s arrived from the United States at Yokota AB, Japan. By the time the entire group completed its deployment on July 13, its aircraft had already flown a leaflet mission to Seoul and a combat mission against the Wonsan marshaling yards in North Korea. Under control of FEAF Bomber Command (Provisional) until October 20, the 92d bombed factories, refineries, iron works, hydroelectric plants, airfields, bridges, tunnels, troop concentrations, barracks, marshaling yards, road junctions, rail lines, supply dumps, docks, vehicles, and other strategic and interdiction targets. The 92d BG returned to Spokane AFB, Washington, in late October into November 1950.

Combat Components.
325th Bombardment Squadron: duration.
326th Bombardment Squadron: duration.
327th Bombardment Squadron: duration.

Station.
Yokota AB, Japan, mid-July–October 29, 1950.
Commander.
Col. Claude E. Putnam, Jr., duration.
Campaign Streamers.
UN Defensive; UN Offensive.
Decorations.
None.

98th Bombardment Group and Wing

Azure, a bend indented between a dexter mailed hand couped at the wrist, in bend, grasping a drop bomb and an olive wreath, all Or. Motto: FORCE FOR FREEDOM. Approved for 98th Group on July 29, 1942. Not formally approved for the 98th Wing until 1956.

98th Bombardment Group, Medium

The first B–29s and crews of the 98th BG, detached from the 98th BW in Spokane AFB, Washington, arrived at Yokota AB, Japan, on August 5, 1950. Two days later, they flew against marshaling yards at Pyongyang, North Korea. The 98th BG engaged primarily in interdiction of enemy communications centers and also supported UN ground forces. Interdiction targets included marshaling yards, oil centers, rail facilities, bridges, roads, troop concentrations, airfields, and military installations. Although not formally inactivated until June 1952, group headquarters became an unmanned unit on April 1, 1951, when control of tactical operations passed to the 98th BW.
Combat Components.
343d Bombardment Squadron: to April 1, 1951.
344th Bombardment Squadron: to April 1, 1951.
345th Bombardment Squadron: to April 1, 1951.
Station.
Yokota AB, Japan, *c.* August 5, 1950–June 16, 1952.
Commander.
Col. Richard H. Carmichael, to April 1, 1951.
Campaign Streamers.
UN Defensive; UN Offensive; CCF Intervention; First UN Counteroffensive.
Decoration.
Republic of Korea Presidential Unit Citation for the period August 7, 1950–
    March 31, 1951.

98th Bombardment Wing, Medium

On April 1, 1951, the 98th BW deployed "on paper" without personnel or equipment to Yokota AFB, Japan, where it assumed the tactical role of the 98th BG. Interdiction of enemy communications, support of UN ground forces, and propaganda leaflet drops constituted the B–29 wing's missions. In January 1952, to avoid daylight interception by enemy fighters, the 98th BW began to fly night missions almost exclusively. In the spring, its B–29s attacked railway installations and airfields, and then in the summer, industrial targets. The wing's last bombing mission, flown on July 25, 1953, was followed on the last day of the war with a propaganda-leaflet drop.

Combat Components.

98th Bombardment Group: assigned but not operational, April 1, 1951–June 16, 1952.

343d Bombardment Squadron: attached April 1, 1951–June 15, 1952, assigned June 16, 1952–.

344th Bombardment Squadron: attached April 1, 1951–June 15, 1952, assigned June 16, 1952–.

345th Bombardment Squadron: attached April 1, 1951–June 15, 1952, assigned June 16, 1952–.

Station.

Yokota AB, Japan, April 1, 1951–.

Commanders.

Col. David Wade, April 1, 1951; Col. Edwin F. Harding, Jr., c. September 15, 1951; Col. Lewis A. Curtis, November 1951; Col. Winton R. Close, May 1952; Col. Charles B. Westover, October 26, 1952; Col. Edgar S. Davis, June 17, 1953; Col. George L. Robinson, July 6, 1953–.

Campaign Streamers.

First UN Counteroffensive; CCF Spring Offensive; UN Summer-Fall Offensive; Second Korean Winter; Korea, Summer-Fall 1952; Third Korean Winter; Korea, Summer 1953.

Decorations.

Distinguished Unit Citation for actions December 1, 1952–April 30, 1953.

Republic of Korea Presidential Unit Citation for the period April 1, 1951–July 27, 1953.

307th Bombardment Group and Wing

Azure, a four-petalled dogwood bloom slipped Or.
Approved for the 307th Group on December 21, 1942,
and for the 307th Wing on December 23, 1952.

307th Bombardment Group, Medium

On August 1, 1950, the 307th BG with its B–29s deployed from MacDill AFB, Florida, to Kadena AB, Okinawa. One week later the Superfortresses went into action over Korea. From August through September, they attacked strategic objectives in North Korea, such as the enemy's transportation system and industrial facilities. Following a campaign in November 1950 against bridges over the Yalu River into Manchuria, the B–29s struck interdiction targets including communications and supply centers, and supported UN ground forces by hitting gun emplacements and troop concentrations. Not officially inactivated until June 1952, the 307th Group became an unmanned organization on February 10, 1951, replaced by the 307th BW.

Combat Components.
370th Bombardment Squadron: to February 10, 1951.
371st Bombardment Squadron: to February 10, 1951.
372d Bombardment Squadron: to February 10, 1951.

Station.
Kadena AB, Okinawa, August 8, 1950–June 16, 1952.

Commander.
Col. John A. Hilger, to February 10, 1951.

Campaign Streamers.
UN Defensive; UN Offensive; CCF Intervention; First UN Counteroffensive.

Decoration.
Republic of Korea Presidential Unit Citation for period [August] 1950–
[February 9, 1951].

307th Bombardment Wing, Medium

The 307th BW moved without personnel or equipment to Kadena AB, Okinawa, on February 10, 1951, and absorbed the resources of the 307th BG. For the next few months the wing's bombers participated in FEAF's bridge-busting campaign, flying numerous missions against key spans. The 307th BW also helped UN ground forces blunt a communist spring offensive. On May 23, it participated in a tremendous nighttime close air support effort, shredding enemy positions along the entire battlefront with radar-aimed fragmentation bombs. Until the end of the war, it continued attacks against industrial targets, bridges, troop concentrations, airfields, supply dumps, rail yards, enemy frontline positions, and lines of communications. By late 1952, the 307th BW usually flew night short-range navigation missions, with enemy airfields and dams as primary targets. As the truce talks neared conclusion in July 1953, the wing helped spoil an enemy ground offensive, earning a Distinguished Unit Citation. By the end of hostilities, the 307th BW and 307th BG combined had flown over 5,800 combat missions.

Combat Components.

307th Bombardment Group: assigned but not operational, February 10, 1951–June 16, 1952.

370th Bombardment Squadron: attached February 10, 1951–June 15, 1952, assigned June 16, 1952–.

371st Bombardment Squadron: attached February 10, 1951–June 15, 1952, assigned June 16, 1952–.

372d Bombardment Squadron: attached February 10, 1951–June 15, 1952, assigned June 16, 1952–.

Station.

Kadena AB, Okinawa, February 10, 1951–.

Commanders.

Col. John A. Hilger, February 10, 1951; Col. John M. Reynolds, March 15, 1951; Col. William H. Hanson, August 20, 1951; Col. John C. Jennison, Jr., February 4, 1952; Brig. Gen. Raymond L. Winn, May 8, 1952; Col. Charles S. Overstreet, *c.* October 1, 1952; Col. Austin J. Russell, December 29, 1952–.

Campaign Streamers.

First UN Counteroffensive; CCF Spring Offensive; UN Summer-Fall Offensive; Second Korean Winter; Korea, Summer-Fall 1952; Third Korean winter; Korea, Summer 1953.

Decorations.

Distinguished Unit Citation for actions July 11–27, 1953.

Republic of Korea Presidential Unit Citation for period February 10, 1951–July 27, 1953.

Reconnaissance

543d Tactical Support Group

At the outset of the Korean War, the only tactical reconnaissance squadron (TRS) available in the Far East, the 8th TRS began flying RF–80 daylight reconnaissance missions over Korea. A few days before the Inchon landings in September 1950, it provided photography for the U.S. Navy to show high- and low-tide heights of the seawalls and to orient landing crews. Meanwhile, the 162d TRS, flying RB–26s, and the photo-processing 363d Reconnaissance Technical Squadron (RTS) moved from the United States to Japan and began operations in August. Requests for photoreconnaissance were so extensive that in September FEAF activated the 543d Tactical Support Group (TSG) to control the reconnaissance squadrons already engaged and to form a visual reconnaissance squadron. Except for the 45th TRS, the group's headquarters and tactical squadrons moved to Korea in early October. It encountered difficulties in command arrangements, physical separation from the supporting 363d RTS, and other problems. Then, the Chinese intervention required temporary withdrawal to Japan in December of all but advanced echelons. In late December the 45th TRS began operations with T–6s and F–51s. Col. Karl "Pop" Polifka, one of the USAF pioneers in the field of aerial reconnaissance, worked for a wing-level organization to replace the 543d TSG.

Combat Components.

8th Tactical Reconnaissance Squadron, Photographic: September 26, 1950–February 25, 1951.

45th Tactical Reconnaissance Squadron: September 26, 1950–February 25, 1951.

162d Tactical Reconnaissance Squadron, Night Photographic: attached September 26–October 10, 1950, assigned October 10, 1950–February 25, 1951.

6166th Air Weather Reconnaissance Flight: December 25, 1950–January 26, 1951.

Stations.

Itazuke AB, Japan, September 26, 1950; Taegu AB, South Korea, *c.* October 10, 1950; Komaki AB, Japan, January 26–February 25, 1951.

Commanders.

Lt. Col. Bert M. Smiley, September 26, 1950; Lt. Col. Jacob W. Dixon (temporary), October 4, 1950; Col. Bert M. Smiley, October 20, 1950–February 25, 1951.

Campaign Streamers.

UN Defensive (8th and 162d Squadrons only); UN Offensive; CCF Intervention; First UN Counteroffensive.

Decoration.

Republic of Korea Presidential Unit Citation for period [February 10–25, 1951].

67th Tactical Reconnaissance Wing

On a shield per bend sinister, sky proper and Azure between a lightning bolt Gules, fimbriated Sable, in bend sinister, the quarter section of a sun, issuing from the dexter chief, Or, fimbriated Sable, in sinister four stars Argent, one, two, and one, all the shield within a diminutive bordure Sable. Motto: LUX EX TENEBRIS—Light from darkness. Approved on March 20, 1952.

67th Tactical Reconnaissance Wing

Activated on February 25, 1951, the 67th TRW replaced the inactivated 543d TSG. By August, the wing had consolidated its subordinate elements at Kimpo AB. Gradually overcoming difficulties, it soon was providing adequate aerial intelligence for both air and ground units. However, organizational changes could not solve fundamental problems—the lack of suitable aircraft, appropriate photographic equipment, and sufficient numbers of trained personnel. The 67th TRW sought in-theater remedies for these problems, including special classes and on-the-job training; creative experimentation with aircraft, cameras, night lighting, and photographic techniques; and the modification of six Sabres to the RF–86 configuration for reconnaissance work. Other aircraft flown on reconnaissance missions included the RB–26, RF–51, and RF–80. For visual reconnaissance, the 67th TRW relied on T–6s and C–47s for a short time. It also performed weather reconnaissance on a regular basis, using the unarmed WB–26s of the attached 6166th Air Weather Reconnaissance Flight.

Combat Components.
67th Tactical Reconnaissance Group: February 25, 1951–.
6166th Air Weather Reconnaissance Flight: attached February 25, 1951–.

Stations.
Komaki AB, Japan, February 25, 1951; Taegu AB, South Korea, March 21, 1951; Kimpo AB, South Korea, August 20, 1951–.

Commanders.
Col. Karl L. Polifka, February 25, 1951; Col. Bert M. Smiley, July 1, 1951; Col. Vincent Howard, July 4, 1951; Col. Edwin S. Chickering, October 31, 1951; Col. Russell A. Berg, August 13, 1952; Col. Charles F. Knierim, July 1953–.

Campaign Streamers.
First UN Counteroffensive; CCF Spring Offensive; UN Summer-Fall Offensive; Second Korean Winter; Korea, Summer-Fall 1952; Third Korean Winter; Korea, Summer 1953.

Decoration.
Republic of Korea Presidential Unit Citation for period February [25], 1951–March 31, 1953.

67th Tactical Reconnaissance Group

The 67th TRG activated on February 25, 1951, with resources from the inactivated 543d Tactical Support Group. The 12th and 15th TRSs replaced and absorbed the resources of the 162d and 8th Squadrons respectively. On a recurring basis, the group provided photographic coverage of all enemy airfields in Korea, as mandated by the FEAF policy of keeping enemy airfields unserviceable. It also flew large-scale frontline block coverage photography for the Eighth Army and provided surveillance for the interdiction of main enemy rail lines, roads, and bridges. New technology permitted it to reconnoiter targets between fighter-bomber attacks, interpret wet negatives, and flash the results and flak locations to the Joint Operations Center in time to assist missions later in the day. During 1951, the 45th TRS routinely flew armed reconnaissance with RF–51s, leading fighter sweeps and directing fighter-bomber strikes. The 67th TRG earned three Distinguished Unit Citations (DUCs). The first was for the period February–April 1951 when the tactical squadrons provided intensive medium- to low-level surveillance of enemy territory as far north as the Yalu River. In conjunction with these missions, the 45th TRS conducted 1,886 fighter sweep sorties, attacking railways, pack animals, roads, vehicles, bridges, and supply dumps. The second DUC recognized contributions to the UN Summer-Fall Offensive, July–November 1951, with the 12th TRS conducting night operations in RB–26s, and the 15th TRS in RF–80s sharing daytime coverage with the 45th TRS. The aircrews flew around-the-clock photo surveillance of enemy activities and provided artillery and naval gun fire direction. The group earned its third DUC during the war's final campaign. Flying continuous close surveillance of enemy activities, the group provided photographic intelligence, visual reconnaissance, and direction of fighter-bomber sweeps to prevent the enemy an opportunity for a last-minute offensive before implementation of the armistice.

Combat Components.

12th Tactical Reconnaissance Squadron: February 25, 1951–.
15th Tactical Reconnaissance Squadron: February 25, 1951–.
45th Tactical Reconnaissance Squadron: February 25, 1951–.

Stations.

Komaki AB, Japan, February 25, 1951; Taegu AB, South Korea, March 1951; Kimpo AB, South Korea, August 1951–.

Commanders.

Col. Jacob W. Dixon, *c.* February 28, 1951; Lt. Col. Stone, *c.* August 29, 1951; Col. Charles C. Andrews, September 1951; Col. Robert R. Smith, May 1952; Lt. Col. George T. Prior, October 1952; Col. John G. Foster, by December 1952–.

Campaign Streamers.

First UN Counteroffensive; CCF Spring Offensive; UN Summer-Fall Offensive; Second Korean Winter; Korea, Summer-Fall 1952; Third Korean Winter; Korea, Summer 1953.

Decorations.
Three Distinguished Unit Citations for actions of February 25–April 21, 1951,
July 9–November 27, 1951, and May 1–July 27, 1953.
Air Force Outstanding Unit Award for period December 1, 1952–April 30,
1953.
Republic of Korea Presidential Unit Citation for period February [25], 1951–
March 31, 1953.

31st Strategic Resonnaissance Squadron

On a black triangle, one point up, bordered white; a skull and crossbones proper. Approved on September 10, 1934.

31st Strategic Reconnaissance Squadron, Photographic

Under the direct operational control of FEAF and with electronic countermeasures as the primary mission, the 31st Strategic Reconnaissance Squadron (SRS) on June 29, 1950, began flying combat missions to provide FEAF Bomber Command with target and bomb-damage assessment photography. By July 12, it had moved to Japan in order to provide developed pictures as quickly as possible. On October 18, foreshadowing the Chinese intervention, a 31st SRS RB–29 crew observed more than 75 enemy fighters parked at Antung Airfield, across the Yalu River. Effective November 15, the 31st SRS moved on paper to join the 5th Strategic Reconnaissance Wing at Beale AFB, California, to be replaced by the 91st SRS.

Stations.
Kadena AB, Okinawa, to July 11, 1950; Yokota AB, Japan, *c.* July 12, 1950;
Johnson AB, Japan, August 14–November 15, 1950.

Campaign Streamers.
UN Defensive; UN Offensive; CCF Intervention.

Decoration.
Republic of Korea Presidential Unit Citation for period July 27–[November
15, 1950].

91st Strategic Reconnaissance Squadron

A mounted knight in armor chasing a devil. Gray armor, green shield with black patriarchal cross piped with white, yellow plume, brown spear, black horse, red devil with brown fork. Approved on February 12, 1924.

91st Strategic Reconnaissance Squadron, Medium, Photographic

On November 15, 1950, the 91st SRS absorbed the personnel and resources of the 31st Strategic Reconnaissance Squadron in Japan. Using RB–29, RB–45, and RB–50 aircraft, it performed target and bomb-damage assessment photo and visual reconnaissance for FEAF Bomber Command, flew other special photographic missions, and conducted electronic "ferret" reconnaissance to determine frequency, location, and other characteristics of enemy ground radar. The squadron also performed shipping surveillance over the Sea of Japan near the Siberian coast and leaflet drops over North Korea. Beginning in late 1952, rotating aircrews of the Philippine-based 581st Air Resupply and Communications Wing augmented the 91st SRS in flying leaflet missions.

Stations.

Johnson AB, Japan, November 15, 1950; Yokota AB, Japan, December 19, 1950–.

Campaign Streamers.

CCF Intervention; First UN Counteroffensive; CCF Spring Offensive; UN Summer-Fall Offensive; Second Korean Winter; Korea, Summer-Fall 1952; Third Korean Winter; Korea, Summer 1953.

Decorations.

Distinguished Unit Citation for actions May 1–July 27, 1953.

Republic of Korea Presidential Unit Citation for period [November 15] 1950–July 27, 1953.

512th Reconnaissance Squadron

On a white disc, a black skull and crossbones surmounting a black three-bladed propeller, one blade to base, within border formed by red counterclockwise, stylized rotation lines from tips of propeller blades. Approved on January 6, 1944.

512th Reconnaissance Squadron, Very Long Range, Weather

Based in Japan at the beginning of the Korean conflict, the 512th RS, flying RB/WB–29s, performed daily strategic weather reconnaissance missions over the combat zone, conducted shipping surveillance and visual reconnaissance, and accomplished electronic countermeasures reconnaissance until February 20, 1951. In the early days of the conflict, the squadron also dropped leaflets. Initially unarmed, and later only lightly armed with two 50-caliber machine guns in the tail turret, the WB–29s flew daily missions over enemy-held territory. During the period June 27 through December 27, 1950, the squadron flew more than 200 combat missions, making over 5,000 vitally needed weather observations. These missions were exceptionally hazardous because of extremely varying weather conditions and exposure to attack over enemy territory. One of the squadron's WB–29s served as an aerial command post and weather station, giving on-the-spot weather data and directions to incoming bombers on the first B–29 strike (July 13, 1950) against North Korean installations. On this and several later such missions, the WB–29 carried Maj. Gen. Emmett O'Donnell, Jr., USAF, Commander, FEAF Bomber Command. The 512th RS was replaced by the 56th SRS in February 1951.

Stations.
Yokota AB, Japan, to August 11, 1950; Misawa AB, Japan, August 11, 1950–February 20, 1951.

Campaign Streamers.
UN Defensive; UN Offensive; CCF Intervention; First UN Counteroffensive.

Decoration.
Air Force Outstanding Unit Award for period June 27–December 27, 1950.

56th Strategic Reconnaissance Squadron

On a disc black, edged red, three concentric circular lines, bisected by one vertical and one horizontal cross hair, representative of the face of a radar scope yellow; superimposed over all a caricatured buzzard gray, "with a Sherlock Holmes manner," face and vest front white, beak and feet yellow, outline and details black, wearing an aviator's helmet brown; the buzzard, smoking a Calabash pipe brown, from which two puffs of smoke white are emitting, and holding in his right hand a dropsonde instrument; in his left hand a magnifying glass white, through which he examines a caricatured representation of a squall-line yellow, in the lower right of the disc. Approved on September 26, 1952.

56th Strategic Reconnaissance Squadron, Medium, Weather

Activated on February 21, 1951, the 56th SRS absorbed the personnel and resources of the 512th RS. Until early June 1952, the squadron flew almost daily strategic weather reconnaissance missions over the combat zone. Through the end of the conflict, the squadron conducted shipping surveillance and flew two reconnaissance tracks to observe and report weather conditions in the area east of the Asian landmass, between Formosa and USSR's Kamchatka Peninsula.

Stations.
Misawa AB, Japan, February 21, 1951; Yokota AB, Japan, September 14, 1951–.

Campaign Streamers.
First UN Counteroffensive; CCF Spring Offensive; UN Summer-Fall Offensive; Second Korean Winter; Korea, Summer-Fall 1952; Third Korean Winter; Korea, Summer 1953.

Decorations.
None.

Rescue

3d Air Rescue Group

The 3d Rescue (later, Air Rescue) Squadron, following the North Korean invasion, deployed detachments to Korea to perform search and rescue. Initially the squadron's primary mission involved intercepting and escorting distressed aircraft over the land areas of Japan and its adjacent seas. Combat operations and a changing tactical situation expanded the mission to include the rescue of stranded personnel behind enemy lines and aeromedical helicopter evacuation. The 3d ARS was regularly augmented with personnel from the 2d ARS (later redesignated 2d Air Rescue Group) based in the Philippines. The aircraft available at the start of the Korean War forced the 3d ARS to confine air rescue flights to short-range rescue. These included the L–5, a highly maneuverable liaison aircraft used in helicopter escort, supply drops, and medical evacuation from small airfields; Sikorsky H–5 helicopters capable of operating in mountainous and rice-paddy terrain; the obsolescent SB–17, a search-and-rescue version of the Flying Fortress bomber; and the SC–47 transport, which aided in searches and hauled critically needed supplies to outlying units. The squadron soon added, while phasing out the SB–17, the SB–29 and the amphibious SA–16. During the UN assault on Pyongyang in October 1950, it evacuated 47 injured paratroopers from drop zones at Sunchon and Sukchon. In March 1951, the squadron tested the new model H–19 helicopter, which proved invaluable in multiple evacuations and greatly extended the operational range for rotary-wing rescues. A significant innovation in the use of the helicopter was medical evacuation. For critically wounded soldiers at frontline aid stations, helicopter medical evacuations reduced a possibly fatal 10- to 14-hour road trip to a one-hour flight to a rear Mobile Army Surgical Hospital (MASH) unit. In December 1951, H–5s participated in a highly successful experiment by flying wounded soldiers directly from frontline aid stations to a hospital ship off the Korean coast. In November 1952, the 3d elevated to group level, and squadrons replaced the detachments. From June 1950 to the end of hostilities in July 1953, it rescued almost 10,000 UN personnel, almost 1,000 from behind enemy lines, and more than 200 from the water. For numerous commendable and heroic rescues, the 3d ARS/ARG earned three Distinguished Unit Citations.

Combat Components.

Flight A (Johnson AB, Japan): to November 14, 1952.

Flight B (Yokota/Misawa/Yokota/Komaki, Japan): to November 14, 1952.

Flight C (Misawa AB, Japan): to November 14, 1952.

Flight D (Ashiya AB, Japan): to November 14, 1952.

Det F/Det 1 (Seoul/Taegu/Yongdong-po/Seoul, South Korea): *c.* September 24, 1950–March 1, 1953.

36th Air Rescue Squadron: November 14, 1952–.

37th Air Rescue Squadron: November 14, 1952–.

38th Air Rescue Squadron: November 14, 1952–.

39th Air Rescue Squadron: November 14, 1952–.

2157th Air Rescue Squadron: March 1, 1953–.

Station.

Johnson AB, Japan, duration.

Commanders.

Lt. Col. David J. Nolan, to July 25, 1950; Maj. Harvey E. Beedy, July 25, 1950; Maj. Theodore P. Tatum, August 16, 1950; Col. Klair E. Back, August 28, 1950; Lt. Col. Robert B. Keck, June 3, 1953; Col. Tracy J. Peterson, July 15, 1953–.

Campaign Streamers.

UN Defensive; UN Offensive; CCF Intervention; First UN Counteroffensive; CCF Spring Offensive; UN Summer-Fall Offensive; Second Korean Winter; Korea, Summer-Fall 1952; Third Korean Winter; Korea, Summer 1953.

Decorations.

Three Distinguished Unit Citations for actions June 25–December 25, 1950; April 22–July 8, 1951; and May 1–July 27, 1953.

Two Republic of Korea Presidential Unit Citations for the periods June 25, 1950–June 30, 1951, and July 1, 1951–March 31, 1953.

Tactical Control

502d Tactical Control Group

Argent, a disk Sable divided into five concentric rings and eight segments by division lines Vert, in dexter chief on and over the disk an aircraft Gules fimbriated of the first, in base on the disk a radar screen of the like and second mounted on a mountain White and of the third, a lightning flash pointed at both ends Or outlined in Black forming an increscent on and over the edge of the disk. Submitted for approval in February 1953 and approved on August 25, 1953.

502d Tactical Control Group

At the beginning of the Korean War, the USAF's only tactical control group was the 502d at Pope AFB, North Carolina. To meet the emergency in the theater, the Fifth Air Force organized the 6132d Tactical Air Control Squadron (later, Group), which established a full-scale Tactical Air Control Center (TACC) at Taegu, South Korea, on July 23, 1950. Less than three months later, the 502d moved to Korea, and in October 1950 it replaced the 6132d in the mission of directing tactical air operations in Korea. Through its 605th Tactical Control Squadron, the group operated the TACC and worked with the U.S. Army in a Joint Operations Center (JOC). Other squadrons operated tactical air direction centers (TADC), which used stationary and mobile radar and communications equipment to guide aircraft on close air support missions. The group also deployed tactical air control parties (TACP), which accompanied ground units to communicate with USAF strike aircraft. The TACPs followed advancing UN troops into North Korea in October and November 1950, but the Chinese Communist offensive soon overran several of them. The 502d headquarters and the TACC, which operated at Seoul in November and part of December, were forced to return to Taegu at the end of the year. During the spring and summer of 1951, the 502d directed night bombing of enemy targets, including troop concentrations, supply dumps, and motor convoys. As UN ground forces drove the enemy back across the 38th parallel, the group, TACC, and JOC returned to Seoul in June. In October, the 502d set up a communications station a hundred miles behind enemy lines on Cho-do (Cho Island), three miles off the North Korean coast. From this location the detachment guided UN fighters against enemy airplanes in MiG Alley, bombers against strategic targets along the Yalu River, and search-and-rescue aircraft toward survivors who had ditched at sea. On June 6, 1952, the 502d was instrumental in the destruction of nine MiG–15 aircraft through highly effective control procedures to maneuver F–86 Sabres into attack positions. The following month, the 502d guided warplanes in devastating attacks on enemy troop formations, which blunted communist offensives until the Korean truce in July 1953.

Mission Components.

605th Tactical Control Squadron: duration.

606th Aircraft Control and Warning Squadron: duration.

607th Aircraft Control and Warning Squadron: duration.

608th Aircraft Control and Warning Squadron: November 2, 1951–.

6132d Aircraft Control and Warning Squadron: October 9, 1950–November 2, 1951.

1st Shoran Beacon Unit (later, Squadron): attached September 27–December 1, 1950, and September 6, 1952–.

Stations.

6132d: Taegu, South Korea, July 23, 1950; Pohang, South Korea, July 28, 1950; Pusan, South Korea, July 30, 1950; Taegu, South Korea, September 24– October 10, 1950.

502d: Pusan, South Korea, September 24, 1950; Taegu, South Korea, October 3, 1950; Seoul, South Korea, October 11, 1950; Taegu, South Korea, December 20, 1950; Seoul, South Korea, June 15, 1951–.

Commanders.

6132d: Unknown.

502d: Col. William P. McBride, to February 18, 1951; Col. Henry Riera, February 18, 1951; Col. Francis R. Delaney, May 3, 1952; Col. Ernest J. White, Jr., July 25, 1952; Col. Hugh C. Moore, June 15, 1953–.

Campaign Streamers.

6132d: UN Defensive; UN Offensive.

502d: UN Offensive; CCF Intervention; First UN Counteroffensive; CCF Spring Offensive; UN Summer-Fall Offensive; Second Korean Winter; Korea, Summer-Fall 1952; Third Korean Winter; Korea, Summer 1953.

Decorations.

Two Distinguished Unit Citations for actions November 3, 1950–April 21, 1951, and May 1–November 30, 1952.

Three Republic of Korea Presidential Unit Citations for periods September 16, 1950–January 25, 1951; January 25, 1951–March 31, 1953; and October 1, 1952–July 27, 1953.

6147th Tactical Control Group

Azure, a caricatured mosquito, wings bendwise Or, cap, gloves, wing tips, and tail Gules, headphone and tail bandage Argent, earpiece and eyes Sable and of the fourth; in chief three aircraft, one and two bend sinisterwise of the last, all within a diminished bordure of the second. Submitted for approval in early 1953 and approved on September 23, 1953.

6147th Tactical Control Group

The 6147th Tactical Control Group originated at Taejon, South Korea, within the "operations section" of the Joint Operations Center—three pilots and two aircraft testing the airborne forward air controller concept. On July 9, 1950, two airborne controllers flew their first mission in L–17s borrowed from the U.S. Army's 24th Infantry Division. Despite attacks from enemy aircraft, each controlled about ten flights of F–80s. The next day, controllers testing T–6s spotted and directed the destruction of 17 enemy tanks. The following day the small group of controllers left for Taegu to organize as a squadron. The 6147th Tactical Control Squadron, Airborne, activated effective August 1 to provide target-spotting information to tactical aircraft in flight. After the UN landings at Inchon in late September, the squadron (its aircraft nicknamed "Mosquitoes") directed air strikes against retreating enemy troops ahead of the advancing UN lines and operated as the eyes of UN ground forces. Squadron controllers also conducted deep penetrations into enemy country, search and rescue, night direction for B–26s, parachute-drop mission coordination, and artillery adjustment. As the enemy fled, the squadron moved to Kimpo AB, where the pilots were within minutes of their working areas but also within range of enemy snipers on takeoffs and landings. By late October, the squadron had moved to Pyongyang, but in December it retreated to Taegu, where it returned to controlling close air support missions. In January 1951, the 6147th TCS gained a C–47 that provided an airborne radio relay between the JOC and controllers, enabling Mosquitoes to adapt to the changing combat situation. In April 1951, the 6147th elevated to group level and organized three squadrons, two of which provided airborne controllers while the third provided the U.S. Army with ground tactical air control parties. A year later, the group moved to Chunchon, from where it directed interdiction missions. In the closing days of the war, it assisted allied aircraft in crushing a last-minute enemy offensive in the vicinity of the Kumsong River. The 6147th TCG earned three Distinguished Unit Citations during the war.

Combat Components.
942d Forward Air Control Squadron: attached June 20, 1953–.
6148th Tactical Control Squadron: April 25, 1951–.
6149th Tactical Control Squadron: April 25, 1951–.

6150th Tactical Control Squadron: April 25, 1951–June 20, 1953.

Stations.

Taegu AB, South Korea, August 1, 1950; Kimpo AB, South Korea, October 5, 1950; Seoul, South Korea, October 18, 1950; Pyongyang East, North Korea, October 28, 1950; Taegu AB, South Korea, late November 1950; Pyongtaek, South Korea, March 12, 1951; Chunchon, South Korea, April 18, 1952–.

Commanders.

Lt. Col. Merrill M. Carlton, August 1, 1950; Col. Timothy F. O'Keefe, March 28, 1951; Col. John C. Watson, *c.* January 1952; Col. Paul Fojtik, January 10, 1953–.

Campaign Streamers.

UN Defensive; UN Offensive; CCF Intervention; First UN Counteroffensive; CCF Spring Offensive; UN Summer-Fall Offensive; Second Korean Winter; Korea, Summer-Fall 1952; Third Korean Winter; Korea, Summer 1953.

Decorations.

Three Distinguished Unit Citations for actions July 9–November 25, 1950; July 9–November 27, 1951; and December 1, 1952–April 30, 1953.

Two Republic of Korea Presidential Unit Citations for the periods July 9–November 25, 1950, and October 1, 1952–April 30, 1953.

Tactical Support (Temporary)

In July 1950 Allied planners did not foresee that the Korean campaign would be of long duration. Consequently, the Fifth Air Force modified its command structure only to meet immediate needs. When the time came to move tactical air units to Korean airfields, Fifth Air Force did not deploy its permanent wings because they were heavily committed to the air defense of Japan. Instead, it utilized temporary air base squadrons and air base units to support tactical units in Korea. By August, the situation called for larger organizations with greater allotments of personnel and equipment, and Fifth Air Force set up five temporary tactical support wings to support the combat groups. Formed to assist in the projection of force to Korea, these temporary wings provided facilities, administration, services, and operational control for assigned and attached combat units. The task was formidable, for the installations the wings controlled were usually "bare-base" operations with no amenities and only marginally serviceable airfields. Logistically, poor roads and rail lines, limited port facilities, and overextended airlift hampered the wings. Organizationally, they were without regular status, such as authorization for personnel and equipment or for promotions. Even with these handicaps and hardships, the tactical support wings performed valiantly. They worked diligently to make combat airfields operable and to provide the support and control required by the combat units. They struggled to keep pace with the dynamically changing battle lines, opening new bases and forward operating locations as needed. Their success bought time for the Fifth Air Force to reorganize, and on December 1, 1950, regular wings replaced them.

6002d Tactical Support Wing

This wing organized effective August 1, 1950, at Taegu AB, to support the 18th Fighter-Bomber Group. Forced to withdraw with its tactical units to Ashi-ya AB, Japan, on August 8, it returned to Korea on September 5 and advanced to Pyongyang on November 22. It retreated to Suwon AB on November 30, where it was replaced on December 1, 1950, by the 18th Fighter-Bomber Wing.
Commander.
Col. Curtis R. Low, August 1–December 1, 1950.

6131st Tactical Support Wing

Organized effective August 8, 1950, at Pohang, to support the 8th Fighter-Bomber Group, the wing moved to Suwon on October 7 and to Kimpo on October 28. On November 25, it advanced to Pyongyang, where it was replaced by the 8th Fighter-Bomber Wing effective December 1, 1950.
Commanders.
Col. Robert W. Whitty, August 8, 1950; Col. Charles W. Stark, *c.* August 16–December 1, 1950.

6133d Tactical Support Wing

This wing organized August 12, 1950, at Iwakuni AB, Japan, to support the 3d Bombardment Group. It was replaced by the 3d Bombardment Wing on December 1.
Commander.
Col. Virgil L. Zoller, August–December 1, 1950.

6149th Tactical Support Wing

Organized September 5, 1950, at Taegu AB to support the 49th Fighter-Bomber Group, this wing was replaced by the 49th Fighter-Bomber Wing effective December 1.
Commander.
Col. Aaron W. Tyer, September 5–December 1, 1950.

6150th Tactical Support Wing

Organized September 5, 1950, at Tsuiki AB, Japan, to support the 35th Fighter-Interceptor Group, the wing moved to Pohang on October 5 and to Yonpo on November 27, where it was replaced by the 35th Fighter-Interceptor Wing on December 1.

Commander.
Col. Frederic C. Gray, Jr., September 5–December 1, 1950.

Troop Carrier

1st Troop Carrier Group (Provisional)

1st TCG was organized at Ashiya AB, Japan, on August 26, 1950, under the operational control of FEAF through the 1st Troop Carrier Task Force (Provisional). The 1st TCG and its provisional squadrons were based at Tachikawa and supported by the 374th TCW. Personnel from units of Thirteenth and Twentieth Air Forces and the Far East Materiel Command manned the 1st TCG. Using C–46s and briefly C–47s, the group began airlifting freight and passengers between Japan and Korea on September 2, 1950. The group transported a U.S. Marine Corps unit to Pyongyang on November 25 and 26, and then flew emergency air evacuations from Sinanju and other forward bases as the Chinese advanced. Leaving Kimpo AB on January 4, the group inactivated effective January 25, with many of its personnel transferring to the 86th TCS of the 437th TCG. In its five months of operation, the group carried more than 28,000 passengers, 7,000 air evacuees, and nearly 12,000 tons of cargo.

Combat Components.
46th Troop Carrier Squadron (P): August 26–October 6, 1950.
47th Troop Carrier Squadron (P): August 26, 1950–January 25, 1951.
48th Troop Carrier Squadron (P): August 26, 1950–January 10, 1951.

Station.
Tachikawa AB, Japan, August 26, 1950–January 25, 1951.

Commanders.
Col. Cecil H. Childre, August 1950; Lt. Col. Edward H. Nigro, October 21, 1950–January 1951.

Campaign Streamers.
UN Defensive; UN Offensive; CCF Intervention.

Decorations.
None.

61st Troop Carrier Group

Barry of six, Or and Azure, a pale nebuly, all counter-changed. Approved on August 20, 1951.

61st Troop Carrier Group, Heavy

From the last week of July until early December 1950, the 61st TCG, equipped with C–54 Skymasters, flew the northern route from McChord AFB, Washington, to Japan, providing airlift of personnel and supplies for UN forces. Flying a total of 253 Pacific trips, it airlifted 368 tons of cargo and transported 5,117 passengers until alerted for movement to Japan. On December 13, three days after the 61st TCG arrived at Ashiya, the squadrons flew their first combat missions, carrying ammunition, supplies and equipment to besieged UN forces fighting their way out of the Hungnam perimeter, and returning wounded personnel and evacuees to South Korea and Japan. The 61st TCG often operated from airstrips that were too primitive for larger transports. In November 1952, the USAF began to phase C–54s out of the Korean airlift. The 61st had accounted for movement of over 67,257 air evacuees, 615,195 passengers, and 152,500 tons of cargo before returning to the United States on November 18.

Combat Components.
4th Troop Carrier Squadron: attached December 17, 1950–July 25, 1951.
14th Troop Carrier Squadron: to *c.* December 5, 1950, and March 26–*c.* November 15, 1952.
15th Troop Carrier Squadron: duration.
53d Troop Carrier Squadron: duration, except detached March 26–September 14, 1952.

Stations.
McChord AFB, Washington, to December 5, 1950; Ashiya AB, Japan, December 10, 1950; Tachikawa AB, Japan, March 26–November 1952.

Commanders.
Col. Frank Norwood, to February 14, 1952; Lt. Col. Hal E. Ercanbrack, Jr., February 14, 1952–.

Campaign Streamers.
CCF Intervention; First UN Counteroffensive; CCF Spring Offensive; UN Summer-Fall Offensive; Second Korean Winter; Korea, Summer-Fall 1952.

Decorations.
Distinguished Unit Citation for period December 13, 1950–April 21, 1951.
Republic of Korea Presidential Unit Citation for period July 1, 1951–November 15, 1952.

314th Troop Carrier Group

Or, on clouds in fess, Azure, two boots passant of the field, ornamented, Gules. Motto: VIRI VENIENTE—Men Will Come. Approved on August 17, 1942.

314th Troop Carrier Group, Medium

Detached from its parent wing, the 314th TCG, with its newly modified C–119 Flying Boxcars, moved from Sewart AFB, Tennessee, to arrive at Ashiya AB, Japan, in late August 1950. From September through November 1950, it dropped ammunition and rations to UN frontline troops as they engaged the North Korean forces. It airlifted the 187th Airborne Regimental Combat Team to Kimpo AB. On October 20, the 314th TCG furnished the bulk of the aircraft in the airborne phase of the UN assault north of Pyongyang. It received a Distinguished Unit Citation for actions from November 28 through December 10, 1950. During this period the Chinese Communist Army encircled regiments of the U.S. 1st Marine and 7th Infantry Divisions near the Changjin Reservoir. The 314th TCG airdropped urgently needed ammunition, gasoline, and rations, as well as an eight-span M–2 treadway bridge, allowing the besieged UN forces to extricate themselves along with their equipment. The group maintained an almost constant shuttle to frontline troops in Korea, delivering supplies, ammunition, and fuel and, at times, moving and airdropping troops. It continued to transport personnel and supplies from Japan to Korea for the remainder of the war and it evacuated UN prisoners of war when they were freed.

Combat Components.

37th Troop Carrier Squadron: attached August 21, 1950–May 8, 1952.

50th Troop Carrier Squadron: duration.

53d Troop Carrier Squadron: attached April 14–c. June 1952.

61st Troop Carrier Squadron: duration.

62d Troop Carrier Squadron: duration.

Station.

Ashiya AB, Japan, September 7, 1950–.

Commanders.

Col. Richard W. Henderson, to August 27, 1951; Col. William H. DeLacey, August 27, 1951; Col. David E. Daniel, September 28, 1951; Lt. Col. Harold L. Sommers, May 1, 1952–.

Campaign Streamers.

UN Defensive; UN Offensive; CCF Intervention; First UN Counteroffensive; CCF Spring Offensive; UN Summer-Fall Offensive 1951; Second Korean Winter; Korea, Summer-Fall 1952; Third Korean Winter; Korea, Summer 1953.

Decorations.

Distinguished Unit Citation for actions November 28–December 10, 1950.

Republic of Korea Presidential Unit Citation for period July 1, 1951–July 27, 1953.

315th Troop Carrier Group

Azure, a winged packing box bend sinisterwise Or. Motto: ADVENIAM—I Will Arrive. Approved for the 315th Group on May 22, 1942; never formally approved for the Wing.

315th Troop Carrier Wing, Medium

The 315th TCW activated on June 10, 1952, at Brady AB, Japan, replacing the 437th TCW, which returned to Reserve status. Over the next year, the C–46-equipped 315th TCW transported between Japan and Korea nearly 55,500,000 pounds of cargo, along with more than 656,000 passengers, paratroopers, and medical evacuees. It also airdropped gasoline, bombs, ammunition, propaganda leaflets, spare engines, flares, rations, fresh vegetables, and other items. It moreover sprayed South Korean cities and installations to fight insect-borne diseases. In all, the 315th TCW flew over one million hours in combat support missions during the Korean War.

Combat Component.

315th Troop Carrier Group: June 10, 1952–.

Station.

Brady AB, Japan, June 10, 1952–.

Commanders.

Col. Kenneth W. Northammer, June 10, 1952; Col. Robert O. Good, July 26, 1953–.

Service Streamer.

Korean Theater.

Decoration.

Republic of Korea Presidential Unit Citation for period [June 10, 1952]–July 27, 1953.

315th Troop Carrier Group, Medium

The 315th TCG inherited C–46 Commando aircraft from the 437th TCG. Following activation on June 10, 1952, it flew troop and cargo airlift, airdrop, leaflet drop, spray, air evacuation, search-and-rescue, and other aerial missions between Japan and Korea. It transported U.S. Army units during exercises in Japan in 1952 and 1953 and airlifted the 187th Airborne Regimental Combat Team and other XVI Corps units to Korea in a series of major combat support operations in June and July 1953. Beginning in March 1953, when C–119s in the theater were grounded by propeller malfunctions, the C–46s of the 315th TCG moved all personnel between Korea and southern Japan until the end of the war.

Combat Components.
19th Troop Carrier Squadron: June 10, 1952–.
34th Troop Carrier Squadron: June 10, 1952–.
43d Troop Carrier Squadron: June 10, 1952–.
344th Troop Carrier Squadron: June 10–December 14, 1952.

Station.
Brady AB, Japan, June 10, 1952–.

Commanders.
Lt. Col. Jack L. Crawford, Jr., June 10, 1952; Lt. Col. Gene I. Martin, December 5, 1952–.

Campaign Streamers.
Korea, Summer-Fall 1952; Third Korean Winter; Korea, Summer 1953.

Decoration.
Republic of Korea Presidential Unit Citation for period [June 10, 1952]–July 27, 1953.

374th Troop Carrier Group and Wing

Per bend Azure and Or, in chief a hand couped in armour, holding a dagger, point upward, issuing from its handle an arrow and a wheat stalk Or, in base a winged foot Azure, all within a diminished bordure of the second. Motto: CELERITER PUGNARE—Swiftly to Fight. Approved for 374th Group on July 3, 1951, and for 374th Wing on December 20, 1951.

374th Troop Carrier Wing, Heavy

In June 1950, the 374th TCW was the only air transport wing assigned to Fifth Air Force. By early September 1950, it was attached to the 1st Troop Carrier Task Force (Provisional) and then on September 10, to the FEAF Combat Cargo Command (Provisional). Reassigned to the 315th Air Division (Combat Cargo), it served with that division from January 1951 through the end of the war. The wing's assigned and attached components flew a variety of aircraft, including C–54s, C–46s, C–47s, C–119s, and C–124s, performing combat airlift, airdrops, and aeromedical evacuation in Korea throughout the war.

Combat Components.

1st Troop Carrier Group, Provisional: attached August 26, 1950–January 10, 1951.

374th Troop Carrier Group: duration.

21st Troop Carrier Squadron: attached June 29, 1951–March 28, 1952.

47th Troop Carrier Squadron, Provisional: attached January 10–26, 1951.

6142d Air Transport Unit: attached August 1–October 1, 1950.

6143d Air Transport Unit: attached July 26–October 1, 1950.

6144th Air Transport Unit: attached July 26–October 1, 1950.

Station.

Tachikawa AB, Japan, duration.

Commanders.

Col. Troy W. Crawford, to September 1951; Col. Charles W. Howe, September 1951; Col. James W. Chapman, Jr., August 9, 1952–.

Campaign Streamers.

UN Defensive; UN Offensive; CCF Intervention; First UN Counteroffensive; CCF Spring Offensive; UN Summer-Fall Offensive; Second Korean Winter; Korea, Summer-Fall 1952; Third Korean Winter; Korea, Summer 1953.

Decoration.

Republic of Korea Presidential Unit Citation for period July 1, 1951–July 27, 1953.

374th Troop Carrier Group, Heavy

When the Korean War began in June 1950, the 374th TCG controlled the 6th and 22d Squadrons based in Japan and equipped with C–54s, and the 21st Squadron based in the Philippines and equipped with C–47s and C–54s. Within 12 hours of the North Korean attack, the group began transporting cargo to Korea and evacuating personnel on return trips. The 374th TCG moved personnel, equipment, ammunition, gasoline, rockets, rations, water, medical items, barbed wire, guns, and other materials from Japan to Suwon and Pusan, South Korea, to supply the U.S. Army. The 21st TCS moved to Japan on June 29 to come under control of FEAF Combat Cargo Command. Between mid-September and mid-December 1950, the group operated mostly from Ashiya AB, Japan; then from October 23 to November 12, it operated from bases in Korea, landing war essentials and other cargo at various small forward airstrips near UN fighting forces. A C–47-equipped squadron of the Royal Thailand Air Force operated with the 374th TCG during this period. After moving back to Tachikawa AB, Japan, in mid-December, the group continued to airlift supplies and personnel in support of UN action in Korea. The 6th and 22d TCSs transitioned from C–54s to C–124s in mid-1952. In Operation Little Switch, the 374th transported the first group of repatriated prisoners of war from Korea to Japan in April 1953, and after the cease-fire, in Operation Big Switch, it airlifted UN personnel who had been the enemy's prisoners.

Combat Components.

4th Troop Carrier Squadron: attached December 2–17, 1950, and July 25–November 16, 1951.

6th Troop Carrier Squadron: duration.

14th Troop Carrier Squadron: attached November 16, 1951–March 26, 1952, and November 15–30, 1952.

21st Troop Carrier Squadron: duration, except detached *c.* September 10, 1950–June 25, 1951, and June 29, 1951–November 30, 1952.

22d Troop Carrier Squadron: duration.

344th Troop Carrier Squadron: attached December 14, 1952–.

Stations.

Tachikawa AB, Japan, duration, except deployed at Ashiya AB, Japan, *c.* September 15–December 17, 1950.

Commanders.

Lt. Col. Benjamin M. Tarver, Jr., to July 22, 1950; Col. Herbert A. Bott, July 22, 1950; Col. Charles W. Howe, July 1951; Col. Edward H. Nigro, September 1951; Lt. Col. James F. Hogan, April 20, 1952; Col. Edward H. Nigro, August 26, 1952; Lt. Col. Frederick C. Johnson, November 11, 1952; Lt. Col. Harold P. Dixon, December 19, 1952; Lt. Col. Frederick C. Johnson, *c.* January 1953; Col. Francis W. Williams, April 24, 1953–.

Campaign Streamers.

UN Defensive; UN Offensive; CCF Intervention; First UN Counteroffensive; CCF Spring Offensive; UN Summer-Fall Offensive; Second Korean Winter; Korea, Summer-Fall 1952; Third Korean Winter; Korea, Summer 1953.

Decorations.

Distinguished Unit Citation for actions June 27–September 15, 1950.

Republic of Korea Presidential Unit Citation for period July 1, 1951–July 27, 1953.

Azure, two hands in bend sinister proper, the upper a dexter hand issuing from a cloud Argent and holding an olive branch of the second, a lightning flash Or and a sword Sable, the lower sinister hand in profile issuing from a fan indented of seven sections (Blue, White, Orange, Black, White, Yellow, and Red), which in turn issue from base, above the cloud four mullets of four points of the third, all within a diminished bordure of the last. Motto: SPECTATE AD CAELUM—Look to the Skies. Approved on January 9, 1953.

403d Troop Carrier Wing, Medium

The personnel of the Reserve 403d Troop Carrier Wing moved from Oregon to Japan in April 1952. At Ashiya AB, in addition to its 403d TCG, the wing gained operational control of the 314th TCG with its three assigned squadrons as well as two separate squadrons. The 314th TCG flew C–119 Flying Boxcars, and the attached squadrons flew C/VC–47s and C–54s. The 403d TCW supported the Far East Command and UN forces. It inactivated on January 1, 1953, returning to Reserve status.

Combat Components.

314th Troop Carrier Group: attached April 14–December 31, 1952.

403d Troop Carrier Group: to January 1, 1953.

21st Troop Carrier Squadron: attached April 14–c. September 12, 1952, and
 further attached to the 314th Troop Carrier Group, April 14–c. June 1952.

6461st Troop Carrier Squadron: attached December 1–31, 1952.

Station.

Ashiya AB, Japan, April 14, 1952–January 1, 1953.

Commanders.

Col. Philip H. Best, April 14, 1952; Col. Maurice F. Casey, Jr., May 15, 1952–
 January 1, 1953.

Service Streamer.

Korean Theater.

Decoration.

Republic of Korea Presidential Unit Citation for period [April 14, 1952]–[January 1] 1953.

403d Troop Carrier Group, Medium

The 403d TCG moved to Ashiya AB, Japan, in April 1952 without aircraft, and for the next month it trained to fly newly acquired C–119s. From then until the end of 1952, it dropped paratroops and supplies, transported personnel and equipment, and evacuated casualties in support of the Far East Command and UN forces. The group flew over 6,300 flights; dropped nearly 10,000 personnel, more than 18,000 tons of cargo, and 380 tons of supplies; and airlifted almost 14,000 medical patients. It returned to Reserve status on January 1, 1953.

Combat Components.
63d Troop Carrier Squadron: to January 1, 1953.
64th Troop Carrier Squadron: to January 1, 1953.
65th Troop Carrier Squadron: to January 1, 1953.
Station.
Ashiya AB, Japan, April 14, 1952–January 1, 1953.
Commanders.
Lt. Col. Henry C. Althaus, to April 22, 1952; Maj. Wallace C. Forsythe, April 22, 1952; Lt. Col. Ernest W. Burton, August 1952–January 1, 1953.
Campaign Streamers.
Korea, Summer-Fall 1952; Third Korean Winter.
Decoration.
Republic of Korea Presidential Unit Citation for period [April 14, 1952]–[January 1] 1953.

437th Troop Carrier Wing, Medium

The 437th TCW, the first Reserve wing called to active duty in the Korean War, moved from the United States to Japan in three echelons in late October and early November 1950. It absorbed most of the personnel and equipment of the provisional 1st TCG in January 1951. In addition to its combat support missions, the wing assumed responsibility for most scheduled courier flights in Japan and Korea. During seven months of Korean service, the 437th TCW carried nearly 66,000 tons of cargo, 6,500 patients, and 240,000 passengers. Inactivated on June 10, 1952, it returned to Reserve status.

Combat Component.
437th Troop Carrier Group: to June 10, 1952.
Station.
Brady Field, Japan, November 8, 1950–June 10, 1952.
Commanders.
Brig. Gen. John P. Henebry, to January 26, 1951; Col. John W. Lacey, January 26, 1951; Col. John R. Roche, February 26, 1951; Col. Kenneth W. Northamer, May–June 10, 1952.
Campaign Streamers.
CCF Intervention; First UN Counteroffensive; CCF Spring Offensive; UN Summer-Fall Offensive; Second Korean Winter; Korea, Summer-Fall 1952.
Decoration.
Republic of Korea Presidential Unit Citation for period July 1, 1951–[June 10, 1952].

437th Troop Carrier Group, Medium

The 437th TCG's C–46 aircraft began arriving in Japan in early November 1950. Almost immediately the group, in three intensive days, helped to deliver combat materiel to UN ground forces at Pyongyang while evacuating personnel and equipment from forward bases in North Korea. During December, the C–46s continued to deliver combat materiel to the front line and evacuate ground forces from Sinanju, Pyongyang, and Yonpo, North Korea, and from Seoul and Suwon, South Korea. In a five-day period in December, it airlifted almost 2,500 patients from Korea to Japan. When the UN forces regained the initiative in early 1951, the 437th TCG began flying airdrop missions to supply Eighth Army frontline troops. In March, it airdropped the 187th Regimental Combat Team and two Ranger companies, along with more than 15 tons of ammunition, food, and signal equipment at Munsan-ni. From June to October 1951 and again in the spring of 1952, the 437th TCG flew insecticide spraying missions to combat disease in South Korea.

Combat Components.
83d Troop Carrier Squadron: to June 10, 1952.
84th Troop Carrier Squadron: to June 10, 1952.
85th Troop Carrier Squadron: to June 10, 1952.
86th Troop Carrier Squadron: January 26, 1951–June 10, 1952.

Station.
Brady AB, Japan, November 8, 1950–June 10, 1952.

Commanders.
Col. John R. Roche, to January 1951; Lt. Col. Edward H. Nigro, January 1951; Lt. Col. George W. Sutcliffe, March 5, 1951; Lt. Col. Jack L. Crawford, Jr., September 5, 1951–June 10, 1952.

Campaign Streamers.
CCF Intervention; First UN Counteroffensive; CCF Spring Offensive; UN Summer-Fall Offensive; Second Korean Winter; Korea, Summer-Fall 1952.

Decoration.
Republic of Korea Presidential Unit Citation for period July 1, 1951–[June 10, 1952].

483d Troop Carrier Wing, Medium

Activated on January 1, 1953, to replace the 403d TCW, 483d TCW controlled the 314th TCG as well as its own 483d TCG. It assumed responsibility for C–119 troop carrier and air transport operations in a large area of the Far East. Using virtually every pilot and aircraft of both groups, it moved approximately 4,000 paratroopers and their equipment from southern Japan to Korea in June through early July 1953.

Combat Components.
314th Troop Carrier Group: attached January 1, 1953–.
483d Troop Carrier Group: January 1, 1953–.
6461st Troop Carrier Squadron: January 1, 1953–.

Station.
Ashiya AB, Japan, January 1, 1953–.

Commander.
Col. Maurice F. Casey, Jr., January 1, 1953–.

Campaign Streamers.

Third Korean Winter; Korea, Summer 1953.

Decorations.

Air Force Outstanding Unit Award for period May 6, 1953–September 10, 1954, partly for transporting supplies to UN forces in Korea to the end of the conflict.

Republic of Korea Presidential Unit Citation for period [January 1]–July 27, 1953.

483d Troop Carrier Group, Medium

The 483d TCG transported personnel and supplies by C–119s from Japan to Korea. During the final months of the conflict, it alternated with the 314th TCG to airdrop supplies to a detachment of the 502d Tactical Control Group, located on a 5,000-foot mountain near Chongmong-ni. In late June 1953, the 483d TCG airlifted reinforcements and cargo to areas behind the western half of the UN line.

Combat Components.

815th Troop Carrier Squadron: January 1, 1953–.

816th Troop Carrier Squadron: January 1, 1953–.

817th Troop Carrier Squadron: January 1, 1953–.

Station.

Ashiya AB, Japan, January 1, 1953–.

Commanders.

Lt. Col. Ernest W. Burton, January 1, 1953; Col. George M. Foster, March 1, 1953–.

Campaign Streamers.

Third Korean Winter; Korea, Summer 1953.

Decorations.

Air Force Outstanding Unit Award for period May 6, 1953–September 10, 1954, partly for transporting supplies to UN forces in Korea until the end of the conflict.

Republic of Korea Presidential Unit Citation for period [January 1]–July 27, 1953.

Other Combat Support

1st Shoran Beacon Squadron

In August 1950 the 1st Shoran Beacon Unit moved to Japan from the United States, and by October 1 it had moved to South Korea. It broadcast short-range navigation (Shoran) signals from ground sites to guide 3d Bombardment Group B–26s and 162d Tactical Reconnaissance Squadron RB–26s on night missions over targets in Korea. The first two sites in South Korea were too far away from the bombline to be effective. In November the unit set up two new sites at Wonsan and Pyongyang in North Korea, but mountains around the

Wonsan site interfered with its signals and a Communist Chinese offensive soon forced evacuation of both sites. Two new beacon sites set up in South Korea in December demonstrated the inadequacy of the unit's equipment. That and the continued advance of enemy troops forced the 1st Shoran Beacon Unit to move temporarily back to Japan at the end of the year, where it recalibrated and refurbished its equipment. In early 1951, it returned to South Korea and set up Shoran beacon sites at several locations, some of which it had to defend periodically against enemy guerrilla assaults. During the year, the unit established four sites, two on islands off the coast of Korea and two on mountaintops just south of the 38th parallel. It also maintained other sites in Japan and Okinawa to train aircrews in Shoran operations. Redesignated the 1st Shoran Beacon Squadron in February 1952, the unit provided electronic signals that guided 3d Bombardment Group B–26 bombardment missions until the armistice in mid-1953.

Stations.

Kimpo AB, South Korea, October 1, 1950; Iwakuni AB, Japan, December 19, 1950; Taegu AB, South Korea, February 20, 1951; Seoul, South Korea, June 16, 1951; Pyongtaek, South Korea, April 24, 1953–.

Campaigns.

UN Offensive; CCF Intervention; First UN Counteroffensive; CCF Spring Offensive; UN Summer-Fall Offensive; Second Korean Winter; Korea, Summer-Fall 1952; Third Korean Winter; Korea, Summer 1953.

Decorations.

Two Distinguished Unit Citations for actions January 25–April 21, 1951, and May 1–November 30, 1952.

Republic of Korea Presidential Unit Citation for period January 24–April 21, 1951.

5th Communications Group

On a shield Azure, within a diminutive border Argent, an antenna mast Argent in pale, resting on a stylized map of Korea Or, in base, two sound waves Argent between the apex of the antenna mast in chief; a dragon Vert, scales and detail Green, Sable and Argent, vomiting flames of fire, entwined around the antenna mast, head to sinister base; over all in fess, Satan's head Gules, facing to sinister and wearing a headset with two small flexible antennas with a sound wave Argent, protruding from each; from the sides of Satan's head a pair of wings Argent. Approved on October 8, 1952

5th Communications Group

The 5th Communications Group activated on November 25, 1951, in Seoul, South Korea, replacing the 934th Signal Battalion, which had carried out communications functions since October 1950. Assigned directly to Fifth Air Force, the 5th Communications Group supported FEAF agencies in Korea by installing, operating, and maintaining radio, telephone, and teletype communications networks that linked USAF and other military installations in Korea with bases in Japan. Composed of the 1st Radio Squadron, 1st Telephone and Carrier Squadron, 2d and 7th Communications Squadrons (Operations), and the 2d Radio Relay Squadron, the group also operated communications centers serving Fifth Air Force headquarters at Seoul and Taegu until well after hostilities ceased.

Station.
Seoul, South Korea, November 25, 1951–.

Commanders.
Col. John M. Maersch, November 25, 1951; Lt. Col. William E. Gegg, by March 1952; Lt. Col. Jeremy K. Schloss, by December 1952 and for the duration.

Campaign Streamers.
UN Summer-Fall Offensive; Second Korean Winter; Korea, Summer-Fall 1952; Third Korean Winter; Korea, Summer 1953.

Decorations.
Two Republic of Korea Presidential Unit Citations for periods [November 25], 1951–September 30, 1952, and October 1, 1952–July 27, 1953.

10th Liaison Squadron

Activated in July 1951 in Seoul, South Korea, the 10th Liaison Squadron supported the 930th and 931st Engineer Aviation Groups, the 6147th Tactical Control Group, and the 17th Bombardment Wing, among others. Using L–5 and L–20 aircraft, the unit surveyed forward areas for airfield, radar, and communications sites and regularly surveyed abandoned air strips. The squadron provided emergency airlift to remote forward positions, transported air liaison officers to forward U.S. Army units, and performed courier service, including the delivery of mail and monthly payrolls to forward Air Force units. It also transported North Korean prisoners on occasion and dropped arms and supplies to guerrillas behind enemy lines.

Station.
Seoul, South Korea, July 25, 1951–.

Campaign Streamers.
UN Summer-Fall Offensive; Second Korean Winter; Korea, Summer-Fall 1952; Third Korean Winter; Korea, Summer 1953.

Decorations.
None.

20th Weather Squadron

On a light turquoise Blue rectangle, long axis horizontal, border Black, the weather gremlin in Red Shoes, coat, and cap, trimmed with Yellow-Orange Belt and Blue buttons, standing with legs arched over aircraft hangar golden Orange, shaded proper, and holding aloft a White cloud formation, outlined dark Blue, with right hand, and resting on the staff of a weather anemometer; two stylized aircraft in sinister side, one of golden Orange, the other of light Red-Violet. Approved on September 15, 1943.

20th Weather Squadron Detachments

When the Korean War broke out in June 1950, the 20th Weather Squadron was already providing meteorological information to FEAF from its headquarters at Nagoya, Japan, and from weather stations scattered around the theater. For the next six months, the 20th furnished crucial combat weather data to the Fifth Air Force, the U.S. Eighth Army, and other UN forces by deploying numerous detachments in Korea. The unit's personnel briefed tactical organizations before missions and sometimes flew on the aircraft of those organizations in order to obtain weather data over enemy-held territory. Forward-deployed weather personnel with frontline troops radioed weather information to rear areas. Some of the unit's meteorological information contributed to the success of the Inchon invasion in September. By November, ten of the squadron's detachments had served at 13 locations in South and North Korea, moving with UN ground troops and operating small mobile weather stations sheltered in tents. The squadron operated a C–47 aircraft to move equipment and supplies to its scattered weather stations in Korea. In mid-November, it turned over its Korean weather responsibilities and operating locations to the 30th Weather Squadron and focused on Japan, where its headquarters had remained.

Station.
Nagoya, Japan, duration.
Campaign Streamers.
None. *Note:* Individual squadron detachments operating in Korea may have received campaign streamers on their own.
Service Streamer.
Korean Theater.

30th Weather Squadron

When the 30th Weather Squadron activated in November 1950, it took over Korean weather stations from the overextended 20th Weather Squadron. The squadron headquarters served at Seoul except for the period from December

1950 to July 1951 when enemy troops in or near the South Korean capital forced it to function at Taegu. The 30th managed many mobile detachments all over Korea to provide weather information to the Fifth Air Force, Eighth Army, and other UN forces. By the end of the war these detachments had served at 20 different locations around Korea, including some in the north when UN troops were there. In addition to the detachments, the squadron deployed a number of two-man teams with portable weather stations. Some of these teams served with UN ground units in forward areas, on islands off the Korean coast, or at airfields where full detachments were not required. In late 1951, the 30th Weather Squadron began training Korean observers and forecasters, whose work eventually allowed the squadron to reduce the number of its detachments. The squadron served the U.S. Eighth Army so well in Korea that the Department of the Army subsequently decided to rely on the Air Force for weather services.

Stations.
Seoul, South Korea, November 16, 1950; Taegu, South Korea, December 22, 1950; Seoul, South Korea, July 3, 1951–.

Campaign Streamers.
CCF Intervention; First UN Counteroffensive; CCF Spring Offensive; UN Summer-Fall Offensive; Second Korean Winter; Korea, Summer-Fall 1952; Third Korean Winter; Korea, Summer 1953.

Decorations.
Three Republic of Korea Presidential Unit Citations for periods November 15, 1950–June 30, 1951; March 16, 1951–September 30, 1952; and October 1, 1952–July 27, 1953.

75th Air Depot Wing

On a shield Or, a stylized aircraft Azure, throughout, in pale, thereon a sword Argent, flamant Gules, fimbriated Or, issuing from the dexter and sinister chief, two gears of the second, all within a diminutive of the bordure Gules. Approved on July 31, 1952.

75th Air Depot Wing

The 75th Air Depot Wing arrived in South Korea from Texas on January 2, 1953, replacing the 6405th Air Support Wing. It operated a major depot at Chinhae until the end of the conflict. Assigned to the Far East Air Logistic Force, the wing received, stored, and transported equipment and supplies such as ammunition, fuel, breathing oxygen, and aircraft parts for combat wings in South Korea. It recovered, reclaimed, and repaired crashed or disabled aircraft in Korea. The wing also maintained and repaired combat aircraft, particularly B–26s, at Iwakuni AB in Japan, working with the 6418th Air Depot Wing stationed there. Among the 75th's other duties were the salvage and disposal of used and surplus war materiel; controlling corrosion of aircraft fuel tanks; maintaining and defending Chinhae Airdrome (K–10); sending traveling teams to maintain and repair aircraft equipment; flying clothing and shop equipment at various bases in Korea; and rehabilitating, storing, and issuing pierced-steel planking for airstrips. In the course of these duties, the wing maintained liaison with port agencies at Pusan and Inchon and with railheads in South Korea for the processing of USAF personnel and materiel, including Air Force special-purpose vehicles.

Station.

Chinhae, South Korea, January 2, 1953–.

Commander.

Col. William C. Sams, duration.

Campaign Streamers.

Third Korean Winter; Korea, Summer 1953.

417th Engineer Aviation Brigade

At the beginning of the Korean War, few airfields in Korea were able to support the modern aircraft of the USAF. Most of the existing facilities had been constructed by the Japanese before 1945 and lacked runways long enough or strong enough to support multiple landings by large, four-engined cargo aircraft such as C–54s or jet fighters such as F–86s. The extensive use of the old runways by World War II–vintage USAF aircraft, like F–51s, also demanded frequent and extensive runway repairs. To correct the problem, FEAF deployed to Korea engineer aviation units manned by Special Category Army Personnel with Air Force (SCARWAF) troops. Although they suffered chronic shortages of adequately trained personnel, as early as July 1950, the 802d and 822d Engineer Aviation Battalions were repairing and extending runways at Pohang and Taegu. By the end of the Korean War, the engineer aviation units in Korea included the 417th Engineer Aviation Brigade with its subordinate units: three groups, ten battalions, three companies, and one detachment. The engineer aviation units repaired, renovated, and expanded air bases all over Korea for the basing and staging of FEAF, Fifth Air Force, and other UN aircraft, including fighters, fighter-bombers, and transports. Among the airfields they repaired or expanded, besides Pohang and Taegu, were Kimpo, Suwon, Pyongyang, Pusan, Hoengsong, Chunchon, Chinhae, Chungju, Kunsan, Seoul, and Pyongtaek. At most of these airfields the engineers laid pierced-steel planking for runways and taxiways and replaced inadequate foundations. They also constructed airfield facilities such as jet fuel storage tanks and hardstands. At airfields captured from the enemy, aviation engineer personnel filled in bomb craters and patched runways. In 1952, the engineer aviation battalions constructed new 9,000-foot concrete or asphalt runways for jet fighters at Taegu, Suwon, and Kunsan. That same year, three of the battalions built a new air base with a fourth 9,000-foot runway at Osan-ni. The new paved runways saved tires, lessened structural damage to aircraft, and reduced the need for jet-assisted takeoff (JATO) units. At Seoul, the aviation engineers strengthened and extended the runways to handle strategic airlift transports. At Pusan and Pyongtaek, they constructed airfield facilities for U.S. Marine Corps air units.

Engineer Aviation Units in Korea as of May 1953:

417th Engineer Aviation Brigade
    420th Engineer Aviation Topographic Detachment
    366th Engineer Aviation Battalion
    733d Engineer Aviation Supply Point Company
    840th Engineer Aviation Battalion
    841st Engineer Aviation Battalion
    1903d Engineer Aviation Battalion
    930th Engineer Aviation Group
        622d Engineer Aviation Maintenance Company
        808th Engineer Aviation Battalion
        822d Engineer Aviation Battalion
    931st Engineer Aviation Group
        809th Engineer Aviation Battalion
        811th Engineer Aviation Battalion
        919th Engineer Aviation Maintenance Company
    934th Engineer Aviation Group
        802d Engineer Aviation Battalion
        839th Engineer Aviation Battalion

801st Medical Air Evacuation Squadron

Three months before the North Koreans invaded South Korea, the 801st Medical Air Evacuation Squadron had moved from Japan to Clark AB in the Philippines, leaving only a flight in Japan. When the conflict began, this flight air-evacuated wounded personnel from Korea, while the rest of the squadron returned to Japan. As American casualties mounted, the 801st, flying on C–47 aircraft, evacuated the wounded from forward airstrips to hospitals in the rear. Following the waterborne invasion by ground forces at Inchon in September 1950 and during the subsequent battle for Seoul, the 801st, under heavy fire from enemy troops, evacuated nearly 1,450 battle casualties from the Suwon and Kimpo airstrips near Seoul. In December, at the Chosin Reservoir in northeast Korea, the squadron evacuated almost 4,700 battle casualties from the Koto-ri and Hagaru-ri airstrips. During these actions, it operated from inadequate airstrips located in an area entirely surrounded by enemy troops, who subjected the aircraft to hostile fire on the ground as well as in the air. For actions during these two periods, the 801st earned a Distinguished Unit Citation. As the conflict dragged on, the 801st, utilizing C–46, C–47, C–54, and C–124 aircraft, flew on intra-Korea, intra-Japan, and Korea-to-Japan medical evacuation missions. For more than a year after the USAF authorized a group-level organization, the service could not obtain the necessary trained personnel to man the unit. Finally on June 18, 1953, the 6481st Medical Air Evacuation Group, a Table of Distribution unit, replaced the 801st, assuming its mission through the end of the war.

Stations.

Tachikawa AB, Japan, September 14, 1950; Ashiya AB, Japan, December 1, 1950; Tachikawa AB, Japan, February 6, 1951–June 18, 1953.

Campaign Streamers.

UN Defensive; UN Offensive; CCF Intervention; First UN Counteroffensive; CCF Spring Offensive; UN Summer-Fall Offensive; Second Korean Winter; Korea, Summer-Fall 1952; Third Korean Winter; Korea, Summer 1953.

Decorations.

Distinguished Unit Citation for actions September 21–30 and December 1–10, 1950.

Republic of Korea Presidential Unit Citation for period July 1, 1951–[June 18] 1953.

3903d Radar Bomb Scoring Group
Detachments C (11), K (5), and N (22)

In September 1950, detachments C, K, and N of Strategic Air Command's 3903d Radar Bomb Scoring Squadron (later, Group) arrived from the United States at Pusan, South Korea. Their mission was to provide radar signals to guide night bomb and flare drops from tactical air support aircraft in Korea. Although the three detachments belonged to the Strategic Air Command, they were attached to the 502d Tactical Control Group. Using mobile equipment mounted on vans, two of the detachments (C and K) moved in November to Pyongyang, North Korea, where they directed bomb drops on enemy troop concentrations. After returning southward in the face of an enemy offensive, detachments C and K arrived by January 1951 at Taegu where they were joined by detachment N from Pusan. Detachments C, K, and N were redesignated respectively as detachments 11, 5, and 22, and each was assigned to accompany a separate U.S. Army corps. Their signals made bomb drops by bombers and fighter-bombers more accurate, enhancing USAF night close support missions. They also guided C–47s dropping flares for night illumination. In October 1951, the three detachments departed Korea, having transferred their radar functions to the 502d Tactical Control Group.

Note: The 3903d as a whole received no Korean campaign or service streamer, but individual detachments operating in Korea received campaign streamers and decorations.

6004th Air Intelligence Service Squadron
12Detachments 1, 2, 3, and 5

By the end of the Korean conflict, the 6004th Air Intelligence Service Squadron, whose headquarters remained in Japan, had deployed four detachments in Korea. Two of these began work in mid-1951. In a search for technical air intelligence information, Detachment 1 interrogated enemy prisoners of war and collected and studied captured enemy materiel, including aircraft wreckage and fragments of expended munitions from enemy aircraft. It maintained teams at major tactical air bases in South Korea to debrief combat crews and review gun-camera film for the same kind of information. Detachment 2 sent subdetachments north of the bombline and behind enemy lines to examine other enemy materiel and interrogate enemy deserters. Beginning in June 1952, the squadron's Detachment 3 undertook management of evasion and escape activities for the recovery of UN airmen shot down over enemy territory. It interrogated U.S. personnel who had successfully escaped the enemy and provided information on successful evasion and escape to tactical units. It also experimented with infrared and radio equipment for locating downed airmen. Prisoner of war exchanges at the end of the Korean conflict led the squadron to deploy Detachment 5 to Korea in June 1953 to interrogate friendly personnel returning from North Korea in order to gather strategic intelligence information.

Station.
Tokyo, Japan, March 2, 1951–.
Campaign Streamers.
None. *Note:* Individual detachments operating in Korea received campaign
streamers and decorations on their own.
Service Streamer.
Korean Theater.
Decorations.
None.

6146th Air Force Advisory Group (ROKAF)

Originally organized as the 6146th Air Base Unit in July 1950, the organization elevated to group-level in August 1952; redesignated to 6146th Air Advisory Group (ROKAF) at that time; and finally redesignated to 6146th Air Force Advisory Group (ROKAF) in July 1953. The organization's primary mission was to train pilots and ground crews for the Republic of Korea's Air Force (ROKAF), but it also flew armed reconnaissance close air support missions. The group maintained its own aircraft and kept operational the airstrip at which it was based, which was often nearer the front lines than any other USAF unit. For part of 1951, a unit detachment trained Korean personnel on the island of Cheju (Cheju-do). At Sachon it trained ROKAF personnel in the operation and maintenance of L–4, L–5, L–16, T–6, and F–51 aircraft. When the group moved to Taegu in early 1953, it left a detachment at Sachon to continue that training. Once trained at Sachon, the Korean pilots deployed to Kangnung near the 38th parallel, where another of the group's detachments had been based since the end of 1951. That detachment earned a Distinguished Unit Citation for the period December 1952 through April 1953 for flying hundreds of close support and interdiction strikes with a wing of the Republic of Korea Air Force. Under the guidance of 6146th Air Force Advisory Group pilots, Koreans flew F–51s from Kangnung to bomb, rocket, and strafe enemy troop concentrations, vehicles, supply dumps, and fuel storage sites.

Stations.

Sachon AB, South Korea, July 27, 1950; Seoul, South Korea, September 26, 1950; Pyongyang East, North Korea, October 28, 1950; Taejon, South Korea, December 6, 1950; Seoul, South Korea, March 22, 1951; Sachon AB, South Korea, June 18, 1951; Taegu, South Korea, January 15, 1953–.

Commanders.

Lt. Col. Dean E. Hess, July 27, 1950; Maj. Harold H. Wilson, May 1951–unknown; Col. Walter W. Berg, July 1952; Lt. Col. Harold T. Babb, May 1953–.

Campaign Streamers.

UN Defensive; UN Offensive; CCF Intervention; First UN Counteroffensive; CCF Spring Offensive; UN Summer-Fall Offensive; Second Korean Winter; Korea, Summer-Fall 1952; Third Korean Winter; Korea, Summer 1953.

Decorations.

Five Republic of Korea Presidential Unit Citations for periods July 27, 1950–January 31, 1951; February 1–October 31, 1951; February 1, 1951–March 31, 1953; March 16, 1951–September 30, 1952; and October 10, 1952–July 27, 1953.

6167th Air Base Group

Originating as the 6153d Air Base Unit in October 1950, this organization operated the Seoul Airdrome except when forced to leave in the face of the Chinese advances in December 1950. From around February 1952, the organization also began flying combat support missions under direct control of Headquarters Fifth Air Force. Flying unarmed, modified C–46, C–47, and B–26 aircraft, the group dropped flares in frontline support and B–26 night interdiction flights. In addition, its aircraft dropped leaflets, and using B–26 and C–47 aircraft fitted with speakers and amplifiers, it flew "voice" psychological warfare missions. Working in close harmony with ground and air intelligence, the 6167th also performed some agent drops and resupply missions deep behind enemy lines during the hours of darkness. The 6167th Operations Squadron received a Distinguished Unit Citation for actions of May–November 1952. Beginning in early 1953, pilots from the 581st Air Resupply and Communications Wing, a special operations organization based in the Philippines, augmented aircrews of the 6167th Air Base Group.

Combat Component.

6167th Operations Squadron: April 1, 1952–.

Stations.

Seoul, South Korea, October 27, 1950; Camp Walker, Taegu, South Korea, *c.* December 15, 1950; Seoul AB, South Korea, *c.* July 15, 1951–.

Commanders.

Capt. Carl V. Hull, by December 1950; Maj. Lee J. Guilbeau, January 1951; Lt. Col. Tyson, July 1951; Lt. Col. Frank E. Lardent, January 1952; Col. Donald R. Conard, December 5, 1952–.

Campaign Streamers.

UN Offensive; CCF Intervention; First UN Counteroffensive; CCF Spring Offensive; UN Summer-Fall Offensive; Second Korean Winter; Korea, Summer-Fall 1952; Third Korean Winter; Korea, Summer 1953.

6204th Photo Mapping Flight Detachment 1

In mid-July 1950, the 6204th Photo Mapping Flight, located at Clark AB, Philippines, deployed the flight's two RB–17 aircraft complete with combat crews and maintenance personnel to Johnson AB, Japan. The FEAF deployment order specified that the two RB–17 aircraft be equipped with normal armament insofar as practicable, not to interfere with the photographic capability of the aircraft. This posed a problem for the flight, since the RB–17s had been flying peacetime missions and were not equipped for combat. However, the 6204th found the necessary gunners and equipment and made the modifications to the aircraft, so that by late August 1950 the detachment began flying photomapping missions over Korea. By the end of November 1950, it had photographed the entire North Korean area at least once and rephotographed some areas as far north as weather conditions permitted. By early December the detachment returned to Clark AB and resumed the flight's mapping program in the Philippine area.

6405th Korea Air Materiel Unit

Shortly after the conflict in Korea began, Far East Air Materiel Command (FEAMCOM) realized that tactical units of Fifth Air Force would need assistance with maintenance and supply until they could get their own base maintenance and supply personnel and equipment to the combat zone. Out of its own materiel resources, FEAF organized the 6405th Korea Air Materiel Unit (KAMU) in July 1950 to exercise operational control of FEAMCOM units in Korea. Organized on paper in Japan, the KAMU quickly moved to Korea, and its field maintenance, depot support, and ammunition-handling units fanned out in support of Fifth Air Force tactical units. Initially KAMU was charged with coordinating Air Force logistics requirements and Army emergency requirements between Fifth Air Force activities in Korea and FEAMCOM, expediting requisitions of emergency aircraft parts and critical items, performing aircraft and ammunition modification projects, and returning Air Force–reparable items to FEAMCOM. It also had responsibility for damaged aircraft in Korea, including salvage, reclamation, and field or depot repair. It soon began operating bomb dumps, aviation ammunition storage, and napalm mixing facilities. In evacuations at Taegu and Pohang in August and September 1950, KAMU personnel continued working on the bases after most of the Fifth Air Force units had left. In the November evacuation from Pyongyang, maintenance personnel kept repairing combat-damaged aircraft, occasionally dodging sniper bullets. Supply personnel worked to evacuate 260- and 500-pound bombs and gasoline, as well as their own gear. In April 1951, KAMU's 543d Ammunition Supply Squadron began operating a pierced-steel planking plant at Pusan East. KAMU also manufactured and issued breathing oxygen to Fifth Air Force tactical units and maintained liaison with the U.S. Army ports in transporting USAF supplies and personnel through these ports. In a paper reorganization, the first 6405th KAMU discontinued in January 1951, replaced by a provisional KAMU, itself replaced in May 1951 by a second 6405th KAMU. In an overall FEAMCOM reorganization in early 1952, the KAMU was elevated to wing-status. After the 75th Air Depot Wing arrived in Korea and settled at Chinhae in January 1953, the KAMU discontinued.

Stations.
6405th KAMU: Taegu AB, South Korea, July 1950; Pusan AB, South Korea; c. August 1950; Seoul AB, South Korea, October 16, 1950; Taegu AB, South Korea, December 15, 1950–January 28, 1951.
KAMU(P): Taegu AB, South Korea, January 28–May 25, 1951.
6405th KAMU (later, 6405th Support Wing; 6405th Air Support Wing): Taegu AB, South Korea, May 25, 1951–February 1, 1953.

Commanders.
6405th KAMU: Col. Marvin Sledge, July 21, 1950–July 28, 1951.
KAMU(P): Col. Marvin Sledge, July 28–May 25, 1951.
6405th KAMU (later, 6405th Support Wing; 6405th Air Support Wing): Col. Marvin Sledge, May 25, 1951; Col. Marion G. Ferguson, Jr., September 7, 1951; Col. Edward J. Perkin, by June 1952; Col. Charles N. Howze, August 26, 1952; Col. William L. Wood, January 25–February 1, 1953.

Campaign Streamers.
6405th KAMU: UN Defensive; UN Offensive; CCF Intervention; First UN Counteroffensive.
KAMU(P): First UN Counteroffensive; CCF Spring Offensive.
6405th KAMU (later, 6405th Support Wing; 6405th Air Support Wing): CCF Spring Offensive; UN Summer-Fall Offensive; Second Korean Winter; Korea, Summer-Fall 1952; Third Korean Winter.

Decorations.
None.

USAF Organizations at Korean Stations, July 1, 1950–July 1, 1953

JULY 1, 1950

No USAF unit listed as based in Korea.

SEPTEMBER 1, 1950

Korea (unspecified location)
1141st Med Svs Sq—OL

Pohang
1st Air Postal Sq—Det 23
35th Ftr-Intcp Gp (35th Ftr-Intcp Wg)
  Hq
    39th Ftr-Intcp Sq
    40th Ftr-Intcp Sq
802d Engr Avn Bn—Co A
6131st Ftr Wg, SE
  Hq & Hq Sq
  6131st Maint & Sup Gp
    Hq
    6131st Maint Sq
    6131st Sup Sq
    6131st Mtr Veh Sq
  6131st Air Base Gp
    Hq & Hq Sq
    6131st Comms Sq
    6131st Air Police Sq
    6131st Food Sv Sq
    6131st Instls Sq
  6131st Sta Med Gp
6144th Air Trans Unit

Pusan
822d Engr Avn Bn
6407th Ammo Handling Unit

Pusan Air Base
1st Air Postal Sq—Det 14

919th Engr Avn Maint Co—Contact Plat

Sachon Air Base
6146th Air Base Unit

Taegu
Fifth Air Force, Adv
  Hq & Hq Sq
440th Sig Avn H Const Bn—Co A
1973d AACS Sq (1809th AACS Gp)
6132d Tac Air Con Gp
6143d Air Trans Unit
6147th Tac Con Sq, Abn
6149th Air Base Unit

Taegu Air Base
67th Ftr-Bmr Sq (18th Ftr-Bmr Gp)
930th Engr Avn Gp
  Hq & Hq & Sv Co (Less Dets)

NOVEMBER 1, 1950

Kimpo
1st Air Postal Sq—Det 24
51st Ftr-Intcp Wg
  Hq & Hq Sq
  51st Ftr-Intcp Gp
    Hq
    16th Ftr-Intcp Sq
    25th Ftr-Intcp Sq
  51st Maint & Sup Gp
    Hq
    51st Maint Sq
    51st Mtr Veh Sq
    51st Sup Sq
  51st Air Base Gp
    Hq & Hq Sq
    51st Comms Sq

51st Air Police Sq
51st Food Sv Sq
51st Instls Sq
51st Med Gp
80th Ftr-Bmr Sq (8th Ftr-Bmr Gp)
6151st Air Base Unit

Pohang

1st Air Postal Sq—Det 23
35th Ftr-Intcp Gp (35th Ftr-Intcp
  Wg)
  Hq
  39th Ftr-Intcp Sq
  40th Ftr Intcp Sq
802d Engr Avn Bn—Co A
6150th Tac Spt Wg
  Hq & Hq Sq
  6150th Maint & Sup Gp
    Hq
    6150th Maint Sq
    6150th Mtr Veh Sq
    6150th Sup Sq
  6150th Air Base Gp
    Hq & Hq Sq
    6150th Comms Sq
    6150th Air Police Sq
    6150th Food Sv Sq
    6150th Instls Sq
  6150th Sta Med Gp

Pusan

2d Rad Relay Sq
502d Tac Con Gp
  Hq (Less Con Det)
  605th Tac Con Sq
  606th AC&W Sq
  607th AC&W Sq
822d Engr Avn Bn (Less OL)
934th Sig Bn, Sep, TAC
1973d AACS Sq—Det 2
3903d RBS Sq—Dets C, K & N
6002d Tac Spt Wg—Port Det 1
6405th Korean Air Mat Unit—OL
6407th Ammo Handling Unit (Less
  OL)

Pusan Air Base

Fifth Air Force—OL
1st Air Postal Sq—Det 14
919th Engr Avn Maint Co—Contact
  Plat

Sachon Air Base

6148th Air Base Unit

Seoul

See: Kimpo Air Base
6146th Air Base Unit

Seoul Airfield

6147th Tac Con Sq, Abn

Suwon

1st Air Postal Sq—Det 4
8th Ftr-Bmr Gp (8th Ftr-Bmr Wg)
  Hq
  35th Ftr-Bmr Sq
  36th Ftr-Bmr Sq
6131st Tac Spt Wg
  Hq & Hq Sq
  6131st Maint & Sup Gp
    Hq
    6131st Maint Sq
    6131st Mtr Veh Sq
    6131st Sup Sq
  6131st Air Base Gp
    Hq & Hq Sq
    6131st Comms Sq
    6131st Air Police Sq
    6131st Food Sv Sq
    6131st Instls Sq
  6131st Med Gp

Taegu

Fifth Air Force, Adv
  Hq & Hq Sq
5th Comms Sq, Comd
8th Tac Recon Sq, Photo-J (543d Tac
  Spt Gp)
9th Stat Svs Unit
49th Ftr-Bmr Gp (49th Ftr-Bmr Wg)
  Hq
  7th Ftr-Bmr Sq
  8th Ftr-Bmr Sq (Less OL)

9th Ftr-Bmr Sq
363d Recon Tech Sq (543d Tac Spt
   Gp)
440th Sig Avn H Const Bn—Co A
1973d AACS Sq (1809th AACS Gp)
   (Less Det)
6132d AC&W Sq (502d Tac Con
   Gp)
6149th Tac Spt Wg
   Hq & Hq Sq
   6149th Maint & Sup Gp
      Hq
      6149th Maint Sq
      6149th Mtr Veh Sq
      6149th Sup Sq
   6149th Air Base Gp
      Hq & Hq Sq
      6149th Comms Sq
      6149th Air Police Sq
      6149th Food Sv Sq
      6149th Instls Sq
   6149th Sta Med Gp
6406th Avn Cargo Unit—OL
6407th Ammo Handling Unit—OL

Taegu Air Base
802d Engr Avn Bn—OL
822d Engr Avn Bn—OL
930th Engr Avn Gp
   Hq & Hq & Sv Co (Less Dets)
6002d AB Gp—OL
6400th Fld Maint Unit—OL

Tongnae
18th Ftr-Bmr Gp (18th Ftr-Bmr Wg)
   Hq
   12th Ftr-Bmr Sq
   67th Ftr-Bmr Sq
6002d Tac Spt Wg
   Hq & Hq Sq (Less Det)
   6002d Maint & Sup Gp
      Hq
      6002d Maint Sq
      6002d Mtr Veh Sq
      6002d Sup Sq
   6002d Air Base Gp

Hq & Hq Sq (Less OL)
6002d Comms Sq
6002d Air Police Sq
6002d Food Sv Sq
6002d Instls Sq
6002d Med Gp

JANUARY 1, 1951
Chinhae
30th Wea Sq—Det 16

Kimpo
1973d AACS Sq—Det 4

Kimpo Air Base
1st Air Postal Sq—Det 24
1st Shoran Beacon Unit—OL
30th Wea Sq—Det 10
440th Sig Avn H Const Bn (Less
   OL)
811th Engr Avn Bn

Korea (unspecified location)
1141st Med Svs Sq—OL

Pohang
1st Air Postal Sq—Det 27
1973d AACS Sq—Det 3
6407th Ammo Handling Unit—OL

Pusan
2d Rad Relay Sq (Less OL)
606th AC&W Sq (502d Tac Con
   Gp) (Less OL)
543d Ammo Sup Sq, Dep—OL
822d Engr Avn Bn—Co A
1973d AACS Sq—Det 2
3903d RBS Sq—Det N
6407th Ammo Handling Unit (Less
   OL)

Pusan Air Base
Fifth Air Force—Port Det 2
1st Air Postal Sq—Dets 14 & 23
20th Wea Sq—Dets 30, 31 & 35

Pusan East Air Base
30th Wea Sq—Det 13
35th Ftr-Intcp Wg
   Hq & Hq Sq

35th Ftr-Intcp Gp
  Hq
  39th Ftr-Intcp Sq
  40th Ftr-Intcp Sq
35th Maint & Sup Gp
  Hq
  35th Maint Sq
  35th Mtr Veh Sq
  35th Sup Sq
35th Air Base Gp
  Hq & Hq Sq
  35th Comms Sq
  35th Air Police Sq
  35th Food Sv Sq
  35th Instls Sq
35th Med Gp
6152d Air Base Unit

Pyongyang
919th Engr Avn Maint Co—Contact
  Plat
822d Engr Avn Bn (Less Co A)
3903d RBS Sq—Dets C & K

Pyongyang Air Base
6148th Air Base Unit

Pyongyang East Airdrome
1st Air Postal Sq—Det 4
6146th Air Base Unit
6147th Tac Con Sq, Abn

Sachon
1973d AACS Sq-Det 6

Seoul
See: Kimpo Air Base
5th Comms Sq, Comd
605th Tac Con Sq (502d Tac Con
  Gp)
607th AC&W Sq (502d Tac Con Gp)
930th Engr Avn Gp
  Hq & Hq & Sv Co (Less Dets)
934th Sig Bn, Sep, TAC

Seoul Air Base
Fifth Air Force
  Hq & Hq Sq (Less Dets)
30th Wea Sq—Det 14

6154th Air Base Gp
  Hq
  6155th Air Police Sq
  6156th Mtr Veh Sq
  6157th Food Sv Sq
  6158th Sup Sq
  6159th Instls Sq
6405th Korean Air Mat Unit

Seoul Airdrome
30th Wea Sq—Det 17
502d Tac Con Gp
  Hq

Seoul Airfield
2d Rad Relay Sq—OL
440th Sig Avn H Const Bn—OL
6153d Air Base Unit
6406th Avn Cargo Unit—OL

Suwon
30th Wea Sq—Det 15
1973d AACS Sq—Det 5
6408th Dep Spt Unit

Suwon Air Base
18th Ftr-Bmr Wg
  Hq & Hq Sq
  18th Ftr-Bmr Gp
    Hq
    12th Ftr-Bmr Sq
    67th Ftr-Bmr Sq
  18th Maint & Sup Gp
    Hq
    18th Maint Sq
    18th Mtr Veh Sq
    18th Sup Sq
  18th Air Base Gp
    Hq & Hq Sq
    18th Comms Sq
    18th Air Police Sq
    18th Food Sv Sq
    18th Instls Sq
6002d Med Sq
6401st Fld Maint Unit

Taegu
1st Air Postal Sq—Det 31

8th Tac Recon Sq, Photo-J (543d Tac
   Spt Gp)
30th Wea Sq (Less Dets)
30th Wea Sq—Dets 11 & 12
162d Tac Recon Sq, Night Photo
   (543d Tac Spt Gp)
363d Recon Tech Sq (543d Tac Spt
   Gp)
1973d AACS Sq (1809th AACS Gp)
   (Less Dets)
6132d AC&W Sq (502d Tac Con
   Gp)

Taegu Air Base
27th Ftr-Escort Gp (27th Ftr-Escort
   Wg)
   Hq
   522d Ftr-Escort Sq
   523d Ftr-Escort Sq
   524th Ftr-Escort Sq
49th Ftr-Bmr Wg
   Hq & Hq Sq
   49th Ftr-Bmr Gp
      Hq
      7th Ftr-Bmr Sq
      8th Ftr-Bmr Sq
      9th Ftr-Bmr Sq
   49th Maint & Sup Gp
      Hq
      49th Maint Sq
      49th Mtr Veh Sq
      49th Sup Sq
   49th Air Base Gp
      Hq & Hq Sq
      49th Comms Sq
      49th Air Police Sq
      49th Food Sv Sq
      49th Instls Sq
   49th Med Gp
543d Tac Spt Gp
   Hq
606th AC&W Sq—OL
6400th Fld Maint Unit—OL

Taejon
30th Wea Sq—Det 18

Urusan Airdrome
802d Engr Avn Bn—Co A
6151st Air Base Unit

MARCH 1, 1951
Chinhae
1st Air Postal Sq—Det 4
18th Ftr-Bmr Wg
   Hq & Hq Sq (Less Det)
   18th Ftr-Bmr Gp
      Hq
      12th Ftr-Bmr Sq
      67th Ftr-Bmr Sq
   18th Maint & Sup Gp
      Hq
      18th Maint Sq
      18th Mtr Veh Sq
      18th Sup Sq
   18th Air Base Gp
      Hq & Hq Sq
      18th Comms Sq
      18th Air Police Sq
      18th Food Sv Sq
      18th Instls Sq
30th Wea Sq—Det 16
6002d Med Sq

Chinhae Airdrome
606th AC&W Sq (502d Tac Con Gp)
6127th Air Terminal Gp—Det 8

Kimpo
1973d AACS Sq—Det 4

Kimpo Air Base
811th Engr Avn Bn (Less Co C)

Korea (unspecified location)
1141st Med Svs Sq—OL

Pohang
1973d AACS Sq—Det 3
6127th Air Terminal Gp—Det 9

Pusan
2d Rad Relay Sq (Less OL)
822d Engr Avn Bn—Co A
1973d AACS Sq—Det 2
3903d RBS Sq—Det N

Pusan Air Base

Fifth Air Force—Det 4
1st Air Postal Sq—Det 14
9th Stat Svs Unit
20th Wea Sq—Dets 30, 31 & 35
30th Wea Sq—Det 10

Pusan East Air Base

5th Mtr Trans Sq, Avn
30th Wea Sq—Det 13
35th Ftr-Intcp Wg
  Hq & Hq Sq
  35th Ftr-Intcp Gp
    Hq
    39th Ftr-Intcp Sq
    40th Ftr-Intcp Sq
  35th Maint & Sup Gp
    Hq
    35th Maint Sq
    35th Mtr Veh Sq
    35th Sup Sq
  35th Air Base Gp
    Hq & Hq Sq
    35th Comms Sq
    35th Air Police Sq
    35th Food Sv Sq
    35th Instls Sq
  35th Med Gp
543d Ammo Sup Sq, Dep—OL
802d Engr Avn Bn—OL
811th Engr Avn Bn—Co C
6127th Air Terminal Gp—Det 4
6148th Air Base Unit
6152d Air Base Unit

Pyongyang

919th Engr Avn Maint Co—Contact
  Plat
822d Engr Avn Bn (Less Co A)
3903d RBS Sq—Dets 5 & 11

Pyongyang East Airdrome

6146th Air Base Unit
6147th Tac Con Sq, Abn

Sachon

1973d AACS Sq—Det 6

Seoul

See: Kimpo Air Base
605th Tac Con Sq (502d Tac Con
  Gp)
607th AC&W Sq (502d Tac Con Gp)
930th Engr Avn Gp
  Hq & Hq & Sv Co (Less Dets)
934th Sig Bn, Sep, TAC

Seoul Air Base

6154th Air Base Gp
  Hq
  6155th Air Police Sq
  6156th Mtr Veh Sq
  6157th Food Sv Sq
  6158th Sup Sq
  6159th Instls Sq

Seoul Airdrome

502d Tac Con Gp
  Hq
6164th Tac Con Sq

Seoul Airfield

6153d Air Base Unit

Suwon Air Base

1st Air Postal Sq—Det 23
18th Ftr-Bmr Wg—Det 1

Taegu

Fifth Air Force
  Hq & Hq Sq (Less Det)
1st Air Postal Sq—Det 31
30th Wea Sq (Less Dets)
30th Wea Sq—Dets 11, 12 & 14
1973d AACS Sq (1809th AACS Gp)
  (Less Dets)
6132d AC&W Sq (502d Tac Con
  Gp)
6165th Rad Relay Sq

Taegu Air Base

1st Rad Sq, Mob—Det 13
1st Shoran Beacon Unit (Less Dets)
2d Rad Relay Sq—OL
3d Air Rsq Sq—Det F
27th Ftr-Escort Gp (27th Ftr-Escort
  Wg)

Hq
522d Ftr-Escort Sq
523d Ftr-Escort Sq
524th Ftr-Escort Sq
30th Wea Sq—Det 14
49th Ftr-Bmr Wg
Hq & Hq Sq
49th Ftr-Bmr Gp
Hq
7th Ftr-Bmr Sq
8th Ftr-Bmr Sq
9th Ftr-Bmr Sq
49th Maint & Sup Gp
Hq
49th Maint Sq
49th Mtr Veh Sq
49th Sup Sq
49th Air Base Gp
Hq & Hq Sq
49th Comms Sq
49th Air Police Sq
49th Food Sv Sq
49th Instls Sq
49th Med Gp
6127th Air Terminal Gp—Det 5

Taejon
30th Wea Sq—Det 18

Taejon Airdrome
6127th Air Terminal Gp—Det 7

Urusan Airdrome
6151st Air Base Unit

MAY 1, 1951
Issue not available

JULY 1, 1951
Issue not available

SEPTEMBER 1, 1951
Cheju Air Base
437th Mtr Veh Sq—OL

Chinhae
1st Air Pstl Sq—Det 4

18th Ftr-Bmr Wg
Hq & Hq Sq (Less Det)
18th Ftr-Bmr Gp
Hq
18th Maint & Sup Gp
Hq
18th Maint Sq
18th Mtr Veh Sq
18th Sup Sq
18th Air Base Gp
Hq & Hq Sq
18th Comms Sq
18th Air Police Sq
18th Food Sv Sq
18th Instls Sq
30th Wea Sq—Det 16
39th Ftr-Inctp Sq (35th Ftr-Intcp Gp)

Chinhae Airdrome
18th Med Gp (18th Ftr-Bmr Wg)
6127th Air Terminal Gp—Det 8

Chunchon
811th Engr Avn Bn—Co C
6127th Air Terminal Gp—OL

Hoengsong
30th Wea Sq—Det 26
811th Engr Avn Bn (Less Cos B & C)
6127th Air Terminal Gp—Det 12
6151st AB Sq—Det 1

Inchon
606th AC&W Sq—Det 1

Kangnumg [Kangnung]
6147th Tac Con Gp—Det 1

Kangnumg [Kangnung] **Airdrome**
6151st Air Base Sq (Less Det)

Kimpo
30th Wea Sq—Det 23

Kimpo Air Base
1st Air Pstl Sq—Det 28
4th Ftr-Intcp Wg
Hq & Hq Sq (Less Det)
4th Ftr-Intcp Gp
Hq

334th Ftr-Intcp Sq
335th Ftr-Intcp Sq
4th Air Base Gp
  Hq & Hq Sq (Less Det)
  4th Comms Sq
  4th Air Police Sq
  4th Food Sv Sq
  4th Instls Sq
4th Med Gp
4th Mtr Veh Sq (4th M&S Gp)
8th Ftr-Bmr Wg
  Hq & Hq Sq
  8th Air Base Gp
    Hq & Hq Sq
    8th Comms Sq
    8th Air Police Sq
    8th Food Sv Sq
    8th Instls Sq
8th Mtr Veh Sq (8th M&S Gp)
8th Sup Sq (8th M&S Gp)
12th Tac Recon Sq, Night Photo
  (67th Tac Recon Gp)
15th Tac Recon Sq, Photo-J (67th
  Tac Recon Gp)
67th Instls Sq (67th AB Gp)
67th Tac Recon Wg
  Hq & Hq Sq
  67th Med Gp
606th AC&W Sq (502d Tac Con
  Gp) (Less Det)
839th Engr Avn Bn
1503d Air Trans Wg—Det 10
1993d AACS Sq (1818th AACS Gp)
6127th Air Terminal Gp—Det 14

Kuksa-bong
1st Shoran Beacon Unit—Det 2

Kunsan
1st Air Pstl Sq—Det 29
440th Sig Avn Const Bn—Co B
808th Engr Avn Bn
6132d AC&W Sq—Det 1

Kwangung Airdrome
607th AC&W Sq—Det 3

Pusan
30th Wea Sq—Det 27
3903d RBS Gp—Det 22

Pusan Air Base
1st Air Pstl Sq—Det 14
30th Wea Sq—Det 10
811th Engr Av Bn—Co B
3497th Mob Tng Sq—Det F–84–5

Pusan East Air Base
1st Shoran Beacon Unit—Det 5
12th Ftr-Bmr Sq (18th Ftr-Bmr Gp)
30th Wea Sq—Det 13
67th Ftr-Bmr Sq (18th Ftr-Bmr Gp)
452d Bomb Wg, L (USAFR EAD)
  Hq & Hq Sq
  452d Bomb Gp, L
    Hq
    728th Bomb Sq, L, Night
      Intruder
    729th Bomb Sq, L, Night
      Intruder
    730th Bomb Sq, L, Night
      Intruder
  452d Maint & Sup Gp
    Hq
    452d Maint Sq
    452d Sup Sq
    452d Mtr Veh Sq
  452d Air Base Gp
    Hq & Hq Sq
    452d Comms Sq
    452d Air Police Sq
    452d Food Sv Sq
    452d Instls Sq
  452d Med Gp
543d Ammo Sup Sq, Dep
822d Engr Avn Bn—Co A
930th Engr Avn Gp
  Hq & Hq & Sv Co (Less Dets)
6127th Air Terminal Gp—Det 4
6401st Fld Maint Unit
6413th Air Base Sq

Pyongtaek Airdrome
1st Air Pstl Sq—Det 30

30th Wea Sq—Det 20
6147th Tac Con Gp
  Hq (Less Det)
  6147th Air Base Sq
  6147th Maint & Sup Sq
  6147th Med Sq
  6148th Tac Con Sq (Air)
  6149th Tac Con Sq (Air)
  6150th Tac Con Sq (Grd)

Pyongyang
919th Engr Avn Maint Co—Contact
    Plat
3903d RBS Gp—Dets 5 & 11

Sachon Airdrome
6146th Air Base Sq

Seoul
See: Kimpo Air Base
30th Wea Sq (Less Dets)
1818th AACS Gp (1808th AACS
    Wg)
  Hq

Seoul Airdrome
Fifth Air Force
  Hq & Hq Sq (Less Det)
1st Air Pstl Sq—Det 31
1st Epidemiological Flt
1st Rad Sq, Mob—OL
1st Shoran Beacon Unit (Less Dets)
9th Stat Svs Flt
30th Wea Sq—Det 18
136th Comms Scty Sq—OL
440th Sig Avn Const Bn (Less Co B)
502d Tac Con Gp
  Hq
  605th Tac Con Sq
934th Sig Bn, Sep TAC (Less Det)
1134th USAF S/A Sq—OL
6004th Air Intel Sv Sq—Det 2
6127th Air Terminal Gp—OL
6153d Air Base Sq (Less Flts)
6153d Air Base Sq—Flts A & B
6154th Air Base Gp
  Hq
  6154th Air Police Sq

6154th Food Sv Sq
6154th Instls Sq
6154th Med Sq
6154th Mtr Veh Sq
6154th Sup Sq

Suwon
30th Wea Sq—Det 21

Suwon Air Base
1st Air Pstl Sq—Det 23
8th Ftr-Bmr Gp (8th Ftr-Bmr Wg)
  Hq
  35th Ftr-Bmr Sq
  36th Ftr-Bmr Sq
  80th Ftr-Bmr Sq
8th Med Gp (8th Ftr-Bmr Wg)
51st Ftr-Intcp Gp (51st Ftr-Intcp
    Wg)
  Hq
  16th Ftr-Intcp Sq
  25th Ftr-Intcp Sq
802d Engr Avn Bn
919th Engr Avn Maint Co (Less
    Contact Plat)
931st Engr Avn Gp
  Hq & Hq & Sv Co
6127th Air Terminal Gp—Det 9

Taegu
30th Wea Sq—Dets 11 & 12
1973d AACS Sq (Mob) (1818th
    AACS Gp)
6132d AC&W Sq (502d Tac Con
    Gp) (Less Det)
6165th Rad Relay Sq

Taegu Air Base
1st Rad Sq, Mob—Det 13
2d Rad Relay Sq
7th Comms Sq, Comd
49th Ftr-Bmr Wg
  Hq & Hq Sq (Less Det)
  49th Ftr-Bmr Gp
    Hq
    7th Ftr-Bmr Sq
    8th Ftr-Bmr Sq
    9th Ftr-Bmr Sq

49th Maint & Sup Gp
Hq
  49th Maint Sq
  49th Sup Sq
  49th Mtr Veh Sq
49th Air Base Gp
  Hq & Hq Sq
  49th Comms Sq
  49th Air Police Sq
  49th Food Sv Sq
  49th Instls Sq
49th Med Gp
67th Tac Recon Gp (67th Tac Recon
  Wg)
Hq
  45th Tac Recon Sq
67th Air Base Gp (67th Tac Recon
  Wg)
  Hq & Hq Sq
  67th Food Sv Sq
748th AF Band
822d Engr Avn Bn (Less Co A)
934th Sig Bn, Sep, TAC—Det 1
3903d RBS Gp—OL
6004th Air Intel Sv Sq—Det 1
6127th Air Terminal Gp—Det 5
6166th Air Wea Recon Flt
6405th Korea Air Mat Unit

Taegu Air Base #2
5th Mtr Trans Sq, Avn (Less Det)
336th Ftr-Intcp Sq (4th Ftr-Intcp Gp)
6152d Air Base Sq

Yongdong-po
1st Air Pstl Sq—OL
3d Air Rsq Sq—Det 1
5th Mtr Trans Sq, Avn—Det 2
10th Ln Sq
18th Ftr-Bmr Wg—Det 1

Yonju
607th AC&W Sq (502d Tac Con
  Gp) (Less Det)

NOVEMBER 1, 1951
Chinhae
1st Air Pstl Sq—Det 4
18th Ftr-Bmr Wg
  Hq & Hq Sq (Less Det)
  18th Ftr-Bmr Gp
    Hq
  18th Maint & Sup Gp
    Hq
    18th Maint Sq
    18th Mtr Veh Sq
    18th Sup Sq
  18th Air Base Gp
    Hq & Hq Sq
    18th Comms Sq
    18th Air Police Sq
    18th Food Sv Sq
    18th Instls Sq
30th Wea Sq—Det 16

Chinhae Airdrome
18th Med Gp (18th Ftr-Bmr Wg)
39th Ftr-Intcp Sq (35th Ftr-Intcp Gp)
6127th Air Terminal Gp—Det 8

Chunchon
811th Engr Avn Bn—Co C
6127th Air Terminal Gp—OL

Chunchon Airdrome
6152d Air Base Sq

E Pyongyang
467th Sig Avn Const Co—OL

Hoengsong
30th Wea Sq—Dets 26 & 28
811th Engr Avn Bn (Less Cos B &
  C)
6151st AB Sq—Det 1

Hoengsong Airdrome
5th Mtr Trans Sq, Avn—Det 2

Inchon
606th AC&W Sq—Det 1

Kangnumg [Kangnung]
1st Shoran Beacon Unit—Det 4
6147th Tac Con Gp—Det 1

Kangnumg [Kangnung] **Airdrome**
6146th Air Base Sq—Det 2
6151st Air Base Sq—(Less Det &
  OL)
Kimpo
30th Wea Sq—Det 23
Kimpo Air Base
1st Air Pstl Sq—Det 28
4th Ftr-Intcp Wg
  Hq & Hq Sq (Less Det)
  4th Ftr-Intcp Gp
    Hq
    334th Ftr-Intcp Sq
    336th Ftr-Intcp Sq
  4th Maint & Sup Gp
    Hq
    4th Maint Sq
    4th Mtr Veh Sq
    4th Sup Sq
  4th Air Base Gp
    Hq & Hq Sq (Less Det)
    4th Comms Sq
    4th Air Police Sq
    4th Food Sv Sq
    4th Instls Sq
  4th Med Gp
67th Maint Sq (67th M&S Gp)
67th Tac Recon Wg
  Hq & Hq Sq
  67th Recon Tech Sq
  67th Tac Recon Gp
    Hq
    12th Tac Recon Sq, Night
      Photo
    15th Tac Recon Sq, Photo-J
    45th Tac Recon Sq
  67th Air Base Gp
    Hq & Hq Sq
    67th Comms Sq
    67th Food Sv Sq (Less OL)
    67th Air Police Sq
    67th Instls Sq
  67th Med Gp

606th AC&W Sq (502d Tac Con
  Gp) (Less Det)
839th Engr Avn Bn (Less OL)
1503d Air Trans Wg—Det 10
1993d AACS Sq (1818th AACS Gp)
6127th Air Terminal Gp—Det 14
6166th Air Wea Recon Flt
Kuksa-bong
1st Shoran Beacon Unit—Det 2
Kunsan
1st Air Pstl Sq—Det 29
3d Bomb Wg, L
  Hq & Hq Sq
  3d Bomb Gp, L
    Hq
    8th Bomb Sq, L, Night
      Intruder
    13th Bomb Sq, L, Night
      Intruder
    90th Bomb Sq, L, Night
      Intruder
  3d Maint & Sup Gp
    Hq
    3d Maint Sq
    3d Mtr Veh Sq
    3d Sup Sq
  3d Air Base Gp
    Hq & Hq Sq
    3d Comms Sq
    3d Air Police Sq
    3d Food Sv Sq
    3d Instls Sq
  3d Med Gp (Less OL)
440th Sig Avn Const Bn—Co B
808th Engr Avn Bn
6127th Air Terminal Gp—OL
6132d AC&W Sq—Det 1
Kwangung Airdrome
607th AC&W Sq—Det 3
Pusan
30th Wea Sq—Det 27
3903d RBS Gp—Det 22

Pusan Air Base
1st Air Pstl Sq—Det 14
30th Wea Sq—Det 10
622d Engr Avn Maint Co
809th Engr Avn Bn
811th Engr Avn Bn—Co B
6151st AB Sq—OL

Pusan East Air Base
12th Ftr-Bmr Sq (18th Ftr-Bmr Gp)
30th Wea Sq—Det 13
67th Ftr-Bmr Sq (18th Ftr-Bmr Gp)
452d Bomb Wg, L (USAFR EAD)
  Hq & Hq Sq
  452d Bomb Gp, L
    Hq
    728th Bomb Sq, L, Night
      Intruder
    729th Bomb Sq, L, Night
      Intruder
    730th Bomb Sq, L, Night
      Intruder
  452d Maint & Sup Gp
    Hq
    452d Maint Sq
    452d Sup Sq
    452d Mtr Veh Sq
  452d Air Base Gp
    Hq & Hq Sq
    452d Comms Sq
    452d Air Police Sq
    452d Food Sv Sq
    452d Instls Sq
  452d Med Gp
543d Ammo Sup Sq, Dep
802d Engr Avn Bn—OL
822d Engr Avn Bn—Co A
930th Engr Avn Gp
  Hq & Hq & Sv Co (Less Dets)
6127th Air Terminal Gp—Det 4
6401st Fld Maint Sq
6413th Air Base Sq

Pyongtaek Airdrome
1st Air Pstl Sq—Det 30
30th Wea Sq—Det 20

6147th Tac Con Gp
  Hq (Less Det)
  6147th Air Base Sq
  6147th Maint & Sup Sq
  6147th Med Sq
  6148th Tac Con Sq (Air)
  6149th Tac Con Sq (Air)
  6150th Tac Con Sq (Grd)

Pyongyang
919th Engr Avn Maint Co—Contact
  Plat
3903d RBS Gp—Dets 5 & 11

Pyongyang East
See: E Pyongyang

Sachon Airdrome
6146th Air Base Sq (Less Det)

Seoul
See: Kimpo Air Base
30th Wea Sq (Less Dets)
1818th AACS Gp (1808th AACS
  Wg)
  Hq

Seoul Airdrome
Fifth Air Force
  Hq & Hq Sq (Less Dets)
1st Air Pstl Sq—Det 31
1st Rad Sq, Mob—OL
1st Shoran Beacon Unit (Less Dets)
30th Wea Sq—Det 18
440th Sig Avn Const Bn (Less Co B
  & OLs)
502d Tac Con Gp
  Hq
  605th Tac Con Sq
934th Sig Bn, Sep TAC (Less Det)
1134th USAF S/A Sq—OL
6004th Air Intel Sv Sq—Det 2
6127th Air Terminal Gp—OL
6153d Air Base Sq (Less Flts)
6153d Air Base Sq—Flts A & B
6154th Air Base Gp
  Hq
  6154th Air Police Sq

6154th Food Sv Sq
6154th Instls Sq
6154th Med Sq
6154th Mtr Veh Sq
6154th Sup Sq

Suwon
30th Wea Sq—Det 21

Suwon Air Base
1st Air Pstl Sq—Det 23
8th Ftr-Bmr Wg
  Hq & Hq Sq
  8th Ftr-Bmr Gp
    Hq
    35th Ftr-Bmr Sq
    36th Ftr-Bmr Sq
    80th Ftr-Bmr Sq
  8th Maint & Sup Gp
    Hq
    8th Maint Sq
    8th Mtr Veh Sq
    8th Sup Sq
  8th Air Base Gp
    Hq & Hq Sq
    8th Comms Sq
    8th Air Police Sq
    8th Food Sv Sq
    8th Instls Sq
  8th Med Gp
51st Ftr-Intcp Wg
  Hq & Hq Sq
  51st Ftr-Intcp Gp
    Hq
    16th Ftr-Intcp Sq
    25th Ftr-Intcp Sq
  51st Maint & Sup Gp
    Hq
    51st Maint Sq
    51st Mtr Veh Sq
    51st Sup Sq
  51st Air Base Gp
    Hq & Hq Sq
    51st Comms Sq
    51st Air Police Sq
    51st Food Sv Sq

51st Instls Sq
51st Med Gp
440th Sig Avn Const Bn—OL
802d Engr Avn Bn (Less OL)
919th Engr Avn Maint Co (Less
    Contact Plat)
931st Engr Avn Gp
  Hq & Hq & Sv Co
6127th Air Terminal Gp—Det 9

Taegu
30th Wea Sq—Dets 11 & 12
1973d AACS Sq (Mob) (1818th
    AACS Gp)
6132d AC&W Sq (502d Tac Con
    Gp)(Less Det)
6165th Rad Relay Sq

Taegu Air Base
Fifth Air Force—Det 1, Rear
1st Air Pstl Sq—OL
1st Epidemiological Flt
1st Rad Sq, Mob—Det 13
2d Rad Relay Sq
3d Air Rsq Sq—OL
7th Comms Sq, Comd
9th Stat Svs Flt
49th Ftr-Bmr Wg
  Hq & Hq Sq (Less Det)
  49th Ftr-Bmr Gp
    Hq
    7th Ftr-Bmr Sq
    8th Ftr-Bmr Sq
    9th Ftr-Bmr Sq
  49th Maint & Sup Gp
    Hq
    49th Maint Sq
    49th Sup Sq
    49th Mtr Veh Sq
  49th Air Base Gp
    Hq & Hq Sq
    49th Comms Sq
    49th Air Police Sq
    49th Food Sv Sq
    49th Instls Sq
  49th Med Gp

136th Ftr-Bmr Gp (ANG EAD)
   (136th Ftr-Bmr Wg)
Hq
  154th Ftr-Bmr Sq
  182d Ftr-Bmr Sq
440th Sig Bn Const Bn—OL
748th AF Band
822d Engr Avn Bn (Less Co A)
934th Sig Bn, Sep, TAC—Det 1
3903d RBS Gp—OL
6004th Air Intel Sv Sq—Det 1
6127th Air Terminal Gp—Det 5
6405th Korea Air Mat Unit

Taegu Air Base #2
5th Mtr Trans Sq, Avn (Less Det)
6152d Air Base Sq

Taejon Airdrome
440th Sig Avn Const Bn—OL

Yongdong-po
3d Air Rsq Sq—Det 1
10th Ln Sq
18th Ftr-Bmr Wg—Det 1

Yonju
607th AC&W Sq (502d Tac Con
  Gp) (Less Det)

JANUARY 1, 1952

Chinhae
1st Air Pstl Sq—Det 4
18th Ftr-Bmr Wg
  Hq & Hq Sq (Less Det)
  18th Ftr-Bmr Gp
    Hq
  18th Maint & Sup Gp
    Hq
    18th Maint Sq
    18th Mtr Veh Sq
    18th Sup Sq
  18th Air Base Gp
    Hq & Hq Sq
    18th Comms Sq
    18th Air Police Sq
    18th Food Sv Sq

  18th Instls Sq
30th Wea Sq—Det 16

Chinhae Airdrome
18th Med Gp (18th Ftr-Bmr Wg)
39th Ftr-Intcp Sq (35th Ftr-Intcp Gp)
6127th Air Terminal Gp—Det 8

Chunchon
811th Engr Avn Bn—Co C
6127th Air Terminal Gp—OL

Chunchon Airdrome
6152d Air Base Sq

Hoengsong
30th Wea Sq—Dets 26 & 28
811th Engr Avn Bn (Less Cos B &
  C)
6151st AB Sq—Det 1

Hoengsong Airdrome
5th Mtr Trans Sq, Avn—Det 2
18th Ftr-Bmr Wg—Det 1

Inchon
606th AC&W Sq—Det 1

Kangnumg [Kangnung]
1st Shoran Beacon Unit—Det 4
6147th Tac Con Gp—Det 1

Kangnumg [Kangnung] **Airdrome**
6146th Air Base Sq—Det 2

Kimpo
30th Wea Sq—Det 23

Kimpo Air Base
1st Air Pstl Sq—Det 28
4th Ftr-Intcp Wg
  Hq & Hq Sq (Less Det)
  4th Ftr-Intcp Gp
    Hq
    334th Ftr-Intcp Sq
    335th Ftr-Intcp Sq
    336th Ftr-Intcp Sq
  4th Maint & Sup Gp
    Hq
    4th Maint Sq
    4th Mtr Veh Sq
    4th Sup Sq

4th Air Base Gp
  Hq & Hq Sq (Less Det)
  4th Comms Sq
  4th Air Police Sq
  4th Food Sv Sq
  4th Instls Sq
4th Med Gp
67th Maint Sq (67th M&S Gp)
67th Tac Recon Wg
  Hq & Hq Sq
  67th Recon Tech Sq
  67th Tac Recon Gp
    Hq
    12th Tac Recon Sq, Night
      Photo
    15th Tac Recon Sq, Photo-J
    45th Tac Recon Sq
  67th Air Base Gp
    Hq & Hq Sq
    67th Comms Sq
    67th Food Sv Sq
    67th Air Police Sq
    67th Instls Sq
  67th Med Gp
606th AC&W Sq (502d Tac Con
  Gp) (Less Dets)
606th AC&W Sq—Det 2
839th Engr Avn Bn (Less OL)
1503d Air Trans Wg—Det 10
1993d AACS Sq (1818th AACS Gp)
6127th Air Terminal Gp—Det 14
6166th Air Wea Recon Flt

Kuksa-bong
1st Shoran Beacon Unit—Det 2

Kunsan
1st Air Pstl Sq—Det 29
3d Bomb Wg, L
  Hq & Hq Sq
  3d Bomb Gp, L
    Hq
    8th Bomb Sq, L, Night
      Intruder
    13th Bomb Sq, L, Night
      Intruder

    90th Bomb Sq, L, Night
      Intruder
  3d Maint & Sup Gp
    Hq
    3d Maint Sq
    3d Mtr Veh Sq
    3d Sup Sq
  3d Air Base Gp
    Hq & Hq Sq
    3d Comms Sq
    3d Air Police Sq
    3d Food Sv Sq
    3d Instls Sq
  3d Med Gp (Less OLs)
808th Engr Avn Bn
6127th Air Terminal Gp—OL

Kwangung Airdrome
607th AC&W Sq—Det 3

Pusan
30th Wea Sq—Det 27

Pusan Air Base
1st Air Pstl Sq—Det 14
30th Wea Sq—Det 10
622d Engr Avn Maint Co
809th Engr Avn Bn
811th Engr Avn Bn—Co B

Pusan East Air Base
12th Ftr-Bmr Sq (18th Ftr-Bmr Gp)
30th Wea Sq—Det 13
67th Ftr-Bmr Sq (18th Ftr-Bmr Gp)
452d Bomb Wg, L (USAFR EAD)
  Hq & Hq Sq
  452d Bomb Gp, L
    Hq
    728th Bomb Sq, L, Night
      Intruder
    729th Bomb Sq, L, Night
      Intruder
    730th Bomb Sq, L, Night
      Intruder
  452d Maint & Sup Gp
    Hq
    452d Maint Sq
    452d Sup Sq

452d Mtr Veh Sq
452d Air Base Gp
  Hq & Hq Sq
  452d Comms Sq
  452d Air Police Sq
  452d Food Sv Sq
  452d Instls Sq
452d Med Gp
543d Ammo Sup Sq, Dep
802d Engr Avn Bn—OL
822d Engr Avn Bn—Co A
930th Engr Avn Gp
  Hq & Hq & Sv Co (Less Dets)
6127th Air Terminal Gp—Det 4
6401st Fld Maint Sq
6413th Air Base Sq

Pyongtaek Airdrome
1st Air Pstl Sq—Det 30
30th Wea Sq—Det 20
6147th Tac Con Gp
  Hq (Less Det)
  6147th Air Base Sq
  6147th Maint & Sup Sq
  6147th Med Sq
  6148th Tac Con Sq (Air)
  6149th Tac Con Sq (Air)
  6150th Tac Con Sq (Grd)

Pyongyang
919th Engr Avn Maint Co—Contact
  Plat

Sachon Airdrome
6146th Air Base Sq—Det 1

Seoul
See: Kimpo Air Base
3d Air Rsq Sq—Det 1
5th Comms Gp
  Hq
  1st Rad Sq
  1st Tp & Carr Sq
  2d Comms Sq, Oprs
30th Wea Sq (Less Dets)
1818th AACS Gp (1808th AACS
  Wg)
  Hq

Seoul Airdrome
Fifth Air Force
  Hq & Hq Sq (Less Dets)
1st Air Pstl Sq—Det 27
1st Air Pstl Sq—Det 31
1st Rad Sq, Mob—OL
1st Shoran Beacon Unit (Less Dets)
30th Wea Sq—Det 18
440th Sig Avn Const Bn (Less OLs)
502d Tac Con Gp
  Hq
  605th Tac Con Sq (Less Det)
605th Tac Con Sq—Det 3
1134th USAF S/A Sq—OL
6004th Air Intel Sv Sq—Det 2
6127th Air Terminal Gp—OL
6153d Air Base Sq (Less Flts & Det)
6153d Air Base Sq—Flts A & B
6154th Air Base Gp
  Hq
  6154th Air Police Sq
  6154th Food Sv Sq
  6154th Instls Sq
  6154th Med Sq
  6154th Mtr Veh Sq
  6154th Sup Sq

Suwon
30th Wea Sq—Det 21

Suwon Air Base
1st Air Pstl Sq—Det 23
8th Ftr-Bmr Wg
  Hq & Hq Sq
  8th Ftr-Bmr Gp
    Hq
    35th Ftr-Bmr Sq
    36th Ftr-Bmr Sq
    80th Ftr-Bmr Sq
  8th Maint & Sup Gp
    Hq
    8th Maint Sq
    8th Mtr Veh Sq
    8th Sup Sq
  8th Air Base Gp
    Hq & Hq Sq

8th Comms Sq
8th Air Police Sq
8th Food Sv Sq
8th Instls Sq
8th Med Gp
51st Ftr-Intcp Wg
Hq & Hq Sq
51st Ftr-Intcp Gp
Hq
16th Ftr-Intcp Sq
25th Ftr-Intcp Sq
51st Maint & Sup Gp
Hq
51st Maint Sq
51st Mtr Veh Sq
51st Sup Sq
51st Air Base Gp
Hq & Hq Sq
51st Air Police Sq
51st Comms Sq
51st Food Sv Sq
51st Instls Sq
51st Med Gp
440th Sig Avn Const Bn—OL
802d Engr Avn Bn (Less OL)
919th Engr Avn Maint Co (Less
Contact Plat)
931st Engr Avn Gp
Hq & Hq & Sv Co
6127th Air Terminal Gp—Det 9

Taegu
30th Wea Sq—Dets 11 & 12
1973d AACS Sq (Mob) (1818th
AACS Gp)
6146th Air Base Sq (Less Dets)
6153d Air Base Sq—Det 1

Taegu Air Base
Fifth Air Force—Det 1, Rear
1st Air Pstl Sq—OL
1st Epidemiological Flt
1st Rad Sq, Mob—Det 13
2d Rad Relay Sq
3d Air Rsq Sq—OL
7th Comms Sq, Oprs

9th Stat Svs Flt
49th Ftr-Bmr Wg
Hq & Hq Sq (Less Det)
49th Ftr-Bmr Gp
Hq
7th Ftr-Bmr Sq
8th Ftr-Bmr Sq
9th Ftr-Bmr Sq
49th Maint & Sup Gp
Hq
49th Maint Sq
49th Sup Sq
49th Mtr Veh Sq
49th Air Base Gp
Hq & Hq Sq
49th Comms Sq
49th Air Police Sq
49th Food Sv Sq
49th Instls Sq
49th Med Gp
136th Ftr-Bmr Wg (ANG EAD)
Hq & Hq Sq
136th Ftr-Bmr Gp
Hq
111th Ftr-Bmr Sq
154th Ftr-Bmr Sq
182d Ftr-Bmr Sq
136th Maint & Sup Gp
Hq
136th Maint Sq
136th Mtr Veh Sq
136th Sup Sq
136th Air Base Gp
Hq & Hq Sq
136th Air Police Sq
136th Comms Sq
136th Food Sv Sq
136th Instls Sq
136th Med Gp
440th Sig Avn Const Bn—OL
608th AC&W Sq (502d Tac Con Gp)
748th AF Band
822d Engr Avn Bn (Less Co A)
3903d RBS Gp—OL
6004th Air Intel Sv Sq-Det 1

6127th Air Terminal Gp—Det 5
6151st Air Base Sq (6154th AB Gp)
(Less Det)
6405th Korean Air Mat Unit

Taegu Air Base #2
5th Mtr Trans Sq, Avn (Less Det)
6152d Air Base Sq

Taejon Airdrome
440th Sig Avn Const Bn—OL

Yongdong-po
10th Ln Sq

Yonju
607th AC&W Sq(502d Tac Con Gp)
(Less Det)

MARCH 1, 1952

Chinhae
1st Air Pstl Sq—Det 4
18th Ftr-Bmr Wg
  Hq & Hq Sq (Less Det)
  18th Ftr-Bmr Gp
    Hq
  18th Maint & Sup Gp
    Hq
    18th Maint Sq
    18th Mtr Veh Sq
    18th Sup Sq
  18th Air Base Gp
    Hq & Hq Sq
    18th Comms Sq
    18th Air Police Sq
    18th Food Sv Sq
    18th Instls Sq
30th Wea Sq—Det 16

Chinhae Airdrome
18th Med Gp (18th Ftr-Bmr Wg)
39th Ftr-Intcp Sq (35th Ftr-Intcp Gp)
6127th Air Terminal Gp—Det 8

Chunchon
811th Engr Avn Bn—Co C
6127th Air Terminal Gp—OL

Chunchon Airdrome
6152d Air Base Sq (Less OL)

Hoengsong
30th Wea Sq—Dets 26 & 28
811th Engr Avn Bn (Less Cos B &
  C)
6151st AB Sq—Det 1

Hoengsong Airdrome
5th Mtr Trans Sq, Avn—Det 2
18th Ftr-Bmr Wg—Det 1

Inchon
606th AC&W Sq—Det 1

Kangnumg [Kangnung]
6147th Tac Con Gp—Det 1

Kangnumg [Kangnung] **Airdrome**
1st Shoran Beacon Sq—Det 4
6146th Air Base Sq—Det 2

Kimpo
30th Wea Sq—Det 23

Kimpo Air Base
1st Air Pstl Sq—Det 28
4th Ftr-Intcp Wg
  Hq & Hq Sq (Less Det)
  4th Ftr-Intcp Gp
    Hq
    334th Ftr-Intcp Sq
    335th Ftr-Intcp Sq
    336th Ftr-Intcp Sq
  4th Maint & Sup Gp
    Hq
    4th Maint Sq
    4th Mtr Veh Sq
    4th Sup Sq
  4th Air Base Gp
    Hq & Hq Sq (Less Det)
    4th Comms Sq
    4th Air Police Sq
    4th Food Sv Sq
    4th Instls Sq
  4th Med Gp
67th Maint Sq (67th M&S Gp)
67th Tac Recon Wg
  Hq & Hq Sq
  67th Recon Tech Sq
  67th Tac Recon Gp

Hq
12th Tac Recon Sq, Night
Photo
15th Tac Recon Sq, Photo-J
45th Tac Recon Sq
67th Air Base Gp
Hq & Hq Sq
67th Comms Sq
67th Food Sv Sq
67th Air Police Sq
67th Instls Sq
67th Med Gp
606th AC&W Sq (502d Tac Con
Gp) (Less Dets)
606th AC&W Sq—Det 2
839th Engr Avn Bn (Less OL)
1993d AACS Sq (1818th AACS Gp)
6127th Air Terminal Gp—Det 14
6166th Air Wea Recon Flt

Korea (unspecified location)
15th Rad Sq, Mob—Det 1

Kuksa-bong
1st Shoran Beacon Unit—Det 2

Kunsan
1st Air Pstl Sq—Det 29
3d Bomb Wg, L
Hq & Hq Sq
3d Bomb Gp, L
Hq
8th Bomb Sq, L, Night
Intruder
13th Bomb Sq, L, Night
Intruder
90th Bomb Sq, L, Night
Intruder
3d Maint & Sup Gp
Hq
3d Maint Sq
3d Mtr Veh Sq
3d Sup Sq
3d Air Base Gp
Hq & Hq Sq
3d Comms Sq
3d Air Police Sq

3d Food Sv Sq
3d Instls Sq
3d Med Gp
808th Engr Avn Bn
6127th Air Terminal Gp—OL

Kwangung Airdrome
607th AC&W Sq—Det 3

Pusan
30th Wea Sq—Det 27

Pusan Air Base
1st Air Pstl Sq—Det 14
622d Engr Avn Maint Co
809th Engr Avn Bn
811th Engr Avn Bn—Co B
1903d Engr Avn Bn

Pusan East Air Base
12th Ftr-Bmr Sq (18th Ftr-Bmr Gp)
30th Wea Sq—Det 13
67th Ftr-Bmr Sq (18th Ftr-Bmr Gp)
452d Bomb Wg, L (USAFR EAD)
Hq & Hq Sq
452d Bomb Gp, L
Hq
728th Bomb Sq, L, Night
Intruder
729th Bomb Sq, L, Night
Intruder
730th Bomb Sq, L, Night
Intruder
452d Maint & Sup Gp
Hq
452d Maint Sq
452d Sup Sq
452d Mtr Veh Sq
452d Air Base Gp
Hq & Hq Sq
452d Comms Sq
452d Air Police Sq
452d Food Sv Sq
452d Instls Sq
452d Med Gp
543d Ammo Sup Sq, Dep
547th Ammo Sup Sq, Dep
802d Engr Avn Bn—OL

822d Engr Avn Bn—Co A
930th Engr Avn Gp
    Hq & Hq & Sv Co (Less Dets)
6127th Air Terminal Gp—Det 4
6401st Fld Maint Sq

Pyongtaek Airdrome

1st Air Pstl Sq—Det 30
30th Wea Sq—Det 20
6147th Tac Con Gp
    Hq (Less Det)
    6147th Air Base Sq
    6147th Maint & Sup Sq
    6147th Med Sq
    6148th Tac Con Sq (Air)
    6149th Tac Con Sq (Air)
    6150th Tac Con Sq (Grd)

Pyongyang

919th Engr Avn Maint Co—Contact
    Plat

Sachon Airdrome

6146th Air Base Sq—-Det 1

Seoul

See: Kimpo Air Base
1st Shoran Beacon Sq—Dets 7 & 8
3d Air Rsq Sq—Det 1
5th Comms Gp
    Hq
    1st Rad Sq
    1st Tp & Carr Sq
    2d Comms Sq, Oprs
30th Wea Sq (Less Dets)
1818th AACS Gp (1808th AACS
    Wg)
    Hq

Seoul Airdrome

Fifth Air Force
    Hq & Hq Sq (Less Dets)
1st Air Pstl Sq—Dets 27 & 31
1st Rad Sq, Mob—OL
1st Shoran Beacon Sq (Less Dets)
30th Wea Sq—Det 18
440th Sig Avn Const Bn (Less OL)
502d Tac Con Gp

Hq
    605th Tac Con Sq (Less Det)
605th Tac Con Sq—Det 3
1134th USAF S/A Sq—OL
6004th Air Intel Sv Sq—Det 2
6153d Air Base Sq (Less Flts & Det)
6153d Air Base Sq—Flts A & B
6154th Air Base Gp
    Hq
    6154th Air Police Sq
    6154th Food Sv Sq
    6154th Instls Sq
    6154th Med Sq
    6154th Mtr Veh Sq
    6154th Sup Sq

Suwon

30th Wea Sq—Det 21

Suwon Air Base

1st Air Pstl Sq—Det 23
8th Ftr-Bmr Wg
    Hq & Hq Sq
    8th Ftr-Bmr Gp
        Hq
        35th Ftr-Bmr Sq
        36th Ftr-Bmr Sq
        80th Ftr-Bmr Sq
    8th Maint & Sup Gp
        Hq
        8th Maint Sq
        8th Mtr Veh Sq
        8th Sup Sq
    8th Air Base Gp
        Hq & Hq Sq
        8th Comms Sq
        8th Air Police Sq
        8th Food Sv Sq
        8th Instls Sq
    8th Med Gp
51st Ftr-Intcp Wg
    Hq & Hq Sq
    51st Ftr-Intcp Gp
        Hq
        16th Ftr-Intcp Sq
        25th Ftr-Intcp Sq

51st Maint & Sup Gp
  Hq
  51st Maint Sq
  51st Mtr Veh Sq
  51st Sup Sq
51st Air Base Gp
  Hq & Hq Sq
  51st Air Police Sq
  51st Comms Sq
  51st Food Sv Sq
  51st Instls Sq (Less OL)
51st Med Gp
802d Engr Avn Bn (Less OL)
919th Engr Avn Maint Co (Less
  Contact Plat)
931st Engr Avn Gp
  Hq & Hq & Sv Co
6127th Air Terminal Gp—Det 9

Taegu
30th Wea Sq—Dets 11 & 12
1973d AACS Sq (Mob) (1818th
  AACS Gp)
6146th Air Base Sq (Less Dets)
6153d Air Base Sq—Det 1

Taegu Air Base
Fifth Air Force—Det 1, Rear
1st Air Pstl Sq—OL
1st Epidemiological Flt
2d Rad Relay Sq
3d Air Rsq Sq—OL
7th Comms Sq, Oprs
9th Stat Svs Flt
49th Ftr-Bmr Wg
  Hq & Hq Sq (Less Det)
  49th Ftr-Bmr Gp
    Hq
    7th Ftr-Bmr Sq
    8th Ftr-Bmr Sq
    9th Ftr-Bmr Sq
  49th Maint & Sup Gp
    Hq
    49th Maint Sq
    49th Sup Sq
    49th Mtr Veh Sq

49th Air Base Gp
  Hq & Hq Sq
  49th Comms Sq
  49th Air Police Sq
  49th Food Sv Sq
  49th Instls Sq
49th Med Gp
136th Ftr-Bmr Wg (ANG EAD)
  Hq & Hq Sq
  136th Ftr-Bmr Gp
    Hq
    111th Ftr-Bmr Sq
    154th Ftr-Bmr Sq
    182d Ftr-Bmr Sq
  136th Maint & Sup Gp
    Hq
    136th Maint Sq
    136th Mtr Veh Sq
    136th Sup Sq
  136th Air Base Gp
    Hq & Hq Sq
    136th Air Police Sq
    136th Comms Sq
    136th Food Sv Sq
    136th Instls Sq
  136th Med Gp
440th Sig Avn Const Bn—OL
608th AC&W Sq (502d Tac Con Gp)
748th AF Band
822d Engr Avn Bn (Less Co A)
6004th Air Intel Sv Sq—Det 1
6127th Air Terminal Gp—Det 5
6151st Air Base Sq (6154th AB Gp)
  (Less Det)
6405th Korea Air Mat Unit

Taegu Air Base #2
5th Mtr Trans Sq, Avn (Less Det)
6152d Air Base Sq

Yongdong-po
10th Ln Sq

Yonju
607th AC&W Sq (502d Tac Con
  Gp) (Less Det)

APRIL 1, 1952

Chinhae
1st Air Pstl Sq—Det 4
18th Ftr-Bmr Wg
  Hq & Hq Sq (Less Det)
  18th Ftr-Bmr Gp
  Hq
  18th Maint & Sup Gp
  Hq
  18th Maint Sq
  18th Mtr Veh Sq
  18th Sup Sq
  18th Air Base Gp
  Hq & Hq Sq
  18th Comms Sq
  18th Air Police Sq
  18th Food Sv Sq
  18th Instls Sq
30th Wea Sq—Det 16

Chinhae Airdrome
18th Med Gp (18th Ftr-Bmr Wg)
39th Ftr-Intcp Sq (35th Ftr-Intcp Gp)
6127th Air Terminal Gp—Det 8

Chunchon
811th Engr Avn Bn—Co C

Chunchon Airdrome
6152d Air Base Sq

Hoengsong
30th Wea Sq—Dets 26 & 28
811th Engr Avn Bn (Less Cos B & C
  & OLs)
6151st AB Sq—Det 1

Hoengsong Airdrome
5th Mtr Trans Sq, Avn—Det 2
18th Ftr-Bmr Wg—Det 1

Inchon
606th AC&W Sq—Det 1

Kangnumg [Kangnung]
6147th Tac Con Gp—Det 1

Kangnumg [Kangnung] Airdrome
1st Shoran Beacon Sq—Det 4
6146th Air Base Sq—Det 2

Kimpo
30th Wea Sq—Det 23

Kimpo Air Base
1st Air Pstl Sq—Det 28
4th Ftr-Intcp Wg
  Hq & Hq Sq (Less Det)
  4th Ftr-Intcp Gp
  Hq
  334th Ftr-Intcp Sq
  335th Ftr-Intcp Sq
  336th Ftr-Intcp Sq
  4th Maint & Sup Gp
  Hq
  4th Maint Sq
  4th Mtr Veh Sq
  4th Sup Sq
  4th Air Base Gp
  Hq & Hq Sq (Less Det)
  4th Comms Sq
  4th Air Police Sq
  4th Food Sv Sq
  4th Instls Sq
4th Med Gp
67th Maint Sq (67th M&S Gp)
67th Tac Recon Wg
  Hq & Hq Sq
  67th Recon Tech Sq
  67th Tac Recon Gp
  Hq
  12th Tac Recon Sq, Night
    Photo
  15th Tac Recon Sq, Photo-J
  45th Tac Recon Sq
  67th Air Base Gp
  Hq & Hq Sq
  67th Comms Sq
  67th Food Sv Sq
  67th Air Police Sq
  67th Instls Sq
67th Med Gp
606th AC&W Sq (502d Tac Con
  Gp) (Less Dets)
606th AC&W Sq—Det 2
839th Engr Avn Bn (Less OL)

1993d AACS Sq (1818th AACS Gp)
6127th Air Terminal Gp—Det 14
6166th Air Wea Recon Flt

Korea (unspecified location)
15th Rad Sq, Mob—Det 1

Kuksa-bong
1st Shoran Beacon Unit—Det 2

Kunsan
1st Air Pstl Sq—Det 29
3d Bomb Wg, L
  Hq & Hq Sq
  3d Bomb Gp, L
    Hq
    8th Bomb Sq, L, Night
      Intruder
    13th Bomb Sq, L, Night
      Intruder
    90th Bomb Sq, L, Night
      Intruder
  3d Maint & Sup Gp
    Hq
    3d Maint Sq
    3d Mtr Veh Sq
    3d Sup Sq
  3d Air Base Gp
    Hq & Hq Sq
    3d Comms Sq
    3d Air Police Sq
    3d Food Sv Sq
    3d Instls Sq
  3d Med Gp
808th Engr Avn Bn
6127th Air Terminal Gp—OL

Kwangung Airdrome
607th AC&W Sq—Det 3

Pusan
30th Wea Sq—Det 27

Pusan Air Base
1st Air Pstl Sq—Det 14
622d Engr Avn Maint Co
809th Engr Avn Bn
811th Engr Avn Bn—Co B
1903d Engr Avn Bn

Pusan East Air Base
12th Ftr-Bmr Sq (18th Ftr-Bmr Gp)
30th Wea Sq—Det 13
67th Ftr-Bmr Sq (18th Ftr-Bmr Gp)
452d Bomb Wg, L (USAFR EAD)
  Hq & Hq Sq
  452d Bomb Gp, L
    Hq
    728th Bomb Sq, L, Night
      Intruder
    729th Bomb Sq, L, Night
      Intruder
    730th Bomb Sq, L, Night
      Intruder
  452d Maint & Sup Gp
    Hq
    452d Maint Sq
    452d Sup Sq
    452d Mtr Veh Sq
  452d Air Base Gp
    Hq & Hq Sq
    452d Comms Sq
    452d Air Police Sq
    452d Food Sv Sq
    452d Instls Sq
  452d Med Gp
543d Ammo Sup Sq, Dep
547th Ammo Sup Sq, Dep
802d Engr Avn Bn—OL
822d Engr Avn Bn—Co A
930th Engr Avn Gp
  Hq & Hq & Sv Co (Less Dets)
6127th Air Terminal Gp—Det 4
6401st Fld Maint Sq

Pyongtaek Airdrome
1st Air Pstl Sq—Det 30
30th Wea Sq—Det 20
6147th Tac Con Gp
  Hq (Less Det)
  6147th Air Base Sq
  6147th Maint & Sup Sq
  6147th Med Sq
  6148th Tac Con Sq (Air)
  6149th Tac Con Sq (Air)

6150th Tac Con Sq (Grd)

Pyongyang

919th Engr Avn Maint Co—Contact
    Plat

Seoul

See: Kimpo Air Base

1st Shoran Beacon Sq—Dets 7 & 8

3d Air Rsq Sq—Det 1

5th Comms Gp

    Hq

    1st Rad Sq

    1st Tp & Carr Sq

    2d Comms Sq, Oprs

30th Wea Sq (Less Dets)

811th Engr Avn Bn—OL

1818th AACS Gp (1808th AACS
    Wg)

    Hq

Seoul Airdrome

Fifth Air Force

    Hq (Less Dets)

1st Air Pstl Sq—Dets 27 & 31

1st Rad Sq, Mob—OL

1st Shoran Beacon Sq (Less Dets)

30th Wea Sq-Det 18

440th Sig Avn Const Bn (Less OL)

502d Tac Con Gp

    Hq

    605th Tac Con Sq (Less Det)

605th Tac Con Sq—Det 3

1134th USAF S/A Sq—OL

6004th Air Intel Sv Sq—Det 2

6153d Air Base Sq (Less Flts & Det)

6153d Air Base Sq—Flts A & B

6154th Air Base Gp

    Hq

    6154th Air Police Sq

    6154th Food Sv Sq

    6154th Instls Sq

    6154th Med Sq

    6154th Mtr Veh Sq

    6154th Sup Sq

Suwon

30th Wea Sq—Det 21

Suwon Air Base

1st Air Pstl Sq—Det 23

8th Ftr-Bmr Wg

    Hq & Hq Sq

    8th Ftr-Bmr Gp

        Hq

        35th Ftr-Bmr Sq

        36th Ftr-Bmr Sq

        80th Ftr-Bmr Sq

    8th Maint & Sup Gp

        Hq

        8th Maint Sq

        8th Mtr Veh Sq

        8th Sup Sq

    8th Air Base Gp

        Hq & Hq Sq

        8th Comms Sq

        8th Air Police Sq

        8th Food Sv Sq

        8th Instls Sq

    8th Med Gp

51st Ftr-Intcp Wg

    Hq & Hq Sq

    51st Ftr-Intcp Gp

        Hq

        16th Ftr-Intcp Sq

        25th Ftr-Intcp Sq

    51st Maint & Sup Gp

        Hq

        51st Maint Sq

        51st Mtr Veh Sq

        51st Sup Sq

    51st Air Base Gp

        Hq & Hq Sq

        51st Air Police Sq

        51st Comms Sq

        51st Food Sv Sq

        51st Instls Sq

    51st Med Gp

802d Engr Avn Bn (Less OL)

919th Engr Avn Maint Co (Less
    Contact Plat)

931st Engr Avn Gp

    Hq & Hq & Sv Co

6127th Air Terminal Gp—Det 9

Taegu
30th Wea Sq—Dets 11 & 12
1973d AACS Sq (Mob) (1818th
    AACS Gp)
6146th Air Base Sq (Less Det)
6153d Air Base Sq—Det 1

Taegu Air Base
Fifth Air Force—Det 1, Rear
1st Air Pstl Sq—OL
1st Epidemiological Flt
2d Rad Relay Sq
3d Air Rsq Sq—OL
7th Comms Sq, Oprs
9th Stat Svs Flt
49th Ftr-Bmr Wg
  Hq & Hq Sq (Less Det)
  49th Ftr-Bmr Gp
    Hq
    7th Ftr-Bmr Sq
    8th Ftr-Bmr Sq
    9th Ftr-Bmr Sq
  49th Maint & Sup Gp
    Hq
    49th Maint Sq
    49th Sup Sq
    49th Mtr Veh Sq
  49th Air Base Gp
    Hq & Hq Sq
    49th Comms Sq
    49th Air Police Sq
    49th Food Sv Sq
    49th Instls Sq
  49th Med Gp
136th Ftr-Bmr Wg (ANG EAD)
  Hq & Hq Sq
  136th Ftr-Bmr Gp
    Hq
    111th Ftr-Bmr Sq
    154th Ftr-Bmr Sq
    182d Ftr-Bmr Sq
  136th Maint & Sup Gp
    Hq
    136th Maint Sq
    136th Mtr Veh Sq

    136th Sup Sq
  136th Air Base Gp
    Hq & Hq Sq
    136th Air Police Sq
    136th Comms Sq
    136th Food Sv Sq
    136th Instls Sq
  136th Med Gp
440th Sig Avn Const Bn—OL
608th AC&W Sq (502d Tac Con Gp)
748th AF Band
811th Engr Avn Bn—OL
822d Engr Avn Bn (Less Co A)
3497th Mob Tng Sq—Det F–84-6
6004th Air Intel Sv Sq—Det 1
6127th Air Terminal Gp—Det 5
6151st Air Base Sq (6154th AB Gp)
    (Less Det)
6405th Spt Wg
  Hq

Taegu Air Base #2
5th Mtr Trans Sq, Avn (Less Det)
6152d Air Base Sq

Yongdong-po
10th Ln Sq
811th Engr Avn Bn—OL

Yonju
607th AC&W Sq (502d Tac Con
  Gp) (Less Det)

MAY 1, 1952

Chinhae
1st Air Pstl Sq—Det 4
18th Ftr-Bmr Wg
  Hq & Hq Sq (Less Det)
  18th Ftr-Bmr Gp
    Hq
  18th Maint & Sup Gp
    Hq
    18th Maint Sq
    18th Mtr Veh Sq
    18th Sup Sq
  18th Air Base Gp
    Hq & Hq Sq

18th Comms Sq
18th Air Police Sq
18th Food Sv Sq
18th Instls Sq
30th Wea Sq—Det 16

Chinhae Airdrome
18th Med Gp (18th Ftr-Bmr Wg)
39th Ftr-Intcp Sq (35th Ftr-Intcp Gp)
6127th Air Terminal Gp—Det 8

Chunchon
1st Air Pstl Sq—Det 30
30th Wea Sq—Det 29
809th Engr Avn Bn—Cos B & C
811th Engr Avn Bn—Co C
6147th Tac Con Gp
   Hq (Less Det)
   6147th Air Base Sq
   6147th Maint & Sup Sq
   6147th Med Sq
   6148th Tac Con Sq (Air)
   6149th Tac Con Sq (Air)
   6150th Tac Con Sq (Grd)

Hoengsong
30th Wea Sq—Dets 26 & 28
811th Engr Avn Bn (Less Cos B, C,
      Det 1 of Co A & OLs)
6151st AB Sq—Det 1

Hoengsong Airdrome
5th Mtr Trans Sq, Avn—Det 2
18th Ftr-Bmr Wg—Det 1

Inchon
606th AC&W Sq—Det 1

Kangnumg [Kangnung]
6147th Tac Con Gp—Det 1

Kangnumg [Kangnung] Airdrome
1st Shoran Beacon Sq—Det 4
811th Engr Avn Bn—Det 1, Co A
811th Engr Avn Bn—Det 1, Co B
6146th Air Base Sq—Det 2
6152d Air Base Sq

Kimpo
30th Wea Sq—Det 23

Kimpo Air Base
1st Air Pstl Sq—Det 28
4th Ftr-Intcp Wg
   Hq & Hq Sq (Less Det)
   4th Ftr-Intcp Gp
      Hq
      334th Ftr-Intcp Sq
      335th Ftr-Intcp Sq
      336th Ftr-Intcp Sq
   4th Maint & Sup Gp
      Hq
      4th Maint Sq
      4th Mtr Veh Sq
      4th Sup Sq
   4th Air Base Gp
      Hq & Hq Sq (Less Det)
      4th Comms Sq
      4th Air Police Sq
      4th Food Sv Sq
      4th Instls Sq
   4th Med Gp
67th Tac Recon Wg
   Hq & Hq Sq
   67th Recon Tech Sq
   67th Tac Recon Gp
      Hq
      12th Tac Recon Sq, Night
         Photo
      15th Tac Recon Sq, Photo-J
      45th Tac Recon Sq
   67th Maint & Sup Gp
      Hq
      67th Maint Sq
      67th Mtr Veh Sq
      67th Sup Sq
   67th Air Base Gp
      Hq & Hq Sq
      67th Comms Sq
      67th Food Sv Sq
      67th Air Police Sq
      67th Instls Sq
   67th Med Gp
606th AC&W Sq (502d Tac Con Gp)
   (Less Dets)

606th AC&W Sq—Det 2
1993d AACS Sq (1818th AACS Gp)
6127th Air Terminal Gp—Det 14
6166th Air Wea Recon Flt

Korea (unspecified location)
15th Rad Sq, Mob—Det 1

Kuksa-bong
1st Shoran Beacon Unit—Det 2

Kunsan
1st Air Pstl Sq—Det 29
3d Bomb Wg, L
  Hq & Hq Sq
  3d Bomb Gp, L
    Hq
    8th Bomb Sq, L, Night
      Intruder
    13th Bomb Sq, L, Night
      Intruder
    90th Bomb Sq, L, Night
      Intruder
  3d Maint & Sup Gp
    Hq
    3d Maint Sq
    3d Mtr Veh Sq
    3d Sup Sq
  3d Air Base Gp
    Hq & Hq Sq
    3d Comms Sq
    3d Air Police Sq
    3d Food Sv Sq
    3d Instls Sq
  3d Med Gp
808th Engr Avn Bn
6127th Air Terminal Gp—OL

Kwangung Airdrome
607th AC&W Sq—Det 3

Osan-ni
839th Engr Avn Bn (Less OL)

Pohang Airdrome
1903d Engr Avn Bn—Co C

Pusan
30th Wea Sq—Det 27

Pusan Air Base
1st Air Pstl Sq—Det 14
622d Engr Avn Maint Co
809th Engr Avn Bn (Less Cos B & C)
811th Engr Avn Bn—Co B (Less Det 1)
1903d Engr Avn Bn (Less Co C)

Pusan East Air Base
12th Ftr-Bmr Sq (18th Ftr-Bmr Gp)
30th Wea Sq—Det 13
67th Ftr-Bmr Sq (18th Ftr-Bmr Gp)
452d Bomb Wg, L (USAFR EAD)
  Hq & Hq Sq
  452d Bomb Gp, L
    Hq
    728th Bomb Sq, L, Night
      Intruder
    729th Bomb Sq, L, Night
      Intruder
    730th Bomb Sq, L, Night
      Intruder
  452d Maint & Sup Gp
    Hq
    452d Maint Sq
    452d Sup Sq
    452d Mtr Veh Sq
  452d Air Base Gp
    Hq & Hq Sq
    452d Comms Sq
    452d Air Police Sq
    452d Food Sv Sq
    452d Instls Sq
  452d Med Gp
543d Ammo Sup Sq, Dep
547th Ammo Sup Sq, Dep
802d Engr Avn Bn—OL
822d Engr Avn Bn—Co A
930th Engr Avn Gp
  Hq & Hq & Sv Co (Less Dets)
6127th Air Terminal Gp—Det 4
6401st Fld Maint Sq

Pyongtaek Airdrome
30th Wea Sq—Det 20

Pyongyang
919th Engr Avn Maint Co—Contact
    Plat

Seoul
See: Kimpo Air Base
1st Shoran Beacon Sq—Dets 7 & 8
3d Air Rsq Sq—Det 1
5th Comms Gp
    Hq
    1st Rad Sq
    1st Tp & Carr Sq
    2d Comms Sq, Oprs
30th Wea Sq (Less Dets)
811th Engr Avn Bn—OL
1818th AACS Gp (1808th AACS
    Wg)
    Hq

Seoul Air Base
Fifth Air Force
    Hq (Less Dets)
1st Air Pstl Sq—Dets 27 & 31
1st Rad Sq, Mob—OL
1st Shoran Beacon Sq (Less Dets)
10th Ln Sq
30th Wea Sq—Det 18
440th Sig Avn Const Bn (Less OL)
502d Tac Con Gp
    Hq
    605th Tac Con Sq (Less Det)
605th Tac Con Sq—Det 3
1134th USAF S/A Sq—OL
6004th Air Intel Sv Sq—Det 2
6154th Air Base Gp
    Hq
    6154th Air Police Sq
    6154th Food Sv Sq
    6154th Instls Sq
    6154th Med Sq
    6154th Mtr Veh Sq
    6154th Sup Sq
6167th Air Base Gp
    Hq (Less Flts & Det)
6167th Air Base Gp—Flts A & B

Suwon
30th Wea Sq—Det 21

Suwon Air Base
1st Air Pstl Sq—Det 23
8th Ftr-Bmr Wg
    Hq & Hq Sq
    8th Ftr-Bmr Gp
        Hq
        35th Ftr-Bmr Sq
        36th Ftr-Bmr Sq
        80th Ftr-Bmr Sq
    8th Maint & Sup Gp
        Hq
        8th Maint Sq
        8th Mtr Veh Sq
        8th Sup Sq
    8th Air Base Gp
        Hq & Hq Sq
        8th Comms Sq
        8th Air Police Sq
        8th Food Sv Sq
        8th Instls Sq
    8th Med Gp
51st Ftr-Intcp Wg
    Hq & Hq Sq
    51st Ftr-Intcp Gp
        Hq
        16th Ftr-Intcp Sq
        25th Ftr-Intcp Sq
    51st Maint & Sup Gp
        Hq
        51st Maint Sq
        51st Mtr Veh Sq
        51st Sup Sq
    51st Air Base Gp
        Hq & Hq Sq
        51st Air Police Sq
        51st Comms Sq
        51st Food Sv Sq
        51st Instls Sq
    51st Med Gp
319th Ftr-Intcp Sq
802d Engr Avn Bn (Less OL)
919th Engr Avn Maint Co (Less

Contact Plat)
931st Engr Avn Gp
  Hq & Hq & Sv Co
6127th Air Terminal Gp—Det 9

Taegu
30th Wea Sq—Dets 11 & 12
1973d AACS Sq (Mob) (1818th
  AACS Gp)
6146th Air Base Sq (Less Det)
6153d Air Base Gp—Det 1

Taegu Air Base
Fifth Air Force—Det 1, Rear
1st Air Pstl Sq—OL
2d Mat Recovery Sq
2d Rad Relay Sq
3d Air Rsq Sq—OL
7th Comms Sq, Oprs
9th Stat Svs Flt
49th Ftr-Bmr Wg
  Hq & Hq Sq (Less Det)
  49th Ftr-Bmr Gp
    Hq
    7th Ftr-Bmr Sq
    8th Ftr-Bmr Sq
    9th Ftr-Bmr Sq
  49th Maint & Sup Gp
    Hq
    49th Maint Sq
    49th Sup Sq
    49th Mtr Veh Sq
  49th Air Base Gp
    Hq & Hq Sq
    49th Comms Sq
    49th Air Police Sq
    49th Food Sv Sq
    49th Instls Sq
  49th Med Gp
136th Ftr-Bmr Wg (ANG EAD)
  Hq & Hq Sq
  136th Ftr-Bmr Gp
    Hq
    111th Ftr-Bmr Sq
    154th Ftr-Bmr Sq
    182d Ftr-Bmr Sq

136th Maint & Sup Gp
  Hq
  136th Maint Sq
  136th Mtr Veh Sq
  136th Sup Sq
136th Air Base Gp
  Hq & Hq Sq
  136th Air Police Sq
  136th Comms Sq
  136th Food Sv Sq
  136th Instls Sq
136th Med Gp
440th Sig Avn Const Bn—OL
608th AC&W Sq (502d Tac Con Gp)
748th AF Band
811th Engr Avn Bn—OL
822d Engr Avn Bn (Less Co A)
3497th Mob Tng Sq—Det F–84-6
6004th Air Intel Sv Sq—Det 1
6127th Air Terminal Gp—Det 5
6149th Hosp Gp
6151st Air Base Sq (6154th AB Gp)
  (Less Det)
6405th Spt Wg
  Hq

Taegu Air Base #2
5th Mtr Trans Sq, Avn (Less Det)
6152d Air Base Sq

Uijongbu
607th AC&W Sq (502d Tac Con
  Gp) (Less Det)

Yongdong-po
1st Epidemiological Flt
811th Engr Avn Bn—OL
6167th Base Sv Sq (6167th AB Gp)
6167th Maint & Sup Sq (6167th AB
  Gp)
6167th Oprs Sq (6167th AB Gp)

JULY 1, 1952

Chinhae
1st Air Pstl Sq—Det 4
18th Ftr-Bmr Wg

Hq (Less Det)
  18th Ftr-Bmr Gp
    Hq
  18th Maint & Sup Gp
    Hq
    18th Maint Sq
    18th Mtr Veh Sq
    18th Sup Sq
  18th Air Base Gp
    Hq
    18th Comms Sq
    18th Air Police Sq
    18th Food Sv Sq
    18th Instls Sq
30th Wea Sq—Det 16

Chinhae Airdrome
18th Med Gp (18th Ftr-Bmr Wg)
6127th Air Terminal Gp—Det 8

Chunchon
1st Air Pstl Sq—Det 30
30th Wea Sq—Det 29
809th Engr Avn Bn—Cos B & C
6147th Tac Con Gp
  Hq (Less Det)
  6147th Air Base Sq
  6147th Maint & Sup Sq
  6147th Med Sq
  6148th Tac Con Sq (Air)
  6149th Tac Con Sq (Air)
  6150th Tac Con Sq (Grd)

Hoengsong
30th Wea Sq—Dets 26 & 28
811th Engr Avn Bn (Less Cos B, C,
  Det 1 of Co A & OLs)
6151st AB Sq—Det 1

Hoengsong Airdrome
5th Mtr Trans Sq, Avn—Det 2
18th Ftr-Bmr Wg—Det 1

Inchon
606th AC&W Sq—Det 1
934th Engr Avn Gp
  Hq & Hq Co
840th Engr Avn Bn

Kangnumg [Kangnung]
6147th Tac Con Gp—Det 1

Kangnumg [Kangnung] Airdrome
1st Shoran Beacon Sq—Det 4
811th Engr Avn Bn—Det 1, Co A
811th Engr Avn Bn—Det 1, Co B
6146th Air Base Sq—Det 2
6152d Air Base Sq

Kimpo
30th Wea Sq—Det 23

Kimpo Air Base
1st Air Pstl Sq—Det 28
4th Ftr-Intcp Wg
  Hq & Hq Sq (Less Det)
  4th Ftr-Intcp Gp
    Hq
    334th Ftr-Intcp Sq
    335th Ftr-Intcp Sq
    336th Ftr-Intcp Sq
  4th Maint & Sup Gp
    Hq
    4th Maint Sq
    4th Mtr Veh Sq
    4th Sup Sq
  4th Air Base Gp
    Hq & Hq Sq (Less Det)
    4th Comms Sq
    4th Air Police Sq
    4th Food Sv Sq
    4th Instls Sq
  4th Med Gp
67th Tac Recon Wg
  Hq
  67th Recon Tech Sq
  67th Tac Recon Gp
    Hq
    12th Tac Recon Sq, Night
      Photo
    15th Tac Recon Sq, Photo-J
    45th Tac Recon Sq
  67th Maint & Sup Gp
    Hq
    67th Maint Sq
    67th Mtr Veh Sq

67th Sup Sq
67th Air Base Gp
  Hq
  67th Comms Sq
  67th Food Sv Sq
  67th Air Police Sq
  67th Instls Sq
67th Med Gp
606th AC&W Sq (502d Tac Con
  Gp) (Less Dets)
606th AC&W Sq—Det 2
839th Engr Avn Bn—OL
1993d AACS Sq (1818th AACS Gp)
6127th Air Terminal Gp—Det 14
6166th Air Wea Recon Flt

Korea (unspecified location)
15 Rad Sq, Mob—Det 151

Kuksa-bong
1st Shoran Beacon Unit—Det 2

Kunsan
1st Air Pstl Sq—Det 29
3d Bomb Wg, L
  Hq
  3d Bomb Gp, L
    Hq
    8th Bomb Sq, L, Night
      Intruder
    13th Bomb Sq, L, Night
      Intruder
    90th Bomb Sq, L, Night
      Intruder
  3d Maint & Sup Gp
    Hq
    3d Maint Sq
    3d Mtr Veh Sq
    3d Sup Sq
  3d Air Base Gp
    Hq
    3d Comms Sq
    3d Air Police Sq
    3d Food Sv Sq
    3d Instls Sq
  3d Med Gp
808th Engr Avn Bn

6127th Air Terminal Gp—OL

Kwangung Airdrome
607th AC&W Sq—Det 3

Osan-ni
839th Engr Avn Bn (Less OL)
841st Engr Avn Bn

Pohang Airdrome
1903d Engr Avn Bn (NG EAD)—Co
  C

Pusan
30th Wea Sq—Det 27

Pusan Air Base
1st Air Pstl Sq—Det 14
366th Engr Avn Bn
622d Engr Avn Maint Co
809th Engr Avn Bn (Less Cos B &
  C)
811th Engr Avn Bn—Co B (Less
  Det 1)
1903d Engr Avn Bn (NG EAD)
  (Less Co C & OL)

Pusan East Air Base
12th Ftr-Bmr Sq (18th Ftr-Bmr Gp)
17th Bomb Wg, L
  Hq
  17th Bomb Gp, L
    Hq
    34th Bomb Sq, L, Night
      Intruder
    37th Bomb Sq, L, Night
      Intruder
    95th Bomb Sq, L, Night
      Intruder
  17th Maint & Sup Gp
    Hq
    17th Maint Sq
    17th Mtr Veh Sq
    17th Sup Sq
  17th Air Base Gp
    Hq
    17th Air Police Sq
    17th Comms Sq
    17th Food Sv Sq

17th Instls Sq
17 Med Gp
30th Wea Sq—Det 13
67th Ftr-Bmr Sq (18th Ftr-Bmr Gp)
543d Ammo Sup Sq, Dep
547th Ammo Sup Sq, Dep
802d Engr Avn Bn—OL
822d Engr Avn Bn—Co A
930th Engr Avn Gp
   Hq & Hq & Sv Co (Less Dets)
6127th Air Terminal Gp—Det 4
6401st Fld Maint Sq

Pusan West Airdrome
1903d Engr Avn Bn (NG EAD)—
   OL

Pyongtaek Airdrome
30th Wea Sq—Det 20

Pyongyang
919th Engr Avn Maint Co—Contact
   Plat

Seoul
See: Kimpo Air Base
Fifth Air Force
   Hq (Less Dets)
1st Air Pstl Sq—Det 31
1st Shoran Beacon Sq (Less Dets)
1st Shoran Beacon Sq—Dets 7 & 8
3d Air Rsq Sq—Det 1
5th Comms Gp
   Hq
   1st Rad Sq
   1st Tp & Carr Sq
   2d Comms Sq, Oprs
   2d Rad Relay Sq
30th Wea Sq (Less Dets)
440th Sig Avn Const Bn (Less OL)
502d Tac Con Gp
   Hq
   605th Tac Con Sq (Less Det)
811th Engr Avn Bn—OL
1818th AACS Gp (1808th AACS
   Wg)
   Hq
6154th Air Base Gp

Hq
6154th Air Police Sq
6154th Food Sv Sq
6154th Instls Sq
6154th Med Sq
6154th Mtr Veh Sq
6154th Sup Sq

Seoul Air Base
1st Air Pstl Sq—Det 27
1st Epidemiological Flt
1st Rad Sq, Mob—OL
10th Ln Sq
30th Wea Sq—Det 18
605th Tac Con Sq—Det 3
811th Engr Avn Bn—Co C
6004th Air Intel Sv Sq—Det 2
6167th Air Base Gp
   Hq (Less Flts & Det)
   6167th Base Sv Sq
   6167th Maint & Sup Sq
   6167th Oprs Sq
6167th Air Base Gp—Flts A & B

Seoul Airdrome
748th AF Band

Suwon
30th Wea Sq—Det 21

Suwon Air Base
1st Air Pstl Sq—Det 23
8th Ftr-Bmr Wg
   Hq
   8th Ftr-Bmr Gp
      Hq
      35th Ftr-Bmr Sq
      36th Ftr-Bmr Sq
      80th Ftr-Bmr Sq
   8th Maint & Sup Gp
      Hq
      8th Maint Sq
      8th Mtr Veh Sq
      8th Sup Sq
   8th Air Base Gp
      Hq
      8th Comms Sq
      8th Air Police Sq

8th Food Sv Sq
8th Instls Sq
8th Med Gp
39th Ftr-Intcp Sq (35th Ftr-Intcp Gp)
51st Ftr-Intcp Wg
Hq
  51st Ftr-Intcp Gp
  Hq
    16th Ftr-Intcp Sq
    25th Ftr-Intcp Sq
  51st Maint & Sup Gp
  Hq
    51st Maint Sq
    51st Mtr Veh Sq
    51st Sup Sq
  51st Air Base Gp
  Hq
    51st Air Police Sq
    51st Comms Sq
    51st Food Sv Sq
    51st Instls Sq
  51st Med Gp
319th Ftr-Intcp Sq
802d Engr Avn Bn (Less OL)
919th Engr Avn Maint Co (Less
    Contact Plat)
931st Engr Avn Gp
  Hq & Hq & Sv Co
6127th Air Terminal Gp—Det 9

Taegu
30th Wea Sq—Dets 11 & 12
1973d AACS Sq (Mob) (1818th
    AACS Gp)
6146th Air Base Sq (Less Det)
6153d Air Base Gp-Det 1

Taegu Air Base
Fifth Air Force—Det 1, Rear
1st Air Pstl Sq—OL
2d Mat Recovery Sq (6400th Sup
    Gp)
3d Air Rsq Sq—OL
7th Comms Sq, Oprs
9th Stat Svs Flt
49th Ftr-Bmr Wg

Hq (Less Det)
49th Ftr-Bmr Gp
  Hq
    7th Ftr-Bmr Sq
    8th Ftr-Bmr Sq
    9th Ftr-Bmr Sq
  49th Maint & Sup Gp
  Hq
    49th Maint Sq
    49th Sup Sq
    49th Mtr Veh Sq
  49th Air Base Gp
  Hq
    49th Comms Sq
    49th Air Police Sq
    49th Food Sv Sq
    49th Instls Sq
  49th Med Gp
136th Ftr-Bmr Wg (ANG EAD)
  Hq
  136th Ftr-Bmr Gp
  Hq
    111th Ftr-Bmr Sq
    154th Ftr-Bmr Sq
    182d Ftr-Bmr Sq
  136th Maint & Sup Gp
  Hq
    136th Maint Sq
    136th Mtr Veh Sq
    136th Sup Sq
  136th Air Base Gp
  Hq
    136th Air Police Sq
    136th Comms Sq
    136th Food Sv Sq
    136th Instls Sq
  136th Med Gp
417th Engr Avn Brig
  Hq & Hq Co
420th Engr Avn Topo Det
440th Sig Avn Const Bn—OL
608th AC&W Sq (502d Tac Con Gp)
811th Engr Avn Bn—OL
822d Engr Avn Bn (Less Co A)
6004th Air Intel Sv Sq—Det 1

6127th Air Terminal Gp—Det 5
6149th Hosp Gp
    Hq
6151st Air Base Sq (6154th AB Gp)
    (Less Det)
6405th Spt Wg
    Hq

Taegu Air Base #2
5th Mtr Trans Sq, Avn (Less Det)
6152d Air Base Sq

Uijongbu
607th AC&W Sq (502d Tac Con
    Gp) (Less Det)

Yongdong-po
811th Engr Avn Bn—OL

SEPTEMBER 1, 1952

Chinhae
1st Air Pstl Sq—Det 4
18th Ftr-Bmr Wg
    Hq (Less Det)
    18th Ftr-Bmr Gp
        Hq
    18th Maint & Sup Gp
        Hq
        18th Maint Sq
        18th Mtr Veh Sq
        18th Sup Sq
    18th Air Base Gp
        Hq
        18th Comms Sq
        18th Air Police Sq
        18th Food Sv Sq
        18th Instls Sq
30th Wea Sq—Det 16

Chinhae Airdrome
18th Med Gp (18th Ftr-Bmr Wg)
6127th Air Terminal Gp—Det 8

Chunchon
1st Air Pstl Sq—Det 30
30th Wea Sq—Det 29
809th Engr Avn Bn—Cos B & C
6147th Tac Con Gp

Hq (Less Det)
6147th Air Base Sq
6147th Maint & Sup Sq
6147th Med Sq
6148th Tac Con Sq (Air)
6149th Tac Con Sq (Air)
6150th Tac Con Sq (Grd)

Hoengsong
30th Wea Sq—Dets 26 & 28
811th Engr Avn Bn (Less Cos B, C,
    Det 1 of Co A & OLs)
6151st AB Sq—Det 1

Hoengsong Airdrome
5th Mtr Trans Sq, Avn—Det 2
18th Ftr-Bmr Wg—Det 1

Inchon
606th AC&W Sq—Det 1
934th Engr Avn Gp
    Hq & Hq Co
840th Engr Avn Bn

Kangnumg [Kangnung]
6147th Tac Con Gp—Det 1

Kangnumg [Kangnung] **Airdrome**
1st Shoran Beacon Sq—Det 4
811th Engr Avn Bn—Det 1, Co A
811th Engr Avn Bn—Det 1, Co B
6146th Air Base Sq—Det 2
6152d Air Base Sq

Kimpo
30th Wea Sq—Det 23

Kimpo Air Base
1st Air Pstl Sq—Det 28
4th Ftr-Intcp Wg
    Hq (Less Det)
    4th Ftr-Intcp Gp
        Hq
        334th Ftr-Intcp Sq
        335th Ftr-Intcp Sq
        336th Ftr-Intcp Sq
    4th Maint & Sup Gp
        Hq
        4th Maint Sq
        4th Mtr Veh Sq

4th Sup Sq
4th Air Base Gp
  Hq (Less Det)
  4th Comms Sq
  4th Air Police Sq
  4th Food Sv Sq
  4th Instls Sq
4th Med Gp
67th Tac Recon Wg
  Hq (Less OL)
  67th Recon Tech Sq
  67th Tac Recon Gp
    Hq
    12th Tac Recon Sq, Night
      Photo
    15th Tac Recon Sq, Photo-J
    45th Tac Recon Sq
  67th Maint & Sup Gp
    Hq
    67th Maint Sq
    67th Mtr Veh Sq
    67th Sup Sq
  67th Air Base Gp
    Hq
    67th Comms Sq
    67th Food Sv Sq
    67th Air Police Sq
    67th Instls Sq
  67th Med Gp
606th AC&W Sq (502d Tac Con
  Gp) (Less Dets)
606th AC&W Sq—Det 2
839th Engr Avn Bn—OL
1993d AACS Mob Comms Sq
  (1818th AACS Mob Comms
  Gp)
6127th Air Terminal Gp—Det 14
6166th Air Wea Recon Flt

Korea (unspecified location)
15th Rad Sq, Mob—Det 151
1038th USAF Aud Gen Sq—OL

Kuksa-bong
1st Shoran Beacon Unit—Det 2

Kunsan
1st Air Pstl Sq—Det 29
3d Bomb Wg, L
  Hq
  3d Bomb Gp, L
    Hq
    8th Bomb Sq, L, Night
      Intruder
    13th Bomb Sq, L, Night
      Intruder
    90th Bomb Sq, L, Night
      Intruder
  3d Maint & Sup Gp
    Hq
    3d Maint Sq
    3d Mtr Veh Sq
    3d Sup Sq
  3d Air Base Gp
    Hq
    3d Comms Sq
    3d Air Police Sq
    3d Food Sv Sq
    3d Instls Sq
  3d Med Gp
808th Engr Avn Bn
6127th Air Terminal Gp—OL

Kunsan Airdrome
474th Ftr-Bmr Wg
  Hq
  474th Ftr-Bmr Gp
    Hq

Kwangung Airdrome
607th AC&W Sq—Det 3

Osan-ni
839th Engr Avn Bn (Less OL)
840th Engr Avn Bn—OL
841st Engr Avn Bn

Pohang Airdrome
1903d Engr Avn Bn (NG EAD)—Co
  C

Pusan
30th Wea Sq—Det 27

Pusan Air Base

1st Air Pstl Sq—Det 14
366th Engr Avn Bn
622d Engr Avn Maint Co
809th Engr Avn Bn (Less Cos B & C)
811th Engr Avn Bn—Co B (Less Det 1)
1903d Engr Avn Bn (NG EAD) (Less Co C & OLs)

Pusan East Air Base

12th Ftr-Bmr Sq (18th Ftr-Bmr Gp)
17th Air Base Gp (17th Bomb Wg)
  Hq
  17th Comms Sq
  17th Air Police Sq
  17th Food Sv Sq
  17th Instls Sq
17th Bomb Gp, L (17th Bomb Wg)
  Hq
  34th Bomb Sq, L, Night Intruder
  37th Bomb Sq, L, Night Intruder
  95th Bomb Sq, L, Night Intruder
17th Med Gp (17th Bomb Wg)
17th Mtr Veh Sq (17th M&S Gp)
17th Sup Sq (17th M&S Gp)
30th Wea Sq—Det 13
67th Ftr-Bmr Sq (18th Ftr-Bmr Gp)
543d Ammo Sup Sq, Dep
547th Ammo Sup Sq, Dep
802d Engr Avn Bn—OL
822d Engr Avn Bn—Co A
930th Engr Avn Gp
  Hq & Hq & Sv Co (Less Dets)
1903d Engr Avn Bn (NG EAD)— OL
6127th Air Terminal Gp—Det 4
6401st Fld Maint Sq

Pusan West Airdrome

1903d Engr Avn Bn (NG EAD)— OL

Pyongtaek Airdrome

30th Wea Sq—Det 20

Pyongyang

919th Engr Avn Maint Co—Contact Plat

Sachon

30th Wea Sq—Det 30

Seoul

See: Kimpo Air Base
Fifth Air Force
  Hq (Less Dets)
1st Air Pstl Sq—Det 31
1st Shoran Beacon Sq (Less Dets)
1st Shoran Beacon Sq—Dets 7 & 8
3d Air Rsq Sq—Det 1
5th Comms Gp
  Hq
  1st Rad Sq
  1st Tp & Carr Sq
  2d Comms Sq, Oprs
  2d Rad Relay Sq
30th Wea Sq (Less Dets)
440th Sig Avn Const Bn (Less OL)
502d Tac Con Gp
  Hq
  605th Tac Con Sq (Less Det)
811th Engr Avn Bn—OL
1818th AACS Mob Comms Gp (1808th AACS Wg)
  Hq
6154th Air Base Gp
  Hq
  6154th Air Police Sq
  6154th Food Sv Sq
  6154th Instls Sq
  6154th Med Sq
  6154th Mtr Veh Sq
  6154th Sup Sq

Seoul Air Base

1st Air Pstl Sq—Det 27
1st Epidemiological Flt
10th Ln Sq
30th Wea Sq—Det 18
605th Tac Con Sq—Det 3
748th AF Band
811th Engr Avn Bn—Co C

6004th Air Intel Sv Sq—Det 2
6167th Air Base Gp
  Hq (Less Flts & Det)
  6167th Base Sv Sq
  6167th Maint & Sup Sq
  6167th Oprs Sq
6167th Air Base Gp—Flts A & B

Suwon
30th Wea Sq—Det 21

Suwon Air Base
1st Air Pstl Sq—Det 23
8th Ftr-Bmr Wg
  Hq
  8th Ftr-Bmr Gp
    Hq
    35th Ftr-Bmr Sq
    36th Ftr-Bmr Sq
    80th Ftr-Bmr Sq
  8th Maint & Sup Gp
    Hq
    8th Maint Sq
    8th Mtr Veh Sq
    8th Sup Sq
  8th Air Base Gp
    Hq
    8th Comms Sq
    8th Air Police Sq
    8th Food Sv Sq
    8th Instls Sq
  8th Med Gp
39th Ftr-Intcp Sq (35th Ftr-Intcp Gp)
51st Ftr-Intcp Wg
  Hq
  51st Ftr-Intcp Gp
    Hq
    16th Ftr-Intcp Sq
    25th Ftr-Intcp Sq
  51st Maint & Sup Gp
    Hq
    51st Maint Sq
    51st Mtr Veh Sq
    51st Sup Sq
  51st Air Base Gp
    Hq

51st Air Police Sq
51st Comms Sq
51st Food Sv Sq
51st Instls Sq
  51st Med Gp
319th Ftr-Intcp Sq
802d Engr Avn Bn (Less OL)
919th Engr Avn Maint Co (Less
    Contact Plat)
931st Engr Avn Gp
  Hq & Hq & Sv Co
6127th Air Terminal Gp—Det 9

Taegu
1st Air Pstl Sq—OL
30th Wea Sq—Dets 11 & 12
1973d AACS Mob Comms Sq
    (1818th AACS Mob Comms
    Gp)
6146th Air Base Sq (Less Det)
6153d Air Base Gp—Det 1

Taegu Air Base
Fifth Air Force—Det 1, Rear
1st Air Pstl Sq—OL
3d Air Rsq Sq—OL
7th Comms Sq, Oprs
9th Stat Svs Flt
49th Ftr-Bmr Wg
  Hq (Less Det)
  49th Ftr-Bmr Gp
    Hq
    7th Ftr-Bmr Sq
    8th Ftr-Bmr Sq (Less OL)
    9th Ftr-Bmr Sq
  49th Maint & Sup Gp
    Hq
    49th Maint Sq
    49th Sup Sq
    49th Mtr Veh Sq
  49th Air Base Gp
    Hq
    49th Comms Sq
    49th Air Police Sq
    49th Food Sv Sq
    49th Instls Sq

49th Med Gp
58th Ftr-Bmr Wg
  Hq
  58th Ftr-Bmr Gp
    Hq
    69th Ftr-Bmr Sq
    310th Ftr-Bmr Sq
    311th Ftr-Bmr Sq
  58th Maint & Sup Gp
    Hq
    58th Maint Sq
    58th Mtr Veh Sq
    58th Sup Sq
  58th Air Base Gp
    Hq
    58th Comms Sq
    58th Air Police Sq
    58th Food Sv Sq
    58th Instls Sq
  58th Med Gp
67th Tac Recon Wg—OL
417th Engr Avn Brig
  Hq & Hq Co
420th Engr Avn Topo Det
440th Sig Avn Const Bn—OL
608th AC&W Sq (502d Tac Con Gp)
811th Engr Avn Bn—OL
822d Engr Avn Bn (Less Co A)
840th Engr Avn Bn—OL
6004th Air Intel Sv Sq—Det 1
6127th Air Terminal Gp—Det 5
6151st Air Base Sq (6154th AB Gp)
  (Less Det)
6405th Air Spt Wg
  Hq
  2d Mat Recovery Sq

Taegu Air Base #2
5th Mtr Trans Sq, Avn (Less Det)
6152d Air Base Sq

Uijongbu
607th AC&W Sq (502d Tac Con
  Gp) (Less Det)

Yongdong-po
811th Engr Avn Bn—OL

NOVEMBER 1, 1952

Anyang
809th Engr Avn Bn—Co A

Chinhae
1st Air Pstl Sq—Det 4
18th Ftr-Bmr Wg
  Hq (Less Det)
  18th Ftr-Bmr Gp
    Hq
  18th Maint & Sup Gp
    Hq
    18th Maint Sq
    18th Mtr Veh Sq
    18th Sup Sq
  18th Air Base Gp
    Hq
    18th Comms Sq
    18th Air Police Sq
    18th Food Sv Sq
    18th Instls Sq
30th Wea Sq—Det 16

Chinhae Airdrome
18th Med Gp (18th Ftr-Bmr Wg)
6127th Air Terminal Gp—Det 8

Chunchon
1st Air Pstl Sq—Det 30
30th Wea Sq—Det 29
809th Engr Avn Bn—Cos B & C
6147th Tac Con Gp
  Hq (Less Det)
  6147th Air Base Sq
  6147th Maint & Sup Sq
  6147th Med Sq
  6148th Tac Con Sq (Air)
  6149th Tac Con Sq (Air)
  6150th Tac Con Sq (Grd)

Goryudo
931st Engr Avn Gp
  Hq & Hq & Sv Co

Hoengsong
30th Wea Sq—Dets 26 & 28
811th Engr Avn Bn—Co A (Less
  Det 1)

6151st AB Sq—Det 1

Hoengsong Airdrome
5th Mtr Trans Sq, Avn—Det 2
18th Ftr-Bmr Wg—Det 1

Inchon
606th AC&W Sq—Det 1
934th Engr Avn Gp
  Hq & Hq Co
840th Engr Avn Bn (Less OL)

Kangnumg [Kangnung]
6147th Tac Con Gp—Det 1

Kangnumg [Kangnung] **Airdrome**
1st Shoran Beacon Sq—Det 4
811th Engr Avn Bn—Det 1, Co A
811th Engr Avn Bn—Det 1, Co B
6146th Air Advisory Gp—Det 2
6152d Air Base Sq

Kimpo
30th Wea Sq—Det 23

Kimpo Air Base
1st Air Pstl Sq—Det 28
4th Ftr-Intcp Wg
  Hq (Less Det)
  4th Ftr-Intcp Gp
    Hq
    334th Ftr-Intcp Sq
    335th Ftr-Intcp Sq
    336th Ftr-Intcp Sq
  4th Maint & Sup Gp
    Hq
    4th Maint Sq
    4th Mtr Veh Sq
    4th Sup Sq
  4th Air Base Gp
    Hq (Less Det)
    4th Comms Sq
    4th Air Police Sq
    4th Food Sv Sq
    4th Instls Sq
  4th Med Gp
67th Tac Recon Wg
  Hq
  67th Recon Tech Sq

67th Tac Recon Gp
  Hq
  12th Tac Recon Sq, Night
    Photo
  15th Tac Recon Sq, Photo-J
  45th Tac Recon Sq
67th Maint & Sup Gp
  Hq
  67th Maint Sq
  67th Mtr Veh Sq
  67th Sup Sq
67th Air Base Gp
  Hq
  67th Comms Sq
  67th Food Sv Sq
  67th Air Police Sq
  67th Instls Sq
67th Med Gp
606th AC&W Sq (502d Tac Con
  Gp) (Less Dets)
606th AC&W Sq—Det 2
839th Engr Avn Bn—OL
1993d AACS Mob Comms Sq
  (1818th AACS Mob Comms
  Gp)
3497th Mob Tng Sq—Det F–86-11
6127th Air Terminal Gp—Det 14
6166th Air Wea Recon Flt

Korea (unspecified location)
15th Rad Sq, Mob—Det 151
1038th USAF Aud Gen Sq—OL

Kuksa-bong
1st Shoran Beacon Unit—Det 2

Kunsan
1st Air Pstl Sq—Det 29
3d Bomb Wg, L
  Hq
  3d Bomb Gp, L
    Hq
    8th Bomb Sq, L, Night
      Intruder
    13th Bomb Sq, L, Night
      Intruder

90th Bomb Sq, L, Night
　　Intruder
3d Maint & Sup Gp
　Hq
　3d Maint Sq
　3d Mtr Veh Sq
　3d Sup Sq
3d Air Base Gp
　Hq
　3d Comms Sq
　3d Air Police Sq
　3d Food Sv Sq
　3d Instls Sq
3d Med Gp
808th Engr Avn Bn
809th Engr Avn Bn—OL
6127th Air Terminal Gp—OL

Kunsan Airdrome
474th Ftr-Bmr Wg
　Hq
　474th Ftr-Bmr Gp
　　Hq
　　428th Ftr-Bmr Sq
　　429th Ftr-Bmr Sq
　　430th Ftr-Bmr Sq

Kwangung Airdrome
607th AC&W Sq—Det 3

Osan-ni
839th Engr Avn Bn (Less OL)
840th Engr Avn Bn—OL
841st Engr Avn Bn

Pusan
30th Wea Sq—Det 27
1873d AACS Mob Comms Sq
　(M&S) (1818th AACS Mob
　Comms Gp)
6127th Air Terminal Gp—OL

Pusan Air Base
1st Air Pstl Sq—Det 14
366th Engr Avn Bn
622d Engr Avn Maint Co
809th Engr Avn Bn (Less Cos &
　OL)

811th Engr Avn Bn—Co B (Less
　Det 1)
1903d Engr Avn Bn (NG EAD)
　(Less Co & OLs)

Pusan East Air Base
12th Ftr-Bmr Sq (18th Ftr-Bmr Gp)
17th Bomb Wg, L
　Hq
　17th Maint & Sup Gp
　　Hq
　　17th Mtr Veh Sq
　　17th Sup Sq
　17th Air Base Gp
　　Hq
　　17th Comms Sq
　　17th Air Police Sq
　　17th Food Sv Sq
　　17th Instls Sq
　17th Med Gp
67th Ftr-Bmr Sq (18th Ftr-Bmr Gp)
543d Ammo Sup Sq, Dep
547th Ammo Sup Sq, Dep
822d Engr Avn Bn—Co A
1903d Engr Avn Bn (NG EAD)—
　OL
6127th Air Terminal Gp—Det 4
6401st Fld Maint Sq

Pusan West Airdrome
17th Bomb Gp, L (17th Bomb Wg)
　Hq
　34th Bomb Sq, L, Night Intruder
　37th Bomb Sq, L, Night Intruder
　95th Bomb Sq, L, Night Intruder
30th Wea Sq—Det 31
1903d Engr Avn Bn (NG EAD)—
　OL

Pyongtaek Airdrome
30th Wea Sq—Det 20
1903d Engr Avn Bn (NG EAD)—Co
　C

Sachon
30th Wea Sq—Det 30

Seoul

See: Kimpo Air base
Fifth Air Force
  Hq (Less Dets)
1st Air Pstl Sq—Det 31
1st Shoran Beacon Sq (Less Dets)
1st Shoran Beacon Sq—Dets 7 & 8
3d Air Rsq Sq—Det 1
5th Comms Gp
  Hq
  1st Rad Sq
  1st Tp & Carr Sq
  2d Comms Sq, Oprs
  2d Rad Relay Sq
30th Wea Sq (Less Dets)
440th Sig Avn Const Bn (Less OL)
502d Tac Con Gp
  Hq
  605th Tac Con Sq (Less Det)
811th Engr Avn Bn—OL
1818th AACS Mob Comms Gp
    (1808th AACS Wg)
  Hq
6154th Air Base Gp
  Hq
  6154th Air Police Sq
  6154th Food Sv Sq
  6154th Instls Sq
  6154th Med Sq
  6154th Mtr Veh Sq
  6154th Sup Sq

Seoul Air Base

1st Air Pstl Sq—Det 27
1st Epidemiological Flt
10th Ln Sq
30th Wea Sq—Det 18
605th Tac Con Sq—Det 3
748th AF Band
809th Engr Avn Bn—OL
811th Engr Avn Bn—Co C
1134th USAF S/A Sq—OL
6004th Air Intel Sv Sq—Det 2
6167th Air Base Gp
  Hq (Less Flts & Det)

6167th Base Sv Sq
6167th Maint & Sup Sq
6167th Oprs Sq
6167th Air Base Gp—Flts A & B

Suwon

30th Wea Sq—Det 21

Suwon Air Base

1st Air Pstl Sq—Det 23
8th Ftr-Bmr Wg
  Hq
  8th Ftr-Bmr Gp
    Hq
    35th Ftr-Bmr Sq
    36th Ftr-Bmr Sq
    80th Ftr-Bmr Sq
  8th Maint & Sup Gp
    Hq
    8th Maint Sq
    8th Mtr Veh Sq
    8th Sup Sq
  8th Air Base Gp
    Hq
    8th Comms Sq
    8th Air Police Sq
    8th Food Sv Sq
    8th Instls Sq
  8th Med Gp
39th Ftr-Intcp Sq (35th Ftr-Intcp Gp)
51st Ftr-Intcp Wg
  Hq
  51st Ftr-Intcp Gp
    Hq
    16th Ftr-Intcp Sq
    25th Ftr-Intcp Sq
  51st Air Base Gp
    Hq
    51st Air Police Sq
    51st Comms Sq
    51st Food Sv Sq
    51st Instls Sq
  51st Med Gp
51st Mtr Veh Sq (51st M&S Gp)
319th Ftr-Intcp Sq
802d Engr Avn Bn

919th Engr Avn Maint Co
6127th Air Terminal Gp—Det 9

Taegu
1st Air Pstl Sq—OL
30th Wea Sq-Dets 11 & 12
1973d AACS Mob Comms Sq
  (1818th AACS Mob Comms
  Gp)
6146th Air Advisory Gp (ROK AF)
  Hq (Less Det)
6153d Air Base Gp—Det 1

Taegu Air Base
Fifth Air Force—Det 1, Rear
1st Air Pstl Sq—OL
7th Comms Sq, Oprs
9th Stat Svs Flt
49th Ftr-Bmr Wg
  Hq (Less Det)
  49th Ftr-Bmr Gp
    Hq
    7th Ftr-Bmr Sq
    8th Ftr-Bmr Sq (Less OL)
    9th Ftr-Bmr Sq
  49th Maint & Sup Gp
    Hq
    49th Maint Sq
    49th Sup Sq
    49th Mtr Veh Sq
  49th Air Base Gp
    Hq
    49th Comms Sq
    49th Air Police Sq
    49th Food Sv Sq
    49th Instls Sq
  49th Med Gp
58th Ftr-Bmr Wg
  Hq
  58th Ftr-Bmr Gp
    Hq
    69th Ftr-Bmr Sq
    310th Ftr-Bmr Sq
    311th Ftr-Bmr Sq
  58th Maint & Sup Gp
    Hq

58th Maint Sq
58th Mtr Veh Sq
58th Sup Sq
58th Air Base Gp
  Hq
  58th Comms Sq
  58th Air Police Sq
  58th Food Sv Sq
  58th Instls Sq
58th Med Gp
417th Engr Avn Brig
  Hq & Hq Co
420th Engr Avn Topo Det
440th Sig Avn Const Bn—OL
608th AC&W Sq (502d Tac Con Gp)
822d Engr Avn Bn (Less Co)
3497th Mob Tng Sq—Det F–84-11
6004th Air Intel Sv Sq—Det 1
6127th Air Terminal Gp—Det 5
6151st Air Base Sq (6154th AB Gp)
  (Less Det)
6405th Air Spt Wg
  Hq
  2d Mat Recovery Sq

Taegu Air Base #2
5th Mtr Trans Sq, Avn (Less Det)
930th Engr Avn Gp
  Hq & Hq & Sv Co (Less Dets)
6152d Air Base Sq

Uijongbu
607th AC&W Sq (502d Tac Con
  Gp) (Less Det)

Ulsan
7th Mtr Trans Sq

Yongdong-po
811th Engr Avn Bn (Less Cos)

JANUARY 1, 1953

Anyang
809th Engr Avn Bn—Co A

Chinhae
1st Air Pstl Sq—Det 4
18th Ftr-Bmr Wg

Hq (Less Det)
18th Ftr-Bmr Gp
  Hq
18th Maint & Sup Gp
  Hq
  18th Maint Sq
  18th Mtr Veh Sq
  18th Sup Sq
18th Air Base Gp
  Hq
  18th Comms Sq
  18th Air Police Sq
  18th Food Sv Sq
  18th Instls Sq
30th Wea Sq—Det 16

Chinhae Airdrome
18th Med Gp (18th Ftr-Bmr Wg)
6127th Air Terminal Gp—Det 8

Chunchon
1st Air Pstl Sq—Det 30
30th Wea Sq—Det 29
809th Engr Avn Bn—Cos B & C
6147th Tac Con Gp
  Hq (Less Det)
  6147th Air Base Sq
  6147th Maint & Sup Sq
  6147th Med Sq
  6148th Tac Con Sq (Air)
  6149th Tac Con Sq (Air)
  6150th Tac Con Sq (Grd)

Goryudo
931st Engr Avn Gp
  Hq & Hq Co

Hoengsong
30th Wea Sq—Dets 26 & 28
811th Engr Avn Bn—Co A (Less
  Det 1)
6151st AB Sq—Det 1

Hoengsong Airdrome
5th Mtr Trans Sq, Avn—Det 2
18th Ftr-Bmr Wg—Det 1

Hwangbong-san
1st Shoran Beacon Sq—Det 4

Inchon
606th AC&W Sq—Det 1
840th Engr Avn Bn (Less OL)

Kangnumg [Kangnung]
6147th Tac Con Gp—Det 1

Kangnumg [Kangnung] **Airdrome**
811th Engr Avn Bn—Det 1, Co A
811th Engr Avn Bn—Det 1, Co B
6146th Air Advisory Gp—Det 2
6152d Air Base Sq

Kaya-san
1st Shoran Beacon Sq—Det 9

Kimpo
30th Wea Sq—Det 23

Kimpo Air Base
1st Air Pstl Sq—Det 28
4th Ftr-Intcp Wg
  Hq (Less Det)
  4th Ftr-Intcp Gp
    Hq
    334th Ftr-Intcp Sq
    335th Ftr-Intcp Sq
    336th Ftr-Intcp Sq
  4th Maint & Sup Gp
    Hq
    4th Maint Sq
    4th Mtr Veh Sq
    4th Sup Sq
  4th Air Base Gp
    Hq (Less Det)
    4th Comms Sq
    4th Air Police Sq
    4th Food Sv Sq
    4th Instls Sq
  4th Med Gp
67th Tac Recon Wg
  Hq
  67th Recon Tech Sq
  67th Tac Recon Gp
    Hq
    12th Tac Recon Sq, Night
      Photo
    15th Tac Recon Sq, Photo-J

45th Tac Recon Sq
67th Maint & Sup Gp
  Hq
  67th Maint Sq
  67th Mtr Veh Sq
  67th Sup Sq
67th Air Base Gp
  Hq
  67th Comms Sq
  67th Food Sv Sq
  67th Air Police Sq
  67th Instls Sq
67th Med Gp
606th AC&W Sq (502d Tac Con
  Gp) (Less Dets)
606th AC&W Sq—Det 2
1993d AACS Mob Comms Sq
  (1818th AACS Mob Comms
  Gp)
3497th Mob Tng Sq—Det F–86-11
6127th Air Terminal Gp—Det 14
6166th Air Wea Recon Flt

Korea (unspecified location)
15th Rad Sq, Mob—Det 151

Kuksa-bong
1st Shoran Beacon Sq—Det 2

Kunsan
1st Air Pstl Sq—Det 29
3d Bomb Wg, L
  Hq
  3d Bomb Gp, L
    Hq
    8th Bomb Sq, L, Night
      Intruder
    13th Bomb Sq, L, Night
      Intruder
    90th Bomb Sq, L, Night
      Intruder
  3d Maint & Sup Gp
    Hq
    3d Maint Sq
    3d Mtr Veh Sq
    3d Sup Sq
  3d Air Base Gp

    Hq
    3d Comms Sq
    3d Air Police Sq
    3d Food Sv Sq
    3d Instls Sq
  3d Med Gp
808th Engr Avn Bn
6127th Air Terminal Gp—OL

Kunsan Airdrome
474th Ftr-Bmr Wg
  Hq
  474th Ftr-Bmr Gp
    Hq
    428th Ftr-Bmr Sq
    429th Ftr-Bmr Sq
    430th Ftr-Bmr Sq

Kwangung Airdrome
607th AC&W Sq—Det 3

Osan-ni
839th Engr Avn Bn
840th Engr Avn Bn—OL
841st Engr Avn Bn
934th Engr Avn Gp
  Hq & Hq Co

Paengnyong-do
1st Shoran Beacon Sq—Det 3

Pusan
30th Wea Sq—Det 27
622d Engr Avn Maint Co—OL
1873d AACS Mob Comms Sq
  (M&S) (1818th AACS Mob
  Comms Gp)

Pusan Air Base
1st Air Pstl Sq—Det 14
809th Engr Avn Bn (Less Cos &
  OL)
811th Engr Avn Bn—Co B (Less
  Det 1)

Pusan East Air Base
12th Ftr-Bmr Sq (18th Ftr-Bmr Gp)
17th Bomb Wg, L
  Hq
  17th Maint & Sup Gp

Hq
17th Mtr Veh Sq
17th Sup Sq
17th Air Base Gp
Hq
17th Comms Sq
17th Air Police Sq
17th Food Sv Sq
17th Instls Sq
17th Med Gp
67th Ftr-Bmr Sq (18th Ftr-Bmr Gp)
543d Ammo Sup Sq, Dep
822d Engr Avn Bn—Co A
6127th Air Terminal Gp—Det 4
6401st Fld Maint Sq

Pusan West Airdrome
17th Bomb Gp, L (17th Bomb Wg)
Hq
34th Bomb Sq, L, Night Intruder
37th Bomb Sq, L, Night Intruder
95th Bomb Sq, L, Night Intruder
30th Wea Sq—Det 31
366th Engr Avn Bn

Pyongtaek Airdrome
30th Wea Sq—Det 20
1903d Engr Avn Bn (NG EAD)

Sachon
30th Wea Sq—Det 30

Seoul
See: Kimpo Air Base
Fifth Air Force
Hq (Less Dets)
1st Air Pstl Sq—Det 31
1st Shoran Beacon Sq (Less Dets)
5th Comms Gp
Hq
1st Rad Sq
1st Tp & Carr Sq
2d Comms Sq, Oprs
2d Rad Relay Sq
30th Wea Sq (Less Dets)
440th Sig Avn Const Bn (Less OL)
502d Tac Con Gp
Hq

605th Tac Con Sq (Less Det)
811th Engr Avn Bn (Less OL)
1818th AACS Mob Comms Gp
(1808th AACS Wg)
Hq
6154th Air Base Gp
Hq
6154th Air Police Sq
6154th Food Sv Sq
6154th Instls Sq
6154th Med Sq
6154th Mtr Veh Sq
6154th Sup Sq

Seoul Air Base
1st Air Pstl Sq—Det 27
5th Epidemiological Flt
10th Ln Sq
30th Wea Sq—Det 18
605th Tac Con Sq—Det 3
748th AF Band
811th Engr Avn Bn—Co C
1134th USAF S/A Sq—OL
6004th Air Intel Sv Sq—Det 2
6167th Air Base Gp
Hq (Less Flts & Det)
6167th Base Sv Sq
6167th Maint & Sup Sq
6167th Oprs Sq
6167th Air Base Gp—Flts A & B
6461st Trp Carr Sq, M—Det 1

Suwon Air Base
1st Air Pstl Sq—Det 23
8th Ftr-Bmr Wg
Hq
8th Ftr-Bmr Gp
Hq
35th Ftr-Bmr Sq
36th Ftr-Bmr Sq
80th Ftr-Bmr Sq
8th Maint & Sup Gp
Hq
8th Maint Sq
8th Mtr Veh Sq
8th Sup Sq

8th Air Base Gp
  Hq
  8th Comms Sq
  8th Air Police Sq
  8th Food Sv Sq
  8th Instls Sq
8th Med Gp
30th Wea Sq—Det 21
39th Ftr-Intcp Sq (35th Ftr-Intcp Gp)
51st Ftr-Intcp Wg
  Hq
  51st Ftr-Intcp Gp
    Hq
    16th Ftr-Intcp Sq
    25th Ftr-Intcp Sq
  51st Air Base Gp
    Hq
    51st Air Police Sq
    51st Comms Sq
    51st Food Sv Sq
    51st Instls Sq
  51st Med Gp
51st Mtr Veh Sq (51st M&S Gp)
319th Ftr-Intcp Sq
622d Engr Avn Maint Co (Less OL)
802d Engr Avn Bn
919th Engr Avn Maint Co
6127th Air Terminal Gp—Det 9

Taegu
1st Air Pstl Sq—Det 2
30th Wea Sq—Dets 11 & 12
1038th USAF Aud Gen Sq—OL
1973d AACS Mob Comms Sq
    (1818th AACS Mob Comms
    Gp)
6146th Air Advisory Gp (ROK AF)
  Hq (Less Det)
6153d Air Base Gp—Det 1

Taegu Air Base
Fifth Air Force—Det 1, Rear
7th Comms Sq, Oprs
9th Stat Svs Flt
49th Ftr-Bmr Wg
  Hq (Less Det)

49th Ftr-Bmr Gp
  Hq
  7th Ftr-Bmr Sq
  8th Ftr-Bmr Sq (Less OL)
49th Maint & Sup Gp
  Hq
  49th Maint Sq
  49th Sup Sq
  49th Mtr Veh Sq
49th Air Base Gp
  Hq
  49th Comms Sq
  49th Air Police Sq
  49th Food Sv Sq
  49th Instls Sq
49th Med Gp
58th Ftr-Bmr Wg
  Hq
  58th Ftr-Bmr Gp
    Hq
    69th Ftr-Bmr Sq
    310th Ftr-Bmr Sq
    311th Ftr-Bmr Sq
  58th Maint & Sup Gp
    Hq
    58th Maint Sq
    58th Mtr Veh Sq
    58th Sup Sq
  58th Air Base Gp
    Hq
    58th Comms Sq
    58th Air Police Sq
    58th Food Sv Sq
    58th Instls Sq
  58th Med Gp
417th Engr Avn Brig
  Hq & Hq Co
440th Sig Avn Bn—OL
822d Engr Avn Bn (Less Co)
3497th Mob Tng Sq—Det F–84-11
6004th Air Intel Sv Sq—Det 1
6127th Air Terminal Gp—Det 5
6151st Air Base Sq (Less Det)
6405th Air Spt Wg
  Hq

2d Mat Recovery Sq

Taegu Air Base #2
5th Mtr Trans Sq, Avn (Less Det)
420th Engr Avn Topo Det
930th Engr Avn Gp
  Hq & Hq Co (Less Dets)
6152d Air Base Sq

Tokchok-to
1st Shoran Beacon Sq—Det 1

Uijongbu
607th AC&W Sq (502d Tac Con
  Gp) (Less Det)

Ulsan
7th Mtr Trans Sq
547th Ammo Sup Sq, Dep

Yongdong-po
608th AC&W Sq (502d Tac Con Gp)
809th Engr Avn Bn—OL
811th Engr Avn Bn (Less Cos)

MARCH 1, 1953

Anyang
809th Engr Avn Bn—Co A

Chinhae
1st Air Pstl Sq—Det 4
18th Maint & Sup Gp (18th Ftr-Bmr
  Wg)
  Hq
30th Wea Sq—Det 16

Chinhae Airdrome
75th A/D Wg
  Hq
  7th Stat Svs Flt
  75th Trans Gp, Dep
    Hq
    75th Mtr Veh Sq, Dep
  75th Sup Gp, Dep
    Hq
    75th Recg, Shipping & Svs Sq,
      Dep
    75th Stock Con Sq, Dep
    75th Whs Sq, Dep
  75th Air Base Gp, Dep

Hq
  75th Air Police Sq, Dep
  75th Food Sv Sq, Dep
  75th Instls Sq, Dep
  75th Oprs Sq, Dep
  75th Med Gp
6127th Air Terminal Gp—Det 8

Chunchon
1st Air Pstl Sq—Det 30
30th Wea Sq—Det 29
809th Engr Avn Bn—Cos B & C
6147th Tac Con Gp
  Hq (Less Det)
  6147th Air Base Sq
  6147th Maint & Sup Sq
  6147th Med Sq
  6148th Tac Con Sq (Air)
  6149th Tac Con Sq (Air)
  6150th Tac Con Sq (Grd)

Goryudo
931st Engr Avn Gp
  Hq & Hq Co

Hoengsong
30th Wea Sq—Det 26
811th Engr Avn Bn—Co A (Less
  Det 1)
6151st AB Sq—Det 1
6155th Air Base Sq

Hoengsong Airdrome
5th Mtr Trans Sq, Avn—Det 2
18th Ftr-Bmr Wg—Det 1

Hwangbong-san
1st Shoran Beacon Sq—Det 4

Inchon
606th AC&W Sq—Det 1

Kangnumg [Kangnung]
6147th Tac Con Gp—Det 1

Kangnumg [Kangnung] **Airdrome**
811th Engr Avn Bn—Det 1, Co A
811th Engr Avn Bn—Det 1, Co B
6146th Air Advisory Gp—Det 2
6152d Air Base Sq

Kaya-san
1st Shoran Beacon Sq—Det 9

Kimpo
30th Wea Sq—Det 23

Kimpo Air Base
1st Air Pstl Sq—Det 28
4th Ftr-Intcp Wg
  Hq (Less Det)
  4th Ftr-Intcp Gp
    Hq
    334th Ftr-Intcp Sq
    335th Ftr-Intcp Sq
    336th Ftr-Intcp Sq
  4th Maint & Sup Gp
    Hq
    4th Maint Sq
    4th Mtr Veh Sq
    4th Sup Sq
  4th Air Base Gp
    Hq (Less Det)
    4th Comms Sq
    4th Air Police Sq
    4th Food Sv Sq
    4th Instls Sq
  4th Med Gp
67th Tac Recon Wg
  Hq
  67th Recon Tech Sq
  67th Tac Recon Gp
    Hq
    12th Tac Recon Sq, Night
      Photo
    15th Tac Recon Sq, Photo-J
    45th Tac Recon Sq, Photo-J
  67th Maint & Sup Gp
    Hq
    67th Maint Sq
    67th Mtr Veh Sq
    67th Sup Sq
  67th Air Base Gp
    Hq
    67th Comms Sq
    67th Food Sv Sq
    67th Air Police Sq
    67th Instls Sq
  67th Med Gp
606th AC&W Sq (502d Tac Con
  Gp) (Less Dets)
606th AC&W Sq—Det 2
811th Engr Avn Bn—OL
1993d AACS Mob Comms Sq
  (1818th AACS Mob Comms
  Gp)
6127th Air Terminal Gp—Det 14
6166th Air Wea Recon Flt

Korea (unspecified location)
15th Rad Sq, Mob—Det 151

Kuksa-bong
1st Shoran Beacon Sq—Det 2

Kunsan
1st Air Pstl Sq—Det 29
3d Bomb Wg, L
  Hq
  3d Bomb Gp, L
    Hq
    8th Bomb Sq, L. Night
      Intruder
    13th Bomb Sq, L, Night
      Intruder
    90th Bomb Sq, L, Night
      Intruder
  3d Maint & Sup Gp
    Hq
    3d Maint Sq
    3d Mtr Veh Sq
    3d Sup Sq
  3d Air Base Gp
    Hq
    3d Comms Sq
    3d Air Police Sq
    3d Food Sv Sq
    3d Instls Sq
  3d Med Gp
808th Engr Avn Bn (Less OL)
6127th Air Terminal Gp—OL

Kunsan Airdrome
474th Ftr-Bmr Wg
  Hq

474th Ftr-Bmr Gp
  Hq
  428th Ftr-Bmr Sq
  429th Ftr-Bmr Sq
  430th Ftr-Bmr Sq

Kwangung Airdrome
607th AC&W Sq—Det 3

Osan-ni
1st Air Pstl Sq—Det 33
18th Ftr-Bmr Wg
  Hq (Less Det)
  18th Ftr-Bmr Gp
    Hq
    12th Ftr-Bmr Sq
    67th Ftr-Bmr Sq
  18th Air Base Gp
    Hq
    18th Comms Sq
    18th Air Police Sq
    18th Food Sv Sq
    18th Instls Sq
  18th Med Gp
  18th Maint Sq (18th M&S Gp)
  18th Mtr Veh Sq (18th M&S Gp)
  18th Sup Sq (18th M&S Gp)
30th Wea Sq—Det 32
839th Engr Avn Bn
840th Engr Avn Bn
841st Engr Avn Bn
934th Engr Avn Gp
  Hq & Hq Co
3497th Mob Tng Sq—Det F–86-11

Paengnyong-do
1st Shoran Beacon Sq—Det 3

Pusan
30th Wea Sq—Det 27
1873d AACS Mob Comms Sq
  (M&S) (1818th AACS Mob
  Comms Gp)

Pusan Air Base
1st Air Pstl Sq—Det 14
811th Engr Avn Bn—Co B
  (Less Det 1)

Pusan East Air Base
17th Bomb Wg, L
  Hq
  17th Maint & Sup Gp
    Hq
    17th Mtr Veh Sq
    17th Sup Sq
  17th Air Base Gp
    Hq
    17th Comms Sq
    17th Air Police Sq
    17th Food Sv Sq
    17th Instls Sq
  17th Med Gp
30th Wea Sq—Det 13
543d Ammo Sup Sq, Dep
822d Engr Avn Bn—Co A
6127th Air Terminal Gp—Det 4
6401st Fld Maint Sq

Pusan West Airdrome
17th Bomb Gp, L (17th Bomb Wg)
  Hq
  34th Bomb Sq, L, Night Intruder
  37th Bomb Sq, L, Night Intruder
  95th Bomb Sq, L, Night Intruder
30th Wea Sq—Det 31
366th Engr Avn Bn

Pyongtaek Airdrome
30th Wea Sq—Det 20
808th Engr Avn Bn—OL
809th Engr Avn Bn (Less Cos &
  OL)
822d Engr Avn Bn—OL
1903d Engr Avn Bn (NG EAD)

Sachon
30th Wea Sq—Det 30

Seoul
See: Kimpo Air Base
Fifth Air Force
  Hq (Less Dets)
1st Air Pstl Sq—Det 31
1st Shoran Beacon Sq (Less Dets)
5th Comms Gp
  Hq

1st Rad Sq
1st Tp & Carr Sq
2d Comms Sq, Oprs
2d Rad Relay Sq
30th Wea Sq (Less Dets)
440th Sig Avn Const Bn (Less OL)
502d Tac Con Gp
   Hq
   605th Tac Con Sq (Less Det)
748th AF Band
811th Engr Avn Bn—OL
1818th AACS Mob Comms Gp
      (1808th AACS Wg)
   Hq
6154th Air Base Gp
   Hq
   6154th Air Police Sq
   6154th Food Sv Sq
   6154th Instls Sq
   6154th Med Sq
   6154th Mtr Veh Sq
   6154th Sup Sq

Seoul Air Base

1st Air Pstl Sq—Det 27
5th Epidemiological Flt
10th Ln Sq
30th Wea Sq—Det 18
605th Tac Con Sq—Det 3
608th AC&W Sq (502d Tac Con Gp)
811th Engr Avn Bn—Co C
1134th USAF S/A Sq—OL
2157th Air Rsq Sq (3d Air Rsq Gp)
6004th Air Intel Sv Sq—Det 2
6167th Air Base Gp
   Hq (Less Flts & Det)
   6167th Base Sv Sq
   6167th Maint & Sup Sq
   6167th Oprs Sq
6167th Air Base Gp—Flts A & B
6461st Trp Carr Sq, M (Less Det)

Suwon Air Base

1st Air Pstl Sq—Det 23
8th Ftr-Bmr Wg
   Hq

8th Ftr-Bmr Gp
   Hq (Less OL)
   35th Ftr-Bmr Sq
   36th Ftr-Bmr Sq
   80th Ftr-Bmr Sq
8th Maint & Sup Gp
   Hq
   8th Maint Sq
   8th Mtr Veh Sq
   8th Sup Sq
8th Air Base Gp
   Hq
   8th Comms Sq
   8th Air Police Sq
   8th Food Sv Sq
   8th Instls Sq
8th Med Gp
30th Wea Sq—Det 21
39th Ftr-Intcp Sq (35th Ftr-Intcp Gp)
51st Ftr-Intcp Wg
   Hq
   51st Ftr-Intcp Gp
      Hq
      16th Ftr-Intcp Sq
      25th Ftr-Intcp Sq
   51st Air Base Gp
      Hq
      51st Air Police Sq
      51st Comms Sq
      51st Food Sv Sq
      51st Instls Sq
   51st Med Gp
51st Mtr Veh Sq (51st M&S Gp)
319th Ftr-Intcp Sq
622d Engr Avn Maint Co
802d Engr Avn Bn
919th Engr Avn Maint Co
6127th Air Terminal Gp—Det 9

Taegu

1st Air Pstl Sq—Det 2
7th Comms Sq, Oprs (5th Comms
   Gp)
30th Wea Sq—Dets 11 & 12
417th Engr Avn Brig

Hq & Hq Co
1038th USAF Aud Gen Sq—OL
1973d AACS Mob Comms Sq
    (1818th AACS Mob Comms
    Gp)
3497th Mob Tng Sq—Det F–86-9
6146th Air Advisory Gp (ROK AF)
    Hq (Less Det)
6151st Air Base Sq (Less Det)
6153d Air Base Gp—Det 1

Taegu Air Base
Fifth Air Force—Det 1, Rear
2d Mat Recovery Sq
49th Ftr-Bmr Wg
    Hq (Less Det)
    49th Ftr-Bmr Gp
        Hq
        7th Ftr-Bmr Sq
        8th Ftr-Bmr Sq (Less OL)
    49th Maint & Sup Gp
        Hq
        49th Maint Sq
        49th Sup Sq
        49th Mtr Veh Sq
    49th Air Base Gp
        Hq
        49th Comms Sq
        49th Air Police Sq
        49th Food Sv Sq
        49th Instls Sq
    49th Med Gp
58th Ftr-Bmr Wg
    Hq
    58th Ftr-Bmr Gp
        Hq
        69th Ftr-Bmr Sq
        310th Ftr-Bmr Sq
        311th Ftr-Bmr Sq
    58th Maint & Sup Gp
        Hq
        58th Maint Sq
        58th Mtr Veh Sq
        58th Sup Sq
    58th Air Base Gp

Hq
    58th Comms Sq
    58th Air Police Sq
    58th Food Sv Sq
    58th Instls Sq
    58th Med Gp
440th Sig Avn Const Bn—OL
822d Engr Avn Bn (Less Co & OL)
3497th Mob Tng Sq—Det F–84-11
6004th Air Intel Sv Sq—Det 1
6127th Air Terminal Gp—Det 5

Taegu Air Base #2
420th Engr Avn Topo Det
930th Engr Avn Gp
    Hq & Hq Co (Less Dets)
6152d Air Base Sq

Tokchok-to
1st Shoran Beacon Sq—Det 1

Uijongbu
607th AC&W Sq (502d Tac Con Gp)
    (Less Det)

Ulsan
7th Mtr Trans Sq
547th Ammo Sup Sq, Dep

Yongdong-po
5th Mtr Trans Sq, Avn (Less Det)
809th Engr Avn Bn—OL
811th Engr Avn Bn (Less Cos & OL)

MAY 1, 1953

Anyang
440th Sig Avn Const Bn (Less OL)
809th Engr Avn Bn—Co A

Chinhae
1st Air Pstl Sq—Det 4
18th Maint & Sup Gp (18th Ftr-Bmr
    Wg)
    Hq
30th Wea Sq—Det 16

Chinhae Airdrome
2d Mat Recovery Sq
75th A/D Wg
    Hq

7th Stat Svs Flt
75th Trans Gp, Dep
  Hq
  75th Mtr Veh Sq, Dep
75th Sup Gp, Dep
  Hq
  75th Recg, Shipping & Svs Sq,
    Dep
  75th Stock Con Sq, Dep
  75th Whs Sq, Dep
75th Air Base Gp, Dep
  Hq
  75th Air Police Sq, Dep
  75th Food Sv Sq, Dep
  75th Instls Sq, Dep
  75th Oprs Sq, Dep
75th Med Gp
6127th Air Terminal Gp—Det 8

Chonjin Airdrome
6590th S/A Sq—OL

Chunchon
1st Air Pstl Sq—Det 30
30th Wea Sq—Det 29
809th Engr Avn Bn—Cos B & C
1993d AACS Mob Comms Sq—OL
6147th Tac Con Gp
  Hq (Less Det)
  6147th Air Base Sq
  6147th Maint & Sup Sq
  6147th Med Sq
  6148th Tac Con Sq (Air)
  6149th Tac Con Sq (Air)
  6150th Tac Con Sq (Grd)

Goryudo
931st Engr Avn Gp
  Hq & Hq Co

Hoengsong
30th Wea Sq—Det 26
811th Engr Avn Bn—Co A (Less
  Det 1)
1993d AACS Mob Comms Sq—OL
6151st AB Sq—Det 1
6155th Air Base Sq

Hoengsong Airdrome
5th Mtr Trans Sq, Avn—Det 2
18th Ftr-Bmr Wg—Det 1

Hwangbyong-san
1st Shoran Beacon Sq—Det 4

Inchon
606th AC&W Sq—Det 1

Kangnumg [Kangnung]
6147th Tac Con Gp—Det 1

Kangnumg [Kangnung] **Airdrome**
811th Engr Avn Bn—Det 1, Co A
811th Engr Avn Bn—Det 1, Co B
1993d AACS Mob Comms Sq—OL
6146th Air Advisory Gp—Det 2

Kimpo
30th Wea Sq—Det 23

Kimpo Air Base
1st Air Pstl Sq—Det 28
4th Ftr-Intcp Wg
  Hq (Less Det)
  4th Ftr-Intcp Gp
    Hq
    334th Ftr-Intcp Sq
    335th Ftr-Intcp Sq
    336th Ftr-Intcp Sq
  4th Maint & Sup Gp
    Hq
    4th Maint Sq
    4th Mtr Veh Sq
    4th Sup Sq
  4th Air Base Gp
    Hq (Less Det)
    4th Comms Sq
    4th Air Police Sq
    4th Food Sv Sq
    4th Instls Sq
  4th Med Gp
67th Tac Recon Wg
  Hq
  67th Recon Tech Sq
  67th Tac Recon Gp
    Hq

12th Tac Recon Sq, Night
  Photo
15th Tac Recon Sq, Photo-J
45th Tac Recon Sq, Photo-J
67th Maint & Sup Gp
  Hq
  67th Maint Sq
  67th Mtr Veh Sq
  67th Sup Sq
67th Air Base Gp
  Hq
  67th Comms Sq
  67th Food Sv Sq
  67th Air Police Sq
  67th Instls Sq
67th Med Gp
606th AC&W Sq (502d Tac Con
  Gp) (Less Dets)
606th AC&W Sq—Det 2
811th Engr Avn Bn—OL
1993d AACS Mob Comms Sq
    (1818th AACS Mob Comms
    Gp) (Less OLs)
6127th Air Terminal Gp—Det 14
6166th Air Wea Recon Flt

Korea (unspecified location)
15th Rad Sq, Mob—Det 151

Kuksa-bong
1st Shoran Beacon Sq—Det 2

Kunsan
1st Air Pstl Sq—Det 29
3d Bomb Wg, L
  Hq
  3d Bomb Gp, L
    Hq
    8th Bomb Sq, L, Night
      Intruder
    13th Bomb Sq, L, Night
      Intruder
    90th Bomb Sq, L, Night
      Intruder
  3d Maint & Sup Gp
    Hq
    3d Maint Sq

3d Mtr Veh Sq
3d Sup Sq
3d Air Base Gp
  Hq
  3d Comms Sq
  3d Air Police Sq
  3d Food Sv Sq
  3d Instls Sq
3d Med Gp
808th Engr Avn Bn (Less OL)

Kunsan Airdrome
49th Ftr-Bmr Wg
  Hq (Less Det)
  49th Ftr-Bmr Gp
    Hq
    7th Ftr-Bmr Sq
    8th Ftr-Bmr Sq (Less OL)
6127th Air Terminal Gp—OL

Kwangung Airdrome
607th AC&W Sq—Det 3

Osan-ni
1st Air Pstl Sq—Det 33
18th Ftr-Bmr Wg
  Hq (Less Det)
  18th Ftr-Bmr Gp
    Hq
    12th Ftr-Bmr Sq
    67th Ftr-Bmr Sq
  18th Air Base Gp
    Hq
    18th Comms Sq
    18th Air Police Sq
    18th Food Sv Sq
    18th Instls Sq
  18th Med Gp
18th Maint Sq (18th M&S Gp)
18th Mtr Veh Sq (18th M&S Gp)
18th Sup Sq (18th M&S Gp)
30th Wea Sq—Det 32
839th Engr Avn Bn
841st Engr Avn Bn
934th Engr Avn Gp
  Hq & Hq Co
1993d AACS Mob Comms Sq—OL

Paengnyong-do

1st Shoran Beacon Sq—Det 3

1993d AACS Mob Comms Sq—OL

Pusan

30th Wea Sq—Det 27

1873d AACS Mob Comms Sq
(M&S) (1818th AACS Mob
Comms Gp)

Pusan Air Base

1st Air Pstl Sq—Det 14

811th Engr Avn Bn—Co B (Less
Det 1)

Pusan East Air Base

17th Bomb Wg, L

  Hq

    17th Maint & Sup Gp

      Hq

      17th Mtr Veh Sq

      17th Sup Sq

    17th Air Base Gp

      Hq

      17th Comms Sq

      17th Air Police Sq

      17th Food Sv Sq

      17th Instls Sq

    17th Med Gp

30th Wea Sq—Det 13

543d Ammo Sup Sq, Dep

822d Engr Avn Bn—Co A

6127th Air Terminal Gp—Det 4

6401st Fld Maint Sq

Pusan West Airdrome

17th Bomb Gp, L (17th Bomb Wg)

  Hq

    34th Bomb Sq, L, Night Intruder

    37th Bomb Sq, L, Night Intruder

    95th Bomb Sq, L, Night Intruder

30th Wea Sq—Det 31

366th Engr Avn Bn

6152d Air Base Sq

Pyongtaek Airdrome

30th Wea Sq—Det 20

808th Engr Avn Bn—OL

809th Engr Avn Bn (Less Cos &
OL)

1903d Engr Avn Bn (NG EAD)

Sachon

30th Wea Sq—Det 30

Seoul

See: Kimpo Air Base

Fifth Air Force

  Hq (Less Dets)

1st Air Pstl Sq—Det 31

1st Shoran Beacon Sq (Less Dets)

5th Comms Gp

  Hq

  1st Rad Sq

  1st Tp & Carr Sq

  2d Comms Sq, Oprs

  2d Rad Relay Sq

30th Wea Sq (Less Dets)

502d Tac Con Gp

  Hq

  605th Tac Con Sq (Less Det)

748th AF Band

811th Engr Avn Bn—OL

840th Engr Avn Bn

2157th Air Rsq Sq (3d Air Rsq Gp)

6154th Air Base Gp

  Hq

  6154th Air Police Sq

  6154th Food Sv Sq

  6154th Instls Sq

  6154th Med Sq

  6154th Mtr Veh Sq

  6154th Sup Sq

Seoul Air Base

1st Air Pstl Sq—Det 27

3d Air Rsq Gp—OL

5th Epidemiological Flt

10th Ln Sq

30th Wea Sq—Det 18

605th Tac Con Sq—Det 3

608th AC&W Sq (502d Tac Con Gp)

811th Engr Avn Bn—Co C

1038th USAF Aud Gen Sq—OL

1134th USAF S/A Sq—OL

1993d AACS Mob Comms Sq—OL
6004th Air Intel Sv Sq—Det 2
6167th Air Base Gp
  Hq (Less Flts & Det)
  6167th Base Sv Sq
  6167th Maint & Sup Sq
  6167th Oprs Sq
6167th Air Base Gp—Flts A & B
6461st Trp Carr Sq, M (Less Det)

Song Gumi-ri
1st Shoran Beacon Sq—Det 9

Suwon
1993d AACS Mob Comms Sq—OL

Suwon Air Base
1st Air Pstl Sq—Det 23
8th Ftr-Bmr Wg
  Hq (Less OL)
  8th Ftr-Bmr Gp
    Hq
    35th Ftr-Bmr Sq
    36th Ftr-Bmr Sq
    80th Ftr-Bmr Sq
  8th Maint & Sup Gp
    Hq
    8th Maint Sq
    8th Mtr Veh Sq
    8th Sup Sq
  8th Air Base Gp
    Hq
    8th Comms Sq
    8th Air Police Sq
    8th Food Sv Sq
    8th Instls Sq
  8th Med Gp
30th Wea Sq—Det 21
39th Ftr-Intcp Sq (35th Ftr-Intcp Gp)
51st Ftr-Intcp Wg
  Hq
  51st Ftr-Intcp Gp
    Hq
    16th Ftr-Intcp Sq
    25th Ftr-Intcp Sq
  51st Air Base Gp
    Hq

51st Air Police Sq
51st Comms Sq
51st Food Sv Sq
51st Instls Sq
  51st Med Gp
51st Mtr Veh Sq (51st M&S Gp)
319th Ftr-Intcp Sq
622d Engr Avn Maint Co
802d Engr Avn Bn
919th Engr Avn Maint Co
6127th Air Terminal Gp—Det 9

Taegu
1st Air Pstl Sq—Det 2
7th Comms Sq, Oprs (5th Comms
  Gp)
30th Wea Sq—Dets 11 & 12
417th Engr Avn Brig
  Hq & Hq Co
1038th USAF Aud Gen Sq—OL
1973d AACS Mob Comms Sq
  (1818th AACS Mob Comms
  Gp)
3497th Mob Tng Sq—Det F–86–9
6146th Air Advisory Gp (ROK AF)
  Hq (Less Det)
6151st Air Base Sq (Less Det)
6153d Air Base Gp—Det 1

Taegu Air Base
Fifth Air Force—Det 1, Rear
58th Ftr-Bmr Wg
  Hq
  58th Ftr-Bmr Gp
    Hq
    69th Ftr-Bmr Sq
    310th Ftr-Bmr Sq
    311th Ftr-Bmr Sq
  58th Air Base Gp
    Hq
    58th Comms Sq
    58th Air Police Sq
    58th Food Sv Sq
    58th Instls Sq
  58th Med Gp
58th Mtr Veh Sq (58th M&S Gp)

440th Sig Avn Const Bn—OL
474th Ftr-Bmr Wg
   Hq
   474th Ftr-Bmr Gp
      Hq
      428th Ftr-Bmr Sq
      429th Ftr-Bmr Sq
      430th Ftr-Bmr Sq
   474th Maint & Sup Gp
      Hq
      474th Maint Sq
      474th Mtr Veh Sq
      474th Sup Sq
   474th Air Base Gp
      Hq
      474th Comms Sq
      474th Air Police Sq
      474th Food Sv Sq
      474th Instls Sq
   474th Med Gp
733d Engr Avn Sup Pt Co
822d Engr Avn Bn (Less Co)
1818th AACS Mob Comms Gp
      (1808th AACS Wg)
   Hq
6004th Air Intel Sv Sq—Det 1
6127th Air Terminal Gp—Det 5
6156th Air Base Sq
6157th Air Base Sq

Taegu Air Base #2
420th Engr Avn Topo Det
930th Engr Avn Gp
   Hq & Hq Co (Less Dets)
6152d Air Base Sq

Tokchok-to
1st Shoran Beacon Sq—Det 1

Uijongbu
607th AC&W Sq (502d Tac Con
      Gp) (Less Det)

Ulsan
7th Mtr Trans Sq
547th Ammo Sup Sq, Dep

Yongdong-po
5th Mtr Trans Sq, Avn (Less Det)
809th Engr Avn Bn—OL
811th Engr Avn Bn (Less Cos & OL)

JULY 1, 1953

Anyang
440th Sig Avn Const Bn (Less OL)
809th Engr Avn Bn—Co A

Chinhae
18th Maint & Sup Gp (18th Ftr-Bmr
      Wg)
   Hq
30th Wea Sq—Det 16

Chinhae Airdrome
2d Mat Recovery Sq
6th Mat Recovery Sq
10th Air Pstl Sq—Flt L
75th A/D Wg
   Hq
   75th Trans Gp, Dep
      Hq
      75th Mtr Veh Sq, Dep
   75th Sup Gp, Dep
      Hq
      75th Recg, Shipping & Svs Sq,
         Dep
      75th Stock Con Sq, Dep
      75th Whs Sq, Dep
   75th Air Base Gp, Dep
      Hq
      75th Air Police Sq, Dep
      75th Food Sv Sq, Dep
      75th Instls Sq, Dep
      75th Oprs Sq, Dep
   75th Med Gp, Dep
6127th Air Terminal Gp—Det 8

Chunchon
10th Air Pstl Sq—Flt A
30th Wea Sq—Det 29
809th Engr Avn Bn—Cos B & C
942d Fwd Air Con Sq
6147th Tac Con Gp
   Hq (Less Det)

6147th Air Base Sq
6147th Maint & Sup Sq
6147th Med Sq
6148th Tac Con Sq (Air)
6149th Tac Con Sq (Air)

Goryudo
931st Engr Avn Gp
  Hq & Hq Co

Hoengsong
30th Wea Sq—Det 26
811th Engr Avn Bn—Co A (Less
  Det 1)
6151st AB Sq—Det 1
6155th Air Base Sq

Hoengsong Airdrome
5th Mtr Trans Sq, Avn—Det 2

Hwangbyong-san
1st Shoran Beacon Sq—Det 4

Inchon
606th AC&W Sq—Det 1

Kangnumg [Kangnung]
6147th Tac Con Gp—Det 1

Kangnumg [Kangnung] **Airdrome**
811th Engr Avn Bn—Det 1, Co A
811th Engr Avn Bn—Det 1, Co B
6146th Air Advisory Gp—Det 2

Kimpo
30th Wea Sq—Det 23

Kimpo Air Base
10th Air Pstl Sq—Flt B
4th Ftr-Intcp Wg
  Hq (Less Det)
  4th Ftr-Intcp Gp
    Hq
    334th Ftr-Intcp Sq
    335th Ftr-Intcp Sq
    336th Ftr-Intcp Sq
  4th Maint & Sup Gp
    Hq
    4th Maint Sq
    4th Mtr Veh Sq
    4th Sup Sq

4th Air Base Gp
  Hq (Less Det)
  4th Comms Sq
  4th Air Police Sq
  4th Food Sv Sq
  4th Instls Sq
4th Med Gp
67th Tac Recon Wg
  Hq (Less OL)
  67th Recon Tech Sq
  67th Tac Recon Gp
    Hq
    12th Tac Recon Sq, Night
      Photo
    15th Tac Recon Sq, Photo-J
    45th Tac Recon Sq, Photo-J
  67th Maint & Sup Gp
    Hq
    67th Maint Sq
    67th Mtr Veh Sq
    67th Sup Sq
  67th Air Base Gp
    Hq
    67th Comms Sq
    67th Air Police Sq
    67th Food Sv Sq
    67th Instls Sq
  67th Med Gp
606th AC&W Sq (502d Tac Con
  Gp) (Less Dets)
606th AC&W Sq—Det 2
809th Engr Avn Bn (Less Cos)
811th Engr Avn Bn—OL
1993d AACS Mob Comms Sq
  (1818th AACS Mob Comms
  Gp)
6127th Air Terminal Gp—Det 14
6166th Air Wea Recon Flt

Korea (unspecified location)
15th Rad Sq, Mob—Det 151

Kuksa-bong
1st Shoran Beacon Sq—Det 2

Kunsan
3d Bomb Wg, L

Hq
3d Bomb Gp, L
　Hq
　　8th Bomb Sq, L, Night
　　　Intruder
　　13th Bomb Sq, L, Night
　　　Intruder
　　90th Bomb Sq, L, Night
　　　Intruder
　3d Maint & Sup Gp
　　Hq
　　3d Maint Sq
　　3d Mtr Veh Sq
　　3d Sup Sq
　3d Air Base Gp
　　Hq
　　3d Comms Sq
　　3d Air Police Sq
　　3d Food Sv Sq
　　3d Instls Sq
　3d Med Gp
808th Engr Avn Bn

Kunsan Airdrome
10th Air Pstl Sq—Flt G
49th Ftr-Bmr Wg
　Hq (Less Det)
　49th Ftr-Bmr Gp
　　Hq
　　7th Ftr-Bmr Sq
　　8th Ftr-Bmr Sq
841st Engr Avn Bn—Co B
6127th Air Terminal Gp—OL

Kwangung Airdrome
607th AC&W Sq—Det 3

Osan-ni
10th Air Pstl Sq—Flt F
18th Ftr-Bmr Wg
　Hq
　18th Ftr-Bmr Gp
　　Hq
　　12th Ftr-Bmr Sq
　　67th Ftr-Bmr Sq
　18th Air Base Gp
　　Hq

18th Comms Sq
18th Air Police Sq
18th Food Sv Sq
18th Instls Sq
18th Med Gp
18th Maint Sq (18th M&S Gp)
18th Mtr Veh Sq (18th M&S Gp)
18th Sup Sq (18th M&S Gp)
30th Wea Sq—Det 32
839th Engr Avn Bn
841st Engr Avn Bn (Less Co)
934th Engr Avn Gp
　Hq & Hq Co

Paengnyong-do
1st Shoran Beacon Sq—Det 3

Pusan
30th Wea Sq—Det 27
1873d AACS Mob Comms Sq
　(M&S) (1818th AACS Mob
　Comms Gp)

Pusan Air Base
811th Engr Avn Bn—Co B (Less
　Det 1)

Pusan East Air Base
10th Air Pstl Sq—Flt K
17th Bomb Wg, L
　Hq
　17th Maint & Sup Gp
　　Hq
　　17th Mtr Veh Sq
　　17th Sup Sq
　17th Air Base Gp
　　Hq
　　17th Comms Sq
　　17th Air Police Sq
　　17th Food Sv Sq
　　17th Instls Sq
　17th Med Gp
30th Wea Sq—Det 13
543d Ammo Sup Sq, Dep
822d Engr Avn Bn—Co A
6127th Air Terminal Gp—Det 4
6401st Fld Maint Sq

Pusan West Airdrome
17th Bomb Gp, L (17th Bomb Wg)
  Hq
    34th Bomb Sq, L, Night Intruder
    37th Bomb Sq, L, Night Intruder
    95th Bomb Sq, L, Night Intruder
30th Wea Sq—Det 31
366th Engr Avn Bn
6152d Air Base Sq

Pyongtaek Airdrome
1st Shoran Beacon Sq (Less Dets)
30th Wea Sq—Det 20
1903d Engr Avn Bn (NG EAD)

Sachon
30th Wea Sq—Det 30

Seoul
See: Kimpo Air Base
Fifth Air Force
  Hq (Less Dets)
  1st Air Pstl Sq—Det 31
5th Comms Gp
  Hq
    1st Rad Sq
    1st Tp & Carr Sq
    2d Comms Sq, Oprs
    2d Rad Relay Sq
10th Air Pstl Sq—Flt C
30th Wea Sq (Less Dets)
502d Tac Con Gp
  Hq
    605th Tac Con Sq (Less Det)
748th AF Band
811th Engr Avn Bn—OL
840th Engr Avn Bn
2157th Air Rsq Sq (3d Air Rsq Gp)
6154th Air Base Gp
  Hq
    6154th Air Police Sq
    6154th Food Sv Sq
    6154th Instls Sq
    6154th Med Sq
    6154th Mtr Veh Sq
    6154th Sup Sq

Seoul Air Base
AMC—OL
5th Epidemiological Flt
10th Air Pstl Sq—Flt D
10th Ln Sq
30th Wea Sq—Det 18
605th Tac Con Sq—Det 3
608th AC&W Sq (502d Tac Con Gp)
811th Engr Avn Bn—Co C
1038th USAF Aud Gen Sq—OL
1134th USAF S/A Sq—OL
6004th Air Intel Sv Sq—Det 2
6167th Air Base Gp
  Hq (Less Flts & Det)
  6167th Base Sv Sq
  6167th Maint & Sup Sq
  6167th Oprs Sq
6167th Air Base Gp—Flts A & B
6461st Trp Carr Sq, M (Less Det)

Song Gumi-ri
1st Shoran Beacon Sq—Det 9

Suwon Air Base
8th Ftr-Bmr Wg
  Hq
  8th Ftr-Bmr Gp
    Hq
      35th Ftr-Bmr Sq
      36th Ftr-Bmr Sq
      80th Ftr-Bmr Sq
  8th Maint & Sup Gp
    Hq
      8th Maint Sq
      8th Mtr Veh Sq
      8th Sup Sq
  8th Air Base Gp
    Hq
      8th Comms Sq
      8th Air Police Sq
      8th Food Sv Sq
      8th Instls Sq
  8th Med Gp
10th Air Pstl Sq—Flt E
30th Wea Sq—Det 21
39th Ftr-Intcp Sq (35th Ftr-Intcp Gp)

51st Ftr-Intcp Wg
  Hq
    51st Ftr-Intcp Gp
      Hq
      16th Ftr-Intcp Sq
      25th Ftr-Intcp Sq
    51st Air Base Gp
      Hq
      51st Air Police Sq
      51st Comms Sq
      51st Food Sv Sq
      51st Instls Sq
    51st Med Gp
51st Mtr Veh Sq (51st M&S Gp)
319th Ftr-Intcp Sq
622d Engr Avn Maint Co
802d Engr Avn Bn
919th Engr Avn Maint Co
6127th Air Terminal Gp—Det 9

Taegu
7th Comms Sq, Oprs (5th Comms
  Gp)
10th Air Pstl Sq (6005th Air Pstl
  Gp) (Less Flts)
10th Air Pstl Sq—Flt I
30th Wea Sq—Dets 11 & 12
417th Engr Avn Brig
  Hq & Hq Co
1038th USAF Aud Gen Sq—OL
1973d AACS Mob Comms Sq
    (1818th AACS Mob Comms
    Gp)
6146th Air Advisory Gp (ROK AF)
  Hq (Less Det)
6151st Air Base Sq (Less Det)
6157th Air Base Gp—Det 1

Taegu Air Base
Fifth Air Force—Det 1, Rear
10th Air Pstl Sq—Flt H
58th Ftr-Bmr Wg
  Hq
    58th Ftr-Bmr Gp
      Hq
      69th Ftr-Bmr Sq

      310th Ftr-Bmr Sq
      311th Ftr-Bmr Sq
    58th Air Base Gp
      Hq
      58th Comms Sq
      58th Air Police Sq
      58th Food Sv Sq
      58th Instls Sq
    58th Med Gp
58th Mtr Veh Sq (58th M&S Gp)
440th Sig Avn Const Bn—OL
474th Ftr-Bmr Wg
  Hq
    474th Ftr-Bmr Gp
      Hq
      428th Ftr-Bmr Sq
      429th Ftr-Bmr Sq
      430th Ftr-Bmr Sq
    474th Maint & Sup Gp
      Hq
      474th Maint Sq
      474th Mtr Veh Sq
      474th Sup Sq
    474th Air Base Gp
      Hq
      474th Comms Sq
      474th Air Police Sq
      474th Food Sv Sq
      474th Instls Sq
    474th Med Gp
733d Engr Avn Sup Pt Co
822d Engr Avn Bn (Less Co)
1818th AACS Mob Comms Gp
    (1808th AACS Wg)
  Hq
6004th Air Intel Sv Sq—Det 1
6127th Air Terminal Gp—Det 5
6156th Air Base Sq
6157th Air Base Sq

Taegu Air Base #2
420th Engr Avn Topo Det
930th Engr Avn Gp
  Hq & Hq Co (Less Dets)
6152d Air Base Sq

Tokchok-to
1st Shoran Beacon Sq—Det 1

Tongnae
6004th Air Intel Sv Sq—Det 5

Uijongbu
607th AC&W Sq (502d Tac Con
    Gp) (Less Dets)

Ulsan
7th Mtr Trans Sq
547th Ammo Sup Sq, Dep

Yongdong-po
5th Mtr Trans Sq, Avn (Less Det)
811th Engr Avn Bn (Less Cos &
    OL)

Glossary of
Abbreviations and Acronyms

AACS	Airways & Air Communications Service	Hq	Headquarters
		Hosp	Hospital
AB	Air Base	Instls	Installations
Abn	Airborne	Intel	Intelligence
AC&W	Aircraft Control & Warning	L	Light
		Ln	Liaison
A/D	Air Depot	M	Medium
Adv	Advance	M&S	Maintenance & Supply
AF	Air Force	Maint	Maintenance
AMC	Air Materiel Command	Mat	Materiel
Ammo	Ammunition	Med	Medical
ANG	Air National Guard	Mob	Mobile
Aud	Auditor	Mtr	Motor
Avn	Aviation	NG	National Guard
Bn	Battalion	OL(s)	Operating Location(s)
Bomb	Bombardment	Oprs	Operations
Brig	Brigade	Photo	Photographic
Carr	Carrier	Photo-J	Photographic-Jet
Co(s)	Company(ies)	Plat	Platoon
Comd	Command	Pstl	Postal
Comms	Communications	Pt	Point
Con	Control	Rad	Radio
Const	Construction	RBS	Radar Bomb Scoring
Dep	Depot	Recg	Receiving
Det(s)	Detachment(s)	Recon	Reconnaissance
EAD	Extended Active Duty	ROK AF	Republic of Korea Air Force
Engr	Engineer		
Fld	Field	Rsq	Rescue
Flt(s)	Flight(s)	S/A	Special Activities
Ftr	Fighter	Scty	Security
Ftr-Bmr	Fighter-Bomber	SE	Single Engine
Ftr-Escort	Fighter-Escort	Sep	Separate
Ftr-Intcp	Fighter-Interceptor	Sig	Signal
Fwd	Forward	Spt	Support
Gen	General	Sq	Squadron
Gp	Group	Sta	Station
Grd	Ground	Stat	Statistical
H	Heavy	Sup	Supply

Sv(s)	Service(s)	Trp	Troop
Tac	Tactical	USAF	United States Air Force
TAC	Tactical Air Command	USAFR	United States Air Force
Tech	Technical		Reserve
Tng	Training	Veh	Vehicle
Topo	Topography	Wea	Weather
Tp & Carr	Telephone & Carrier	Whs	Warehouse
Trans	Transport	Wg	Wing

K-Sites

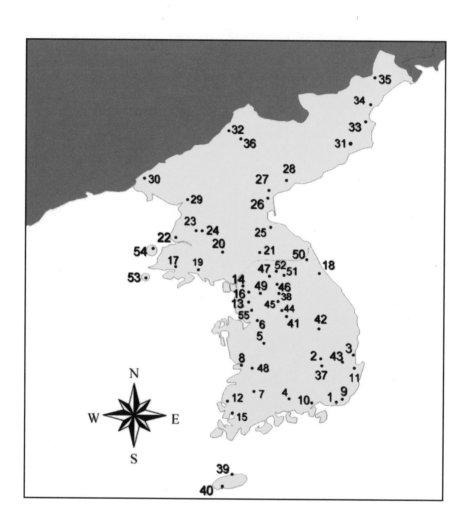

K-Sites By Number

K–1	Pusan West		K–29	Sinanju
K–2	Taegu (Taegu #1)		K–30	Sinuiju
K–3	Pohang		K–31	Kilchu (Kisshu)
K–4	Sachon		K–32	Oesichon-dong
K–5	Taejon		K–33	Hoemun (Kaibun)
K–6	Pyongtaek		K–34	Chongjin (Seishin)
K–7	Kwangju		K–35	Hoeryong (Kainsei)
K–8	Kunsan		K–36	Kanggye
K–9	Pusan East		K–37	Taegu #2
K–10	Chinhae		K–38	Wonju
K–11	Urusan (Ulsan)		K–39	Cheju-do #1
K–12	Mangun		K–40	Cheju-do #2
K–13	Suwon		K–41	Chungju
K–14	Kimpo		K–42	Andong #2
K–15	Mokpo		K–43	Kyongju
K–16	Seoul		K–44	Changhowon–ni
K–17	Ongjin (Oshin)		K–45	Yoju
K–18	Kangnung (Koryo)		K–46	Hoengsong
K–19	Haeju (Kaishu)		K–47	Chunchon
K–20	Sinmak		K–48	Iri
K–21	Pyonggang		K–49	Yangsu-ri
K–22	Onjong–ni		K–50	Sokcho-ri
K–23	Pyongyang		K–51	Inje
K–24	Pyongyang East		K–52	Yanggu
K–25	Wonsan		K–53	Paengyong-do
K–26	Sondok		K–54	Cho-do
K–27	Yonpo		K–55	Osan-ni
K–28	Hamhung West			

K-Sites Alphabetically

ISBN 0-16-050901-7

9 780160 509018

90000